The Bad Catholic's
Guide to the
Catechism

To all those victims, parents, journalists, and others who helped expose the clerical abuse crisis and force overdue reforms in Church discipline—especially Jeffrey M. Bond; and to the many, many faithful and holy priests and religious who have blessed my life—first and foremost, Fr. Angelo Pezzullo.

The Bad Catholic's Guide to the Catechism

by

JOHN ZMIRAK

A Crossroad Book
The Crossroad Publishing Company
New York

The Crossroad Publishing Company
www.CrossroadPublishing.com

In continuation of our 200-year tradition of independent publishing, The Crossroad Publishing Company proudly offers a variety of books with strong, original voices and diverse perspectives. The viewpoints expressed in our books are not necessarily those of The Crossroad Publishing Company, any of its imprints or of its employees. No claims are made or responsibility assumed for any health or other benefit.

Printed in the United States of America.
The text of this book is set in Times
The display face is Brush Script

Project Management by
The Crossroad Publishing Company
Gwendolin Herder

We thank especially:

Cover design: Chris Michalski   Text design: Web Fusion
Development: Gwendolin Herder

Message development, text development, package, and market positioning by
The Crossroad Publishing Company

Cataloging-in-Publication Data is available from the Library of Congress Books published by The Crossroad Publishing Company may be purchased at special quantity discount rates for classes and institutional use. For information, please e-mail info@CrossroadPublishing.com

ISBN 13: 978-0-8245-2680-1

2 3 4 5 6 7 B 16 15 14 13 12

Table of Contents

Preface: In the Footsteps of Fulton Sheen (Sort of . . .)

An early Christian author, Hippolytus, was a staunch defender of Christian teaching. So staunch was he that when a new pope was in office who was seen as being soft on converts, Hippolytus gathered others together and had himself proclaimed pope, the first antipope in history. Later he and the reigning pope, Pontian, were sent away to the same labor camp, where Hippolytus was reconciled to the Church and both were martyred. These days, Pontian and Hippolytus are honored by the Church as saints and martyrs, with a shared feast day.

Much earlier, however, a not yet radical Hippolytus was known for reaching out to dialogue with pagans and fellow Catholics. When there was a need for parchment and papyrus in the years after his death, the ink in which his words had been written was scraped away (probably also due to his antipope status). Thus his teachings are lost to history. In the modern age, techniques were discovered that allowed scholars to recapture his words, and some of those words, notably a description for pagans of the celebration of Holy Mass, are used for the Second Eucharistic Prayer.

A description for pagans of the Holy Mass? How odd that may seem to us. Indeed, most of the early Christian writers and Fathers of the Church were engaged in writing such works addressed to non-Catholics, from Justin Martyr's *Dialogues with Trypho*, to other works by Origen, Clement of Alexandria, Tertullian, and Jerome. This practice was later followed by Augustine, Thomas Aquinas, Blaise Pascal, and Chateaubriand, and in more modern times by G. K. Chesterton, Ronald Knox, and Fulton Sheen.

When most of us hear *catechism*, we think of a systematic statement of belief, normally with questions and answers. Some of us may remember having memorized the short, to-the-point answers in the *Baltimore Catechism*, studied even today. Others may have taken a glance inside a modern catechism and felt a bit overwhelmed, or have memories of being disciplined for not having memorized a lesson in school. (Such memories are revelled in by former Catholic-school students, who like to reminisce about the prison atmosphere they endured, without realizing that public school students of the same era often had it worse, without the ironic comfort of having punishment meted out by a woman wearing medieval garb.) Even non-Catholics will remember memorizing their own central statements of belief as children, from the Heidelberg Catechism to the Augsburg Confession.

If you are looking for short, concise, exhaustive, and taxative statements of belief, *The Bad Catholic's Guide to the Catechism* is probably not for you. *The Bad Catholic's Guide to the Catechism,* indeed, is an effort to dialogue with the postmodern world in contemporary terms, much in the tradition of Hippolytus and Justin Martyr. If you were raised with no faith, were baptized and left alone, went through twelve years of Catholic education with the vague idea that faith was about unicorns and rainbows, or just want a fresh way of understanding many of the teachings of the Church, you will find intelligible yet contemporary explanations in the present work.

Terms such as "the Incarnation, "the Trinity," "the Holy Ghost," and "the Sacraments" can be confusing, even to the most educated, media-savvy modern. The dialogic formula of most catechisms is repeated here to explain those teachings, but with a freshness and occasional drollness unusual in most statements of belief. The text has been vetted, and although expressed in words no modern cleric would use, you will enjoy the presentation and can rest assured that nothing is found that is contrary to the Faith.

Several years ago I was asked to undertake the study of Fulton J. Sheen, to see if he might be canonized someday. Archbishop Sheen, while a young priest teaching at the Catholic University of America, used to speak on a weekly radio show just as radio was getting started. His concern was to use the gifts God had given him to spread the gospel. Over time, as media developed, Archbishop Sheen learned to use whatever innovations he could to address "modern" man. In 1952 this included undertaking a weekly television show, which became an instant hit. Bishop Sheen's show became the highest-rated on television and won him an Emmy. When a comedian challenged his status, Sheen attributed his number one rating to his "better writers, Matthew, Mark, Luke and John."

As my study progressed, I met many people who had known him personally, some even had worked with him. Thousands of people wrote to our offices to tell of ways he had influenced them, the way he had reached them through his use of media. In response I learned more about ways to use social media for my own work with youth in my parish in Princeville, Illinois. I first set up e-mail groups, but when I realized kids were no longer checking e-mail, I got into instant messaging, and then text messaging and Facebook. I drew the line at services like Twitter—do I really want to know what friends are doing every minute?

One of Sheen's great concerns was the alienation and depersonalization of modern man. He always stressed that people are not reducible to categories, that each person is created by God and cannot be reduced to a servant of the state, an instantly classifiable type, or instantly judged because of some category. Because of this, Venerable Fulton was an early opponent of racism, of totalitarian regimes in communist countries such as Russia and China, of Freudian psychology. In other words, a person's background does not determine his or her life.

The challenge in sharing the faith in today's postmodern, media-savvy world is, indeed, that many people embrace their membership in subcultures that tell them they are only important if they are, in fact, members of that group, even if that group is "at odds" with society. People who think of themselves as rebels, for instance, might get a piercing or a tattoo (or several), just like their friends have done, just like they have seen on TV. Sensitive teens might feel their self-esteem bolstered as they are recognized as "emo" or "goth." In their cry for individuality, they become quite the same as everybody else. In their out-of-hand rejection of "uncool" matters of faith, they reject an eternal call that springs from the very depths of their being. New techniques have to be found to reach those who are so filled to the brim with post-modernity that they have closed themselves off to consideration of higher things.

If you find yourself overwhelmed by modernity, *The Bad Catholic's Guide to the Catechism* can help you confront these modern attitudes on their own terms. If you are searching for answers, you will find comprehensive explanations you will understand and be certain the message hasn't been cheapened or dumbed down. Don't be fooled by the title "catechism," though—this work is much more than you might think. Just as Hippolytus, Chesterton, Origen, and Aquinas wrote to explain the Church to moderns of their times, many of Zmirak's illustrations will certainly convince you, on your own terms.

Rev. Msgr. Richard Soseman
Feast of St. James the Apostle, 2012
Vatican City

Introduction: This Is Not a Catechism

As the good Monsignor Soseman, who kindly agreed to vet this book for orthodoxy, informed me, "the word 'catechism' in Canon Law carries with it a laser-focused meaning: a complete compendium of the faith which is aimed at a particular age level. Strictly speaking, a Bishop may publish a catechism for his own Diocese, but any catechism meant for wider circulation is, according to Canon Law, supposed to have Vatican approval."

We don't. And last time I checked, I'm not a bishop. So think of this more along the lines of *The Bartender's Bible* and place it on your bathroom shelf alongside *The Coal Catechism* (1898) and *The Catechism of the History of Newfoundland* (c.1856). It is at once a loving parody of, and a tribute to, the classic Q&A catechisms of the past, especially the many variants of the *Baltimore Catechism*, my favorite being the children's editions, with the "Goofus and Gallant"–style cartoons that taught generations of grubby-necked Ellis Island escapees like my grandparents to see, really *see*, that every time you disobey Sister, it puts another thorn in Jesus's crown.

If you need the official, authoritative answer to a theological question, please pick up that beautifully written brick the *Catechism of the Catholic Church* (*CCC*). It is complete, convincing, and well worth spending a year or two reading slowly from cover to cover.

But it's a very long book, and not the kind of thing you give your smart-aleck teenage nephew or fallen-away best friend. It is my hope that this "catechism," which addresses the fundamental issues of divine revelation, the nature of God, the structure of the Church, and the sacraments, will serve as a tool of apologetics and evangelization. My book isn't nearly so high-minded as the *CCC*, or even as the splendid *Youcat*, aimed at young adults, which I recommend to anyone of any age who hasn't studied academic theology. Think of those two books as the dinner and lunch menus at an exquisite Parisian restaurant. My book is a paper plate full of hot, authentic Tex-Mex served up at a gas station outside Austin. It isn't always pretty, and the spices will clear your sinuses, but it's the last barbacoa for three hundred miles.

So let's begin.

***

Sitting over an overpriced gin and tonic at the Polo Lounge in the Beverly Hills Hotel, I probed the excommunicated bishop about his secret sedevacantism. I didn't toss the issue naked on the table, since he would simply have denied everything. But I knew from several sources that, while the man publicly claimed to accept the legitimacy of then-Pope John Paul II, privately he sowed doubts among his friendlier seminarians. He whispered that the "formal and material heresies" taught by that pope had quite possibly deprived Karol Wojtyla of the throne. That would have left the seat (*sede*) of Peter empty (*vacantes*). A small but intense contingent of traditionalists have held this position for decades, although the public leader of that movement, Archbishop Marcel Lefebvre, always insisted that his resistance to Popes Paul VI and John Paul II amounted to "true" (versus false) obedience, carried out in a grave emergency situation for the Church—akin to the Arian heresy, when St. Athanasius refused commands from the dithering Pope Liberius.

Archbishop Lefebvre's was an emotionally stressful position to hold, since commitment to Catholic tradition encourages us to maximize the authority of the pope— which is hard to do when you're defying direct papal commands and ignoring the bishops he has appointed. One can square this circle neatly by saying instead that Catholics should always obey the pope and that God prevents popes from making decisions catastrophic to the Church—such as the vandalization of the Roman Rite of the Mass. The pope deserves our veneration and our respect. The pope would never allow such a development of doctrine as Vatican II's decree on religious liberty. Therefore, we haven't had a valid pope since Pius XII.

I think that this sad conclusion is encouraged by the happy fact that, since the Counter-Reformation, we have had a very good run of largely prudent, often saintly popes. People tempted by this position need to read a little further back—for example, one of my favorite books for understanding the extent and limits of papal authority, Russell Chamberlain's *The Bad Popes*. This grimly funny chronicle of the felonies of popes in the distant past is a nice corrective to the temptation to treat every papal opinion as dogmatic and to canonize every pontiff on his deathbed. It will vaccinate the reader against the dismal disappointment that comes when one forms a cult of personality around a mere mortal man.

There are plenty of wacky stories about sedevacantists getting valid episcopal orders through squirrelly means, or even electing their own popes—since, hey, it's clear that the Church always needs one! But I'm not here to make fun of such people. If you grant their premises, their conclusions seem to follow. And the pastoral abuse suffered by Catholics for the past four decades at the hands of real live heretical nuns, liturgists, catechists, priests, and bishops was so widespread and egregious that I think Christ will be very forgiving of their traumatized victims.

What I wanted to know from the bishop was this: If you really believe that a validly elected pope has embraced and taught formal heresy, doesn't that shake your faith in the papacy itself? Isn't it kind of a cop-out to make such grand claims for papal authority—and then when a pope seems to misuse it, simply to claim that he's no longer pope? Wouldn't it be more intellectually honest, at some point, to opt out—and become, say, Eastern Orthodox? You'd still have the sacraments and all the Christological councils.

The bishop pointed out that none of Paul VI's or John Paul II's "heretical" statements were pronounced *ex cathedra*. OK, I countered, but what if one of them had been? What if the pope tomorrow were to stand up and proclaim, *ex cathedra*, that abortion was morally licit? Or (to sharpen the point still further) that Mary had not in fact been assumed into heaven? Would that convince him to reject papal authority? What hypothetical circumstance would convince him that the Roman reading of Christ's promises to Peter had in fact been exaggerated?

The bishop was offended by the question. He insisted that such a thing would never happen. I agreed, then said: "But what if it did?" He refused to entertain such a blasphemous hypothetical. I insisted that he must. "Is your position really that the pope teaches infallibly, except when he doesn't—and then he's no longer pope? That seems like a sad kind of a loophole through which to save your faith. We argue for the primacy of Peter by pointing to a perfect historical consistency of doctrinal teaching coming from Rome. If that consistency were broken, would we just look for other arguments instead?" He shook his head and we shook hands.

Another encounter with an apostle who danced with infamy was equally enlightening. The potboiler novelist and one-time Vatican insider Malachi Martin read an ill-advised piece I'd written defending some traditionalists (who'd later prove themselves indefensible) and dropped me an e-mail inviting me to lunch the next time I was in New York City. So during my next trip up there from Baton Rouge (I was still in grad school), I met the elfin Irish ex-priest at Mon Petit Café on Lexington Avenue. I started with preliminary pleasantries, mentioning a Latin Mass priest we knew in common. At that, his finely lined pink face turned suddenly very solemn. The name I had dropped over the vichyssoise provoked him to sadness, and then to the sober, confidential whisper he liked to use when dispensing "inside information" (from sources that surely must have dried up in the late '60s, when he left the priesthood). "John _____ is a very fine man, but I regret to tell you that he is merely a layman." That puzzled me, since this priest of the Newark archdiocese had said the Latin Mass many times at St. Agnes in New York City, at Masses I had attended. Had he never been ordained? Was there some secret impediment not even his bishop had known about?

"Not at all," Martin said, looking left and right then falling to almost a whisper. "The fact is, that the formula for ordaining priests and bishops in the Western Rite that was issued at Vatican II is completely invalid. So no priest under seventy or so—except those ordained by traditionalists—is anything more than a layman. It is a great tragedy for the Faith."

I'd say. If it were true. This set off the sensors in my Heresy Computer, so I sat back for a second, finished most of my veal chop, and formulated the following. "So you don't believe that Paul VI, John Paul II, or even John Paul I were valid popes?"

That puzzled Martin, who raised an ironic whitebrow. "Oh no. Their elections were perfectly valid."

"So you're saying that a valid pope can issue invalid sacraments for more than 90 percent of the Church, drying up the ordinary means of grace for Catholics around the world—and that doesn't affect the indefectibility of the Church, much less the infallibility of the pope?"

He frowned. "I don't see why it would."

I smiled. "Let's have dessert."

Such incidents sparked me to start thinking, intensively for many years, about precisely such blasphemous hypotheticals and troubling counterfactuals, and wondering which ones for me would be "theological deal killers." Just as St. Thomas Aquinas looked for the best arguments against the Faith so he could counter them, I decided to deepen my own faith by considering just what it would take for me decide that the Church had, in fact, been wrong. Or else that I had been mistaken about the nature of the Church and that the Church Christ founded might, in fact, reside somewhere else than I'd been brought up to believe.

It might sound like I'm looking around for a fire exit, finding potential excuses for flouncing off someday into a Tibetan Buddhist temple full of taut-bodied blondes from California. Not at all. Instead, as someone who writes apologetics, I'm trying to keep my arguments honest and make sure I never squirm through loopholes. I also want to be ready to counter the strongest objections to the teachings of the Church and to correct exaggerations that well-meaning people draw from one-sided readings of Church documents. Some of those exaggerated positions are popular among the folks I meet at Latin Mass up here in New England; and to be honest, when I hear what they believe our Church really teaches, I encounter a "theological deal killer." I say to myself, "I don't *think* that the Church teaches that, but I know it can't be *true*." That sends me back to the sources, to read the Church's full teaching in its true context. I think mine is the best response to intellectual doubts.

Of course, some people think it's virtuous to beat their intellects into submission, along the lines of Rex Mottram in Waugh's *Brideshead Revisited*. Rex is an opportunistic convert with an *expansive* notion of the virtue of docility. As the priest trying to instruct Mottram recounts:

> "Yesterday I asked him whether Our Lord had more than one nature. He said: 'Just as many as you say, Father.' Then again I asked him: 'Supposing the Pope looked up and saw a cloud and said "It's going to rain", would that be bound to happen?' 'Oh, yes, Father.' 'But supposing it didn't?' He thought a moment and said, 'I suppose it would be sort of raining spiritually, only we were too sinful to see it.'"

Any Catholic who doesn't have, at least in theory, any theological deal killers is in grave danger of joining Rex Mottram, out in the "rain."

It's important to think through such deal-killer questions because while our Church is, in eternity, the Mystical Bride of Christ, it also has one foot sunk in the squishy earth. It's a real institution—now the oldest one on the planet, given the fall of the Chinese monarchy in 1912—taking part in the messy business of history, making intransigent claims to doing something almost impossibly difficult: proclaiming a single, consistent message about the nature of God, creation, sin, redemption, and the proper ordering of human society, through every culture on earth and every century that passes.

It's a miracle—a literal one, eclipsing all the cast-off crutches at Lourdes and the dancing sun at Fatima —that the Church has stayed "on message" and fought off the heresies that surged in every age, corrupting or quashing every merely human institution. To the Pharisees, she preached the Incarnation; to the pagans, the one true God; to the Gnostics, the goodness of creation; to the Stoics, the sacraments; to the Neoplatonists, God's freedom and transcendence; to the Muslims, the Trinity; to the Albigensians, the holiness of matter and of marriage; to the Latin Averroists, the unity of Truth; to the nominalists, the crucial "analogy" between God's goodness and our own; to the humanists, the role of Christ in raising man above the animals; to the Protestants, the incoherence of scripture without Tradition; to the *philosophes*, the toxic futility of reason stripped of faith; to the socialists, the evil of compelling the Corporal Works of Mercy; to the eugenicists, the sanctity of every flawed and helpless human life; to the racists, the unity of the human race; to the feminists, the supremacy of the family over the individual.

I could go on—and history will go on, firing flaming bags of dog crap at the Faith like shots from a tennis-ball machine that has been possessed by a poltergeist. It is only with mysterious aid from the Holy Spirit that our popes will continue to whack them away, standing unstained in their white mantle of simplicity and truth. Their success is a witness to the truthfulness of the Faith second only to the Resurrection itself. Fail either of these, and we are the greatest of fools.

This staggering, incalculable consistency is the central miracle that makes the Church worth believing in, and the only one that you and I can test for ourselves—by studying history. We can't go back and meet the risen Christ. As my high school religion teacher sneered, biochemists can't verify transubstantiation. (Since modern science looks only at accidents, not substance, the correct response to this was, "Duh!") But we can look at the stunning fact of a single, once-simple gospel exfoliating through history like a many-petalled flower, rising to the sun of truth and growing from the seed Christ planted twenty centuries ago. Through hailstorms, herbicides, and against all the forces of hell, it still grows straight and true.

This, for me, is the reason to believe. If I could not even imagine the plant mutated or dead, I would not be stunned with gratitude at its holiness and health. St. Paul allowed himself to wonder what it would mean if Christ had not been raised from the dead; we likewise must ponder what we would make of a faith that trimmed its creed with every diktat from the zeitgeist.

Our faith alone, and only in its fullest, Catholic form, has taken upon itself the awful challenge of institutional continuity and perfect intellectual consistency. From a purely human point of view, it's a high-wire act performed with no net above the abyss. Yet the beautiful Lady still dances on the wire, almost twenty centuries later.

John Zmirak
The Feast of St. John Bosco, 2012
Manchester, N.H.

Reason and Revelation

1. Who made me?

Selfish DNA made you. But why would it do such a thing? What had you, a bipedal, carbon-based information system of the sort that emerges briefly from biochemical reactions, ever done to DNA to deserve this? Did DNA know that you, the sad sack side effect of brain-flesh and electrical impulses, might someday stare at a rusty late-November sunset over the Hudson recalling your parents' vanished faces and wondering where their ghosts had gone? That you might wake with white knuckles gripping a pillow from a dream in which your frightened grandchildren begged for protection? That the "life" it had callously woken you into might seem instead a death sentence?

Be of good cheer, for DNA knows all these things, and more, though it has neither brain nor motherboard. Verily, it made you to know it, obey it, and serve it by replicating more human beings, who are simply fleshly FedEx envelopes designed to cushion this proto-protein's passage.

Or so the cheerful materialists like to say. If you ask them to connect the dots and explain how some inert substance somehow "arranged" for itself to be reproduced, and devised all the millions of species that exist solely to serve this purpose, developing enormously complex biochemical systems that don't work to promote survival until they're virtually perfect—for instance, eyeballs and feathers—they whisper with touching credulity: *It happened purely by chance, and it took a very, very long time.*

When you point out that physicists say the odds of a universe coming into exist that could support intelligent life, or even amoebas, are infinitesimally tiny, such that it seems the very fundamental forces of this universe, like gravity, were crafted to make possible the emergence of man (cosmologists call this the "anthropic principle"), the materialists must admit that you are right. To explain away this mystery they then say that billions of other universes really must also exist, popping in and out of existence in an infinite, unknowable void, because that way the one that resulted in man is just a fluke. Of course, by definition we can never have any evidence as to whether all these universes are any more real than that money the exiled Nigerian Minister of Petroleum was kind enough to offer you via e-mail, so we'll just have to take all that science on faith.

I, on the other hand, was created by a loving, personal God. That's my story and I'm sticking to it.

2. Who is God? Why settle for only one?

In metaphysics, less is more. The human mind seems to have been designed to look at many complicated, seemingly unrelated or even chaotic occurrences and sort through them until it comes to a simple and clear explanation for all of them. This logical maxim is known to academic philosophers as the "lone gunman" principle. No speculative thinker, from Socrates up through Hegel, would have doubted that a single deity was logically preferable to many. But at some point in the eighteenth century, when it came to talking about religion, philosophers lost the megaphone to *philosophes* (who were really sophists); they cast the question of faith not in terms of ontology but anthropology—as the history of primitive, quaint beliefs.

Starting with the "Enlightenment" (what a PR coup that title was!), unbelieving intellectuals began to theorize as to the origins of religion. Some said that primitive man was terrified and confused by natural phenomena (such as thunder) and so came up with gods (such as thunder gods, not to mention hurricane gods and hemorrhoid gods) to explain everything they saw and to make some sort of sense out of the world. Castes of priests emerged to manage access to these gods, and poets came along to celebrate them. Eventu-

ally, philosophers arose who tried to simplify and rationalize all these figures in the sky—and that's how they got whittled down to one. It is the job of the secular scientist, and the modern freethinking person, to go from one to none.

However, anthropologists in the early twentieth century were disconcerted to find that in nearly every polytheistic tribe they came to study, there was also somewhere in the background a single, highest god. Most tribes said their ancestors used to worship the highest god, but sooner or later they found him too remote to believe in. Or else he didn't answer their prayers promptly enough. So they came up with lower, lesser gods who were more "hands-on" in their interaction with humans, whom they could bribe or flatter into bringing the rains or cursing their enemies. On the Pacific island of Pentecost, for instance, the natives invented bungee jumping as a way to convince the gods to bless their annual harvest of yams. In California, software developers buy clothes made out of hemp because they think it will somehow help "save the rain forest." When you think about it, such magic is just a primitive form of technology, and technology merely a modern, more efficacious kind of magic. Why do you think they used to call the TV science guy "Mr. Wizard"?

3. Who's "Mr. Wizard"?

Never mind. You make me feel old.

4. And who is "God"?

That's a question we try to answer a couple of different ways . . .

5. Pick one.

OK, but wait a minute. This is important: What if the pointy-heads of pre-Revolutionary France who came up with the Just-So story given above about the origins of religion (e.g., the hurricane god) got it wrong? The ancient culture we know the most about, the Hebrews, seems to have started with a simple, noble idea of a single all-powerful God and then fell away from it through impatience (he didn't always do what they asked) and sensuality (they wouldn't worship something they couldn't

picture). Remember when they got tired of moral commands that came from a burning bush and decided instead that what they wanted was milk and honey, which they figured they could squeeze from a golden calf? That reminds me of modern man, who can't be bothered trying to meet his deepest needs through prayer, so he turns instead to a thousand different techniques for beating anxiety and boredom. Are you haunted by a sense of the futility of life and a lingering fear of death? There's an App for That!™

6. OK. Now pick one.

There's a certain amount we can know about God through reason alone ...

7. Says who?

Says the Catholic Church in the First Vatican Council—the one that took place in the 1870s, which was ended by an invading Italian army and didn't accidentally give rise to *Godspell*. The Church has compiled all the things it asserts are true about God and marked off those that pagans have come up with all on their own, without any burning bush or the "still, small voice" within, but just by looking at the world and thinking things through. We call that part of what we believe "natural theology," since it comes from reasoning about nature. In other words, God didn't have to reveal these things to us directly, since we could figure them out for ourselves. In the moral realm, we call the truths we figure out this way "natural law."[1]

8. So there's a realm of theology that doesn't require any faith?

Yes. It's called "mainline Protestantism," and its practitioners devote most of their time to refurbishing ornate, empty buildings in prime locations throughout the country whose original purpose has been lost to history—such as the enormous gothic pile in upper Manhattan known locally as St. John the Simply Divine, which historians theorize was either a native American goth club or an enormous Colonial-era birdhouse.

OK, that's not in fact what natural theology refers to. Sorry. Anglicans inhabiting Gothic churches just gets my Irish up. I remember how they kept all of ours back in the Old Country.

In fact, the realm of natural theology is a real and clearly delimited area of intellectual investigation. It can only go so far, since the Being we're trying to talk about is by definition beyond our capacity to grasp. In the *Summa Contra Gentiles* (*The Complete Goy's Guide to God*), Thomas Aquinas looked at the arguments of pagan philosophers and did the best job of laying out what reason alone can theoretically demonstrate about God. It isn't much, but it's something. Aquinas argues that we know that God exists as the First Cause of the universe—since everything we have ever encountered through science has a cause, and it's irrational to imagine a chain of causes extending infinitely. There has to be a first link in the chain, and it can't itself be caused—or it wouldn't be the first. (The Cause that caused it would.) Such a Cause must be One, or again we're just multiplying links instead of finding the first one. That Cause must be outside of time, since it is what got time started. Since it is the source of all the limited things we know about, it must itself be limitless. In fact, most of what Aquinas said we can know about God just by thinking Him over was stated in the negative: He is *without* beginning, *without* end, *without* flaw, *without* a limited shape or any other kind of shortcoming we could imagine.

---

[1] CCC, 31, 36

9. Really? Then how about this one: Can God make a stone too heavy for Him to lift? Or is He *without* the power to do that?

That argument seems a lot more compelling after you've finished your second joint. But in the cold light of day, when you look in the mirror and try to dab some Visine into your eyes, you realize that this line of thinking is no more attractive than that entire bag of Twinkies you consumed while watching three hours of Mexican hockey . . . naked. So I'll answer this and all such subsequent inquiries in distinctly labeled boxes and large print for those religious seekers who are still trying to "clear their heads" and figure out where they can snag some baby urine to fool their employer's upcoming drug test.

☾☽☾☽☾☽☾☽☾☽☾☽☾☽☾☽☾☽☾☽☾☽☾☽☾☽☾☽☾☽

FAQs from Your Stoner Neighbor #1: Dude, can God make a stone too heavy for him to lift?

On the simplest level, this is not so much an argument as it is a pun, a brainteaser that relies on the squeaky hinges of human thought. This question confuses us at first by disguising a negative as a positive.[2] It admits that God lacks limits. But it claims that a limit is *something*, so God is lacking *something*, and therefore He isn't perfect. You could say the same thing about flaws. Or feathers. Feathers are something, and they're something good—God said so, in a roundabout way, in the Book of Genesis. But God has no feathers.[3] Therefore He isn't perfect. One can imagine a boy in seventh-grade confirmation-prep class substituting "hooters" for feathers. "God has no hooters? But hooters are *awesome* ...." And so on. Such arguments, like Edward Norton in *Fight Club*, seem tough at first but in the end just beat themselves senseless.

Still, there are some sober, adult reflections that come to mind when we think about this. As Pope Benedict XVI reiterated in his bomb-throwing address at Regensburg, Catholics believe that God *is in fact bound* by the laws of logic, which are part of His very nature. He cannot make a square that is also a circle. Nor can He choose to cease existing, go insane, or make what is intrinsically evil good. Furthermore, He cannot betray His promises or reverse His own decisions. Since He made the souls of men immortal, He cannot decide to unmake them. In other words, an eavesdropper on the inner life of the Most Holy Trinity would never hear dialogue like this:

---

[2] CCC, 268
[3] So far as we know.

Father: Do You remember that all-inclusive, no-refund, eternal-salvation-or-damnation initiative I came up with, way back before Vatican II?

Son: Yeah. Honestly, that always struck me as kind of . . . hardcore, Dad.

Holy Spirit: Not terribly Christian, if you ask me. But I'm always the last to be consulted.

Father: Yeah, well, I've been doing a lot of reading, especially back issues of the *National Catholic Reporter*—

Holy Spirit: Are they still publishing that? I guess I lost touch with those people.

Son: They've got pretty good book reviews, but you have to subscribe to the print edition to read them.

Father: And it got Me to thinking. Is it really fair to let fleeting decisions made in time and under duress have eternal results? How many humans really have the backbone to choose heaven or hell?

Holy Spirit: I've been trying to tell You . . .

Father: (grousing) What did I say about "I told You so"?

Holy Spirit: It's Your least favorite sentence. Sorry.

Father: So You know what I'm fixing to do? I'll just keep the saints around so they'll be happy.

Son: What about the sinners?

Father: You can have all the penitent ones, same as ever.

Holy Spirit: And the rest of the poor buggers?

Father: I've decided to momentarily avert My attention from them, and thus cease to maintain their contingent existences in Being. Then poof! They'll wink out into nothingness.

Son: That is so much more compassionate, Dad.

Father: And just to top things off, I'm going to apply this retroactively—so We can call back Michael from guarding the gates of hell. No need!

Son: Wow. Our God *is* an awesome God!

Holy Spirit: What are You going to tell the other angels? And the souls of the Just who have been taking a stern, reluctant pleasure in the execution of divine justice upon the Damned?

Son: We can announce officially that all those souls ran away, and We just couldn't find them.

Holy Spirit: Why not just say that We couldn't care for them any-more, so We brought them to live on a farm, where they can run free and chase squirrels all they want?

Father: All good ideas, Persons. Why don't We retire and attend to the praise and adoration of the saints for a while? Let Us reconvene later to finalize the text of Our statement.

Would the perfections we attribute to God really be enhanced by such a discussion, or the prospect that He could take away our other gifts, such as free will and reason? The "ability" to flip-flop is much like the "ability" to chicken out, procrastinate, or have a panic attack. It's just another way of saying one's will is imperfect, changeable, and subject to new information—in other words, that it isn't God's.[4]

CRBDCRBDCRBDCRBDCRBDCRBDCRBDCRBDCRBDCRBDCRBDCRBDCRBDCRBDCRBDCR

10. So God is just the principle of limitlessness? That sounds more like an implication of grammar than of reality. God is just the term you pop in for "the mostest of the mostest."

That is what literary critic Kenneth Burke said, in his fascinating but finally sterile book *The Rhetoric of Religion*. God is simply the "title of titles," and our idea of Him is not the product of reason or even of revelation, but simply a side effect of the way our brains are wired. St. Anselm of Canterbury agreed, but he pointed the stick the other way. He made the famously clever and unconvincing "ontological argument" for God's existence. It runs like this:

- God is by definition the greatest thing we can possibly conceive.
- *But* if He didn't exist, then we could conceive something greater—namely, something that did.
- *So* for God not to exist is a logical contradiction.
- *Therefore* He exists.

---

[4] CCC, 2086

11. That one belongs in your "Stoner Neighbor" reflections. Just because you define something such that it has to exist doesn't mean your definition points to anything real outside your own mind.

I know. So did St. Thomas Aquinas, which is why he rejected this argument. He hated contradicting a saint, but he put sound logic first. Aquinas's argument undercuts Burke's position, too. Our conceptions of God cannot outrage the laws of logic; finally (like everything else) they are dependent on some evidence from the external world, which we obtain through the senses. What is more, not every culture comes upon even the purely rational truths about God. Most of us aren't philosophers, and most philosophers make mistakes. So God doesn't leave things to chance. He has stepped into history and told us many of these truths we could (in theory) have figured out on our own.

12. But how do you even define "God"?

God is the principle of Being itself. His "essence" (the type of thing that He is) is the same as His "existence" (the fact that He is). We know this because He told us, through Moses: I am Who am.[5] We can say a little more 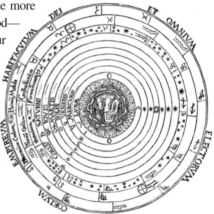 and assert that He is just and rational and good— using our ability to make analogies. But our analogies will always fall short. In fact, without revelation we can't get very far. The most consistent pagan philosopher, Aristotle, got as far as the First Cause, describing him almost as what we'd call a watchmaker. But Aristotle had to stop there because watches hadn't yet been invented. Now that we have precision timepieces, we can go several steps further.

13. Seriously?

No. In fact, natural theology kind of peters out right there, with an abstract notion of a god who is pretty much unimaginable, whose level of involvement with the universe is anybody's guess. This position was revived by the Deists in the eighteenth century, who wanted desperately to deprive the clergy of money and influence—and take it for themselves—so they argued as best they could to banish miracles, revelation, and every other evidence of God's intervention in history to the realm of silly superstition. The most famous American Deist was probably Thomas Jefferson, who went beyond

---

[5] I am always tempted to sing this verse and add "and that's all that I am—I'm Popeye the sailor man, toot toot!" But there is no biblical warrant for asserting this.

the separation of church and state and tried to separate miracles from the Bible. While he was president, he decided that his education in literature and experience managing slaves qualified him to judge which parts of the New Testament were authentic. So he got out his scissors and snipped out every reference to Jesus's healings, the Virgin Birth, the Resurrection, and each place where He claimed to be divine. Jefferson took what was left and pasted it together into what came to be called the "Jefferson Bible," and had it printed at taxpayer expense. Later on, the scholar Rudolf Bultmann used the same principle to found what was called "higher criticism" of the Bible. You start with secular, materialist premises and use those to read the whole thing. Anything that contradicts those premises—from the parting of the Red Sea to the raising of Lazarus from the dead—must have been made up by credulous people later, so you throw it out. This "method," believe it or not, was eventually adopted by the "mainline" (i.e., empty) Protestant churches, and today it dominates theology departments at many Catholic colleges.

14. Yeah, right. Which ones?

The ones with coed dormitories that allow overnight visits so students can more effectively "hook up." Another infallible test is this: If a school (*ahem*) mounts *The Vagina Monologues* on campus, its theology department practices Bultmannian higher criticism. Q.E.D. I can't fully explain it, but there's a 100 percent correlation between those phenomena, which leads me to infer a causal relationship—though I can't say which way it runs. It's possible that Bultmann's influence on campus influences administrators to sponsor feminist plays that celebrate lesbian statutory rape. More likely, traumatic experiences such as enduring Eve Ensler's prose make people doubt the existence of a good and loving God. But again, I'm no philosopher.

15. So that leaves us with an abstract Chain of Being that starts with an utterly perfect, 24-karat link that gradually peters out into 18-karat, 14-karat, then finally tarnished, electroplated jewelry you get at a mall on the Jersey shore—that is, us. Can we know any more about "God" than that?

Yes, but we needed Him to tell us Himself. That's where we move from natural to dogmatic theology. Nowadays it's considered more presentable to call it "systematic" instead of "dogmatic," since modernity is big on systems but sniffs at dogmas. Here we move from reason to revelation—without, of course, switching off that part of our brains

that sorts and measures assertions against each other and the world. When we speak of God as mysterious, we don't mean that He's a muddle. If someone presents us with an assertion about God's nature, and backs it up with snippets of scripture, it's our job to measure it first against all the other things we know about God (through reason alone or because He told us).

The New Atheists like to snark that we Christians might as well be worshiping a Flying Spaghetti Monster, and they have a good reason for saying that: They are insufferable. And sad to say, insecure. Why else would Oxford- or Cambridge-educated, highly paid writers spend thousands of cumulative pages preening about how intelligent and well informed they are, compared to Mexican landscapers with Guadalupe tattoos or elderly Russian ladies lighting candles in front of icons? Some professional atheists (am I a professional nonpolo fan?) have even come up with a title for themselves: the Brights. As in: the people who are *brighter than you*, and too bright even to have to explain why your seedy, sweaty, faintly garlicky beliefs are sad superstitions that the government really should stop you from passing on to your innocent children.[6] The news that functioning adults had taken to calling themselves Brights recalled to my mind many things, each of them sad:

- Lonely sophomore college boys at Renaissance faires, lying to each other about which of the obese Bryn Mawr dropouts at the unicorn jewelry stall they'd bedded the night before. In fluent Klingon.
- Middle-aged men with long nostril hairs attending Mensa meetings in basements of closed-down synagogues, playing angry chess and comparing the scores on their latest IQ tests.
- Aging trophy wives in glamorous houses drying their nails as they snicker at pictures of "people of Walmart."
- Oxbridge academics who read *Brave New World*, decided they were "Alphas," then laid the book aside fondly, never having realized *it was a satire*.

The New Atheists have been too busy congratulating themselves to find out that the Christian tradition insists on using the stern standards of reason and self-consistency in its considerations of God. Aquinas argued, and the Church agrees, that we can know something true and meaningful about God *by analogy* with what we know about lower, smaller, slower-moving things—like the American court system. We know what we

---

[6] But aren't they cute little monkeys! A pity you've had so *many* of them . . . have you measured their carbon footprints?

mean when we say that courts are meant to dispense "justice." They don't just resolve conflicts or prevent contract disputes from ending in duels with pistols—though that does come in handy. No, courts are in the business of trying to embody the abstraction known as justice—which is precisely why we're so often frustrated when they don't. We have a standard against which we judge even the laws of the land, and that sometimes tells us that a given law may be in force but is nevertheless unjust and we won't obey it. Many American Protestants came to say this about slavery, and the result was the Civil War. Catholics saved their indignation for a cause that hit them closer to home—Prohibition—and the result was the emergence of the Mafia and the election of Franklin Roosevelt. (Nobody said you don't pay a price for fighting injustice.)

Yes, God's justice is more perfect than ours, and the difference between our notion of justice and its pristine, divine original is bigger than the similarity. But *justice* as applied to God can't simply be the opposite of what we mean by the word on earth. This kind of thinking is what convinced the Church to condemn a mistake made by one of its greatest theologians, St. Augustine. His reading of the Bible and what it says about the necessity of baptism for salvation convinced him that unbaptized babies who died must go to hell. That conclusion seemed to follow. But the Church took other biblical passages where God

told us that He is just and argued that any "justice" that entailed eternal punishment for souls who'd never committed personal sins would be entirely unhinged from what we mean by *justice*. So why would God even have used the word? Instead of promising us that He is just, He might as well have said that He is made of spaghetti—but God's spaghetti is not our spaghetti.[7]

16. OK, so we're on the same plate, if not the same page. If the best we can do by sheer reason is to end up with a kind of watchmaker god, then the rest of it has to come from "revelation." But there are more religions in the world than you can shake a stick at—and some of them are pretty intolerant, so you'd better hide your stick. Each one makes the same argument: "God is this way, not that way, and we know because He told us so." How in God's name (*heh, heh*) are we supposed to know which one to believe?

First of all, you aren't exactly getting that right about the world religions. Admittedly, it's possible that the one true religion is an obscure little cult that exists in a single mountain valley in Soregonadistan, but that doesn't seem terribly likely. A faith that got reality "right" would by its nature seem destined to make a major impact in the world and attract some followers, so we can start with the major world religions. Now when we look

---

[7] CCC, 271

at them, in fact there are only three that claim to have direct access to revelation from God of what His nature is: Judaism, Christianity, and Islam. What is more, all three of them claim to descend from the very same patriarch, Abraham, who they all agree was the first man to receive explicit instructions from God about how to honor Him.

Buddhism doesn't claim to have a message from God, just a special insight into the nature of ultimate reality—which boils down to the fact that existing in the first place is a kind of curse, and wanting one thing rather than another is a really bad idea because you aren't likely to get it, which will make you unhappy. Since the goal is not to find happiness (that's impossible) but simply to stop the misery, you should learn to quit wanting things, and if you get good enough at this you will eventually stop existing. If Buddhism had a god, and he had a voice, it would be that one inside your head at the dentist's office that tells you to ask for more laughing gas, the risk of a coma be damned. Taoism is a mystical nature cult, and Confucianism a political and ethical philosophy. The latter has so little explicit religious content that when the Jesuits made it to China, they felt they could include Confucian rituals in the Mass, since they didn't even overlap with (much less contradict) Christianity. Hinduism teaches that one of its gods, Krishna, revealed himself to man—only to teach us about many hundreds of different gods, none of which claims omnipotence, and one of which is an elephant. Next!

17. So even if you narrow things down to the religions of revelation, how could someone choose among them?

That is where reason comes in. You compare the claims each of these faiths makes for itself, what they assert about God, what they tell men to do, and what they promise will happen in human history. You look at their track record and judge their effects on human society, comparing their visions of what is good against what your reason has convinced you is true. But mostly, you just check which religion your parents held, and you stick with that.

18. Is that good enough?

Of course not. But it's mighty tempting. Inertia is a major force in religious matters, which is why you'll get atheists in Ireland (like old James Joyce) insisting they are Catholic (not Protestant) atheists, and Jewish Buddhists fervently interested in West Bank land disputes. Some people, of course, assert that God planted each of us where we're supposed to be, so we should just stick with the religion that we've got.

If that were true, the English would still be performing human sacrifices at Stonehenge—instead of gathering overaged Harry Potter fans for Morris dancing, mead-swilling contests, and really bad sex. Those Wiccan nerds' ancestors converted to Christianity for a reason, and the nerds drifted out of it for a reason, too. Whatever tradition we're born into, at some point we test it out for ourselves, and sometimes we see it doesn't work. So no, you shouldn't just bloom where you were planted.

What's the alternative? It would be really nice to spend the time investigating in depth the claims of every variant of every religion that ever came down the pike—from Jainism, which considers the lives of insects sacred, to Norse mythology, which has much more interesting and appealing scriptures than we do and inspires better operas. If each of us lived for thousands of years and had nothing to do but wait for the robots to bring us more margaritas, the "religious seeker" model would work pretty well. Alas, our technology never seems to bring us any closer to that kind of utopia, however many World's Fairs we attend. So we must make our decisions based on limited information and act on them for the brief time we flicker across this earthly stage. Then we hope for the best—hope in particular that if a religion we rejected does turn out to be true, it isn't one of those whose deity punishes people for being sincerely mistaken.

It isn't just laziness that leads people to give the benefit of the doubt to the religion in which they were raised. The whole notion of revelation is based on putting a certain amount of trust in the testimony of witnesses. Whom should we trust before our parents? So our parents pass on to us the story of a certain series of supernatural events and religious precepts, which were passed along to them, going all the way back to the first prophet or founder of that faith. That's what the word *tradition* means, a passing along—like a relay race that goes back for millennia, where the baton keeps getting handed on from one runner to the next. If you're trying to judge which team in the relay race deserves to win, you look to where they started from, and how well they're running the race. Then you compare the actual tenets of those faiths and you look to the verdict of history: what kind of impact is each of those teams having on the world?

19. So are you going to show me why Judaism and Islam are wrong, and Christianity is right?

No. This isn't that kind of book. I'm here to lay out what the Catholic Church says about itself, not to refute the others. Obviously, by saying that this faith is true, I'm asserting that the tenets of other creeds that contradict it would have to be false. God is either a trinity or He isn't. Jesus was either the incarnate Son of God or He wasn't. A law of logic says that two sets of mutually exclusive assertions cannot be simultaneously true. Except in California.

20. What happened to the law of logic there?

Their state supreme court ruled it unconstitutional. It was never very popular anyway—like one of those crazy old laws that says you can't drive your dogcart to the haymarket on the Sabbath unless you're flying the Union Jack.

21. OK, so what is the Christian account of how revelation occurred?

As Elmer Fudd might say, "Vewy, vewy swowly."[8] Divine revelation didn't happen in a blinding flash—such as God dropping the *Summa Theologiae* on top of a mountain and waiting for people to invent the Latin language so they could read it. (Though he could have given them magical spectacles[9] that would translate it for them, but that's another story.) It seems that God preferred to unfold slowly His personality and will for us through the course of messy human history. We might wonder at this and call up the divine customer-service line to ask why in heck human nature arrived in the mail without the instructions. I don't pretend to know what

---

[8] CCC, 53
[9] Obligatory Mormon joke. Sorry, I couldn't resist.

He was thinking here, but I find it aesthetically fitting that our knowledge of God evolved in much the way that animal species did, over a long time and by fits and starts, with sudden leaps whenever God saw fit, until finally the world was ready to receive the final product: in creation, man; in revelation, the Son of Man. God seems to prefer planting seeds to winding up robots.

So we start with traces of a primitive monotheism among some scattered peoples of the world—which might have been long-faded memories of what Adam told his children about the whole "apple incident," combined with crude deductions that boil down to "Nothing comes from nothing." But mankind pretty much wandered around with no more than that for quite some time, and this was when he employed the inductive method to discover the hemorrhoid god.

The first incident in the Jewish-Christian scriptures that suggests God revealed Himself to us after that is the rather discouraging narrative of Noah. According to the story, the human race went so wrong so fast that God decided to backspace over most of it, leaving only a single righteous family, trapped on a stinky boat with way too many pets. When they landed, they had no more idea of what to do with themselves than the cast of *Gilligan's Island*, so God gave them instructions. We call this the Covenant of Noah.[10] The Jews believe that these are the only commandments God gave to the Gentiles—seven of them, instead of 613—and that the rest of us can please God just by keeping them. That's the reason Jews don't generally try to make converts.[11] The Jewish Talmud lists the seven laws of Noah as follows:

- Don't worship idols.
- Don't kill the innocent.
- Don't steal.
- Don't fornicate.
- Don't blaspheme God.
- Don't eat pieces of animals while they're still alive.
- Resolve your disputes through impartial judges.

Most of this sounds fairly obvious and commonsensical—though we might wonder why it was necessary to tell people to stop pulling off pieces of live animals and eating them. They must have gotten into some pretty bad habits while they were still stuck on that ark.

---

[10] CCC, 53
[11] Who are *we* to run around making things *harder* for people? *Feh!*

22. That ark must have been the size of Alabama . . .

I know, I know.

23. . . . to fit all those elephants, hippos, rhinos, tree sloths, polar bears, gorillas, lions and moose . . .

OK, smart guy.

24. . . . not to mention breeding pairs of more than one million species of insects. Sure they're mostly small, but those creepy-crawlies add up.

Spoken like a true-believing member of Campus Crusade for Cthulhu, complete with a bad case of acne and involuntary celibacy. Maybe you should focus on Onan instead of Noah.

Look, there's a reason why Catholics don't read the bible in an exclusively literal sense, and haven't since the time of Origen (+253).[12] The Church looks at the books of scripture according to the genres in which they were written (history, allegory, wisdom, prophecy, and so on). And this story, clearly, was intended as allegory—which means that on top of some historical content (and there's flotsam from flood narratives in the basements of most ancient cultures), the writer piled up details to make a point. Unlike liberal Protestants, we don't use this principle to explain away Jesus's miracles and the moral law. Nor are we fundamental-ists, who take everything in the Bible literally—except for "This is my body" (Luke 22:19), "Thou art Peter" (Matthew 16:18), and "No, your pastor can't get divorced" (Cleopatra 7:14). The Church responded to biblical criticism with ap-propriate skepticism at first, then accepted the useful parts (like reading original languages and looking for ancient manuscripts) without throwing out the tradi-

---

[12] CCC, 115

tional mode of reading the Bible in light of how the Church Fathers traditionally understood it.

25. Why should the Church be the interpreter of the Bible?

In the case of the New Testament, the Church had transcribed the books; shouldn't we own the copyright to our own memoirs? When the list of circulating gospels and epistles was drawn up, there were more surplus candidates milling around than in downtown Manchester, New Hampshire, before a primary—some of them inspirational but probably inauthentic, like the Protoevangelium of James, which tells the story of Mary's childhood; others creepily gnostic, like the Gospel of Thomas, which has Jesus using His "superpowers" to wreak revenge on His schoolmates. (That gospel is always popular, since it shows Jesus doing exactly what each of us would really do in His place.) The decision about which books were divinely inspired was based largely on the evidence of the liturgy: which books had been used in churches for services in the most places for the longest. As I like to tell Jehovah's Witnesses who come to my door: That Bible you're waving at me was codified by a council of Catholic bishops who prayed to Mary and the saints, baptized infants, and venerated the Eucharist.[13] So you could say that as the original, earthly author and editor, the Church has a better claim to knowing how to read it than do the reporters at *National Geographic*—who every Christmas and Easter discover some new and tantalizing scrap of papyrus containing gnostic sex magic tips or Jesus' wedding registry.

In the case of the Old Testament, the Church draws heavily on how Jews traditionally read their own scriptures—but with one important and obvious difference. We are the descendants of the faction of Jews who accepted Christ as the Messiah and evangelized the gentiles, all the while considering themselves the "faithful remnant" who had remained true to the faith of Abraham. So we see throughout the Old Testament foreshadowings of Christ, for instance in Abraham's sacrifice and Isaiah's references to the "suffering servant." The Jews who were skeptical of Jesus believed they were heroically resisting a blasphemous false prophet who'd tempted them to idolatry. As the Church spread and gained political clout, and Christians began to mistreat shamefully the people from whom they'd gotten monotheism in the first place, there surely was genuine heroism

---

[13] CCC, 120

entailed in standing firm. I often wonder how many Jews would be drawn to Jesus if they could separate Him from the sins committed against their great-grandparents in His name ....

The version of the Old Testament that Catholics and Orthodox use is different from what Jews use today. Our version, based on the Septuagint translation into Greek, is somewhat longer and includes some later documents that Jews accepted right up to the time Saint Paul converted—books that illustrate a lot of the mature developments in Judaism that led up to the coming of Christ. The very fact that Christian apostles were using these books may have led the rabbis eventually to reject them. (Since the biblical reference to purgatory can be found in one of these books, Martin Luther and the Anglicans also excluded them.) Ironically, the Book of Maccabees exists in Catholic Bibles but not Jewish ones, and right up until Vatican II we had a Feast of the Maccabees—which means that you could call Hanukkah a Catholic holiday. But don't tell the judges in New York City or they'll pull all the menorahs out of the schools.

CRORRORRORRORRORRORRORRORRORRORRORRORRORRORRORRORRO

FAQs from Your Stoner Neighbor #2
But if the Christian God exists, that means I can't have sex now.

Assuming you aren't validly married, you raise a legitimate point. You have hit upon what is surely the most common intellectual obstacle to Christian faith in our time, and I really don't know how to help you. Most of the potential spouses to whom I might introduce you are themselves Christian believers, who would likely spurn the opportunity to date an unbeliever—or (worse) might decide to take you in hand and try to "fix" you. I've known the temptation myself, reasoning: "It's a whole lot easier to take an attractive pagan and make her into a Catholic than to find a homely Catholic and make her attractive. Apologetics are so much less painful and expensive than plastic surgery; it's much more humane to change the software than the hardware."[14] The hormonally driven form of Christian witness has been known to work, of course. How many noble Romans were lured into the catacombs by infuriatingly chaste young Christian maidens? Who can count the WASP tycoons who found themselves disinherited for wedding their pink-cheeked, papist housemaids? But I don't think this is what you had in mind here.

Nor is sacramental marriage a satisfying answer to the fallen sexual appetite. For one thing, your options are strictly limited . . . to one. Then there is the striking biological reality: For faithful Catholics, sexual activity has been known to carry unwanted, costly, long-lasting side effects bearing medical names like "Patrick," "Pedro," "Bridget," and "Maria." To the average would-be promiscuous modern man, the Christian view of sexuality emits the same allure as the third bowl of stew and plate of bananas on day six of the Cabbage Soup Diet. If one of the nonnegotiable epistemological principles upon which hinges your response to the proposition of God's existence is the license to have sex right away, and for an extended period, with a long list of different people, without producing still more people whom you will someday have to send to Stanford, then I'm afraid you'll have to try another religion. Have you considered Odinism?

CRBOCRBOCRBOCRBOCRBOCRBOCRBOCRBOCRBOCRBOCRBOCRBOCRBOCRBOCR

26. So the point of the Noah allegory is . . .?

That God, at some point after a serious atmospheric disturbance, ratified the contents of the natural law that men could come up with on their own by offering them a revelation of His will that would apply to the whole human race. Also, this story reiterates one of the nonnegotiable facts underlying the allegorical bits of Genesis: that the entire human species is descended from a common ancestor. Regardless of race, we are all a single family—not something everyone wanted to accept at various points in the twentieth century. In *Humani Generis*, which declared that some forms of evolutionary theory could be reconciled with the Catholic faith, Pius XII especially insisted on this point—having seen firsthand, in the thousands of Jewish refugees he sheltered inside the Vatican, the price of denying it. Furthermore, this covenant is with the whole human race, which is the last time in the Old Testament that God evinces direct interest in the morals of our entire species.

With the next event in revelation history, He takes a sharp turn toward the particular,[15] summoning into existence a chosen people who will enjoy His special interest, receive unique protection, and labor under graver responsibilities than the ordinary run of humans, in their role as a "light unto the nations." I say

---

[14] Not my most edifying thoughts, I admit, but I'm not here to convince the reader that I am a saint—only that he's a sinner, too.

[15] CCC, 72

"enjoy," but of course the experience of being chosen wasn't always enjoyable, a fact that's reflected in a wry old Jewish joke. A rabbi catalogs all the sufferings to which the Jews have been subjected, from their captivity in Egypt and exile in Babylon to their occupation under the Romans and two-thousand-year exile from the Promised Land, and asks God why all this had to happen. God answers, "Because you are my chosen people." So the rabbi says, "Isn't it time you chose somebody else?"

27. Indeed. What's up with that?

There's a strange and intimate relationship that seems to be a by-product of the warp and woof of our world since the fall of man—the link between holiness and suffering. It isn't that misery itself is a good or holy thing (pedophiles are miserable in prison, and bully for that); it's that our willingness to endure suffering for the sake of others is the highest expression of love.[16] There's a mystical side to this that we'll get to later, with Christ's redemption, but you can also look at it from a naturalistic perspective: In a world where entropy reigns, and all things tend toward chaos and destruction, a certain quotient of suffering is inevitable. We can lighten our own load by shifting our pain onto other, weaker people, or we can voluntarily shoulder some of their burdens. If we want to work toward a greater good, we have to give up lesser goods along the way. Think of it as not buying scratch-off lottery tickets but instead saving up to go to Vegas.

---

[16] CCC, 1502

28. So what has that got to do with the Jews?

Who was the man who went alone into the desert to scout out the promised land of Las Vegas? Bugsy Siegel. You think that was an accident?

29. Are you insane?

Just trying to make scripture relevant to contemporary concerns. Call it being "pastoral." But let's get back to Abraham—who started off life as Abram, of course, in the land of Ur, which was located in what's currently Iraq. In the next great moment of revelation, God told Abram to get the heck out of Iraq. (That's something most of us can understand as Americans, isn't it?) God promised Abram that if he would pick up from his home country and devote himself to Him, He would make Abram the father of a great people, whose descendants would be as numberless as the stars in the heavens. And He changed Abram's name to Abraham—just as Winona Horowitz changed hers to "Winona Ryder" so she could become a star.

30. Seriously, cut it out.

All right. Speaking seriously, it is from the Jews alone that we inherited the notion of a pure, just, unitary, omnipotent, and benevolent God Whose demands on us are not primarily liturgical but ethical. The Temple in Jerusalem offered the Israelites some means of showing their devotion and atoning for sin; yet the Jewish law was centered on raising up the standard of man's behavior and restoring in him the tarnished image of God that briefly flickered in Adam: "For I desired mercy, and not sacrifice; and the knowledge of God more than burnt offerings" (Hosea 6:6). To appreciate the centrality of the Jewish contribution to the West, compare the moralizing God of the Old Testament with the divine thugs who eat their young in Hesiod, the tyrants who reign in Sophocles—not to mention the fertility gods who came to reign in Carthage, who insisted on eating *our* young (in the form of first-born infants). Ironically, men like Nietzsche who came to hate the Jewish-Christian morality blamed the Jews for yoking together piety and "slave" virtues like kindness and compassion. Literary observers from Jorge Luis Borges ("Deutsches Requiem") to Walker Percy (*The Thanatos Syndrome*) saw in the Nazi vulgarization of Nietzsche a coherent philosophical impulse: to root this morality out, but leave alive and thriving the impulse to bow down and worship power—in the Nazis' case, that of an earthly dictator. As Borges's highly cultured Nazi torturer writes in his diary on the brink of his execution for war crimes:

> The world was dying of Judaism, and of that disease of Judaism that is belief in Christ; we proffered it violence and faith in the sword. . . . There are many things that must be destroyed in order to build a new order; now we know that Germany was one of them. . . . What does it matter that England is the hammer and we the anvil? What matters is that violence, not servile Christian acts of timidity, now rules. . . . My flesh may feel fear; I myself do not.

It's fascinating to contrast pagan tales, like Gilgamesh and Prometheus, where the gods inflict suffering on humans, with the biblical Book of Job. In the pagan tales, the gods are imperfectly just and fight off man's attempts to grab his share of the cosmic pie. At around the same time, the Israelites were developing a much more refined and mystical view of a much more loveable God. According to Jewish tradition, Job wasn't even an Israelite, just a righteous man who followed God (and Noah's laws) whom the devil afflicted with every imaginable suffering on earth to test his faithfulness. All his friends flocked around him with cheap religious advice, pestering him  with pamphlets that "proved" he must be suffering for his sins—otherwise God would not have allowed it. Surely there must be some secret sin (like Oedipus's incest) that justified all Job's misery, or else he would have to admit that the universe was unfair and "curse God and die." The first half of that argument is moralistic (like those TV and megachurch preachers who hawk a "prosperity gospel"), and the second half nihilistic (like college sophomores in black turtlenecks who decided God was dead when they didn't get into Harvard). Job rejected both arguments and maintained in excruciating tension his own innocence and God's justice—though in the end he did ask God for some kind of explanation. What he got was a voice from the whirlwind proclaiming God's utter transcendence and demanding that Job first explain how the universe had been created, uncode all the laws of nature—particularly, for some reason, meteorology—before He would unfold to Job the mystery of suffering.

31. Not a particularly satisfying answer, is it? Along the lines of: "Shut up, He explained."

If you leave things there, it isn't. If Job had been the last book of the bible, we'd all be Muslims—focusing so narrowly on God's omnipotence that we cannot rationally account for His justice, much less mercy. But what about this possibility: The whole of revelation seems to occur in painfully slow stages, almost as if God were gradually weaning us from milk to mashed-up vegetables, then pureed meat, until we finally had the teeth and the digestion to eat some steak. The mystical significance of innocent suffering was something so central to God's own nature and to His plan for redeeming man that it would require many centuries for God's people to be prepared—and even then, many would choke on it. The figures of Abel and then of Job were the first tiny hints of what God had in mind to do for us.[17] The Church calls them "antetypes," which is biblical jargon for what movie critics call foreshadowing. Think of that scene in the first *Spider-Man* film where Peter Parker watches a spider crawl up the wall . . .

32. Why didn't God simply let us know what He expected all at once—in some all-purpose, ready-made, infallible book?

It seems that he wanted to break the news to us gradually. The shape of revelation reminds me of that old joke about the kid in camp whose cat got hit by a car. His parents are afraid of how he'll react when he finds out, so they dribble out the news over several letters. The first one says the cat is up on the roof but won't come down; the second that the fire department is trying to get it down but isn't optimistic; and finally in the third one they write that the cat fell off and is dead. The kid is very sad, but he's able to handle it. Then the next week he gets a letter that starts off, "Your grandma is up on the roof . . ."

33. So revelation was actually *bad* news?

Let's say it was a sobering diagnosis. We learned, through the stories of Cain and Abel, the Tower of Babel, and Noah's flood, just how exalted God is, how bad the

---

[17] CCC, 117

human condition was by contrast, and what kind of major surgery we'd require before we were ready to join Him again.[18] The news kept getting "worse" as God revealed more and more about Himself and upped His demands—proving to us early on in human history that it's risky to negotiate with a Yahwist.

He started small, as we've seen, with the very modest demands made of Noah. I can get along without eating flesh torn from live animals, and apart from some weirdly cruel Japanese, who insist on eating wriggling lobsters, so can most of us. But with the story of Abraham, God shows us the (slightly scary) level of dedication He's ultimately seeking. That's still not enough, and through Moses He issues the Ten Commandments. Next come the elaborate ritual and dietary laws designed to keep His people separate from the fertility-worshiping, human-sacrifice-happy, temple-prostitute-visiting gentiles who surround them . . . until finally Christ comes and on the Cross shows us the true extent of what obeying God's will can entail.

Not to mention the ethical screws that God feels constrained to tighten: At first He reluctantly tolerates things like divorce and polygamy, even slavery and aggressive war. But over the course of time He narrows the conditions for these practices, demanding that the Israelites treat even their pagan captives with kindness, until with the coming of Christ the concessions to fallen human nature are all revoked, either explicitly or implicitly. The oldest and stubbornest of these evils, slavery, took the longest for Christians to renounce outright, but from the beginning the Church tried to mitigate it and restrict it. (Medieval serfs were a privileged class compared to earlier Roman or later Muslim slaves.) It's embarrassing to us Catholics, but our Protestant brethren were the ones who finally launched the movement to abolish slavery outright, which only really took fire in the late eighteenth century. (The best account of this is a book by my old friend Eric Metaxas, *Amazing Grace: William Wilberforce and the Heroic Campaign to End Slavery*.) At the same time that God increases what He requires of His people, He also extends the definition of who can belong to that group. Instead of simply trying to purify a single tribe, He wants the "good news" proclaimed to every nation. So the apostles must confront the fallen, pagan practices of every tribe on the face of the earth, and face the kind of reception most moral reformers provoke: first guffaws of laughter, then simmering resentment, and then a slow, lingering death. The Romans, whose empire by the time of Christ had enslaved some one in three of its residents, found Christian objections to slavery, prostitution, and infanticide merely ridiculous. They laughed us off, until the Christians refused the central practice that held that tenuous empire together: the organized civic religion that divinized Rome's dictatorial emperor. We see that when Christians resist something politically critical like that, and refuse to go through the motions of worshiping the government, well, that's when the empire strikes back.

---

[18] Imagine God as the doctor of the soul. First He showed us those insurance-agency "ideal weight tables" that they drew up in the 1940s, before the invention of television or Doritos. Then He nudged us onto the scale . . .

34. So that's what provoked Darth Vader to send those Imperial Walkers to the ice planet of Hoth? I'd always wondered that.

Well, now you know.

35. But who would that make Yoda—John the Baptist? Was Simon Peter Jar Jar Binks?

Here we press up against the limitations of analogical thinking. Remember what Aquinas wrote: The similarities will always be exceeded by the differences. He further pointed out in his prescient treatise *De Cinema*, that as part of merely contingent nature, which without the consistent attention of their creators tend toward diminishment and corruption unto nothingness, sequels usually suck. The Greco-Roman view was that mankind began with a Golden Age, from which it was sliding inexorably through Silver and Bronze down the periodic table until it finally perishes in the muck. Traces of this nostalgic prejudice remain in classically educated men like St. Augustine—who finally couldn't reconcile it with the contrary theological truth that revelation had progressed instead of regressed, that God had revealed ever more of Himself until He gave us the fullness of truth in Jesus Christ. Even that revelation becomes not more opaque but clearer over the centuries, as the Church unfolds its implications for human life. For Jews who await the Messiah and Christians who wait for His return, history isn't a spiral flowing inexorably downward into the crapper but rather a militant march of God's own people through time, until He finally intervenes decisively and brings about a new heaven and a new earth.[19] And whatever the eschatological form our world finally takes, there is no place for Jar Jar Binks in it. Of that we have God's assurance.

36. So what was God revealing about Himself when he demanded that Abraham sacrifice Isaac? I've always found that part of the Bible not so much inspiring as creepy.

That is one of the flashpoints for controversy among even Christian interpreters of the Bible. One could easily write a book on this episode alone—as Kierkegaard did, in *Fear and Trembling*.

37. What did he have to say?

He regarded Abraham's willingness to transgress the law against killing the innocent out of obedience to God a "teleological suspension of the ethical," a case where a "knight of faith" like Abraham had to push past the evident dictates of human reason, so beloved of Immanuel Kant, to attain a higher stage of existence.

---

[19] CCC, 676

38. Huh?

Exactly. There are dozens of possible takes on this haunting story, but I'll try to sum up the three most apparently cogent:

The traditional-juridical reading: Man had earned death through Original Sin, relinquishing the mysterious immunity to death and decay that God had granted our first parents.[20] Man's immortal spirit now inhabits a body subject to the same law of entropy, the same diseases and accidents that afflict every other animal. So as both our creator and our judge, God is within His rights in demanding our lives of any of us at any time. Our "right to life" is merely a secular way of restating our duty not to murder each other. Or do you think that God is violating our rights when He allows a tornado to sweep through our town, or a virus to slip through that needle we've been sharing?

39. "I brought you into this world . . . I can take you out."

We call God "Father" for a reason.

The juridical reading goes on to say (pointing to the sacrifices of the Old Testament and that of Christ) that "almost all things are by the law purged with blood; and without shedding of blood is no remission" (Hebrews 9:22). (This is one reason why Abel's

---

[20] CCC, 418

animal sacrifice was more pleasing than Cain's gift of grain.) Hence, God would not have been overreaching or unmasking Himself as a monster if He had, in fact, let Abraham complete the sacrifice of Isaac. But He did relent, and thereby revealed still more about Himself. To the Jews, He showed His generous mercy; and the fact that its beneficiary, Isaac, went on to father the Jewish people means that their very presence in the world is a testimony to God's goodness and love. Dad is putting his belt back on, forgiving us, and sending us back to our homework.

Christians agree, and go even further: They see in the ram that God accepted instead of Isaac a figure of Jesus. Not only will God commute the death penalty earned by Adam but He will also send His own son to pay the price of our sins. If blood must be spilled—and for some mysterious reason it must—it will be Christ's, not ours.[21] That sacrifice, for Catholic and Orthodox Christians, will be reenacted on our altars until the end of time, in unbloody form, as more than a memorial but less than a new event: as a window into the eternity where time all happens at once, and Christ is in some sense always on the cross, and always emerging from the tomb. For tee-totaling Baptists, of course, the Eucharist is merely commemorative and features only grape juice in plastic cups. It's less a sacrifice than a Passion play.

40. That's very ecumenical of you.

It's the cold, unvarnished truth. They'll tell you so themselves, if you can hear them over the guitars and drum sets.

41. Oh, and I suppose you never hear that kind of thing in a Catholic parish?

I never hear more than the first couple of notes. After that I head for the nearest confessional (or the crying room) and whip out my headphones. I call up a Haydn Mass on my Android and say the rosary till it's over.

---

[21] CCC, 606

Now where did we leave off? Right, with Isaac trussed up like a goat and Abraham holding the deer knife. Next we have what I'll dub the *liberal / squeamish* exegesis: Of course God doesn't demand blood sacrifices of us. But we in our fallen humanity feel the need to atone for sinning grievously by committing some act of equal weight. Cross-cultural history shows that in many human religions this means sacrificing some living creature—in some cases, even people. On this reading, Abraham was acting not out of faith and obedience but out of a merely human delusion by trussing up Isaac and preparing to sacrifice him. God acted decisively, at the very outset of Jewish history, to show us that this is not the kind of sin offering He wants. However, because man still craved a means to enact his penitence for sin, God allowed the Jews to engage in animal sacrifice—a practice He put a stop to once and for all with the coming of Christ, Whose death on the cross is a final rebuke to the universal human instinct of finding scapegoats for sin. When we go to Mass, it's a communal celebration of the end of the reign of the Law and the advent of the final revelation of God's true will for us. There's no sacrifice at all, no priest standing in the place of Christ offering Himself to the Father for sin, so there's also no reason why you can't fill the sanctuary with laymen in jogging pants and panchos, and instead of bread and wine use carrot cake and Pepsi. Sunday, the "eighth day," becomes instead an everlasting Fat Tuesday that never gives way to Lent.

Except, as parties go, this one isn't much fun. You wouldn't have picked these people to party with (especially that one, sheesh!), you're all sitting in (padded) pews, and the music sounds like what they play in the waiting room at Bellevue. Which just goes to prove what I've always said: Catholicism is a wondrous religion—but a really pathetic hobby.

Image courtesy Wikipedia Commons.

42. You promised a third option. Please tell me that one exists.

It does, but if you're really offended by the idea of Christ's sacrifice for sin, it's not going to satisfy you. That's a part of divine revelation so deeply rooted in scripture, liturgy, and tradition that if you pulled it out, the Church would be left as little more than a self-help group organized to encourage kindness. Kind of like the Rotary Club.[22] The heretic Pelagius tried to remake Christianity that way in the fourth century, and as the novelist Anthony Burgess pointed out in his best novel, *The Wanting Seed*, what Pelagius really invented was milk-and-water British socialism.

Why bother with affirming apparent absurdities, saying that God became incarnate through a virgin and died under torture, then rose from the dead, all so He could walk around ancient Palestine for three years setting a *really good example*? Besides, if that's your standard, Jesus wouldn't be the first choice anyway. (How about Jimmy Stewart instead?) Jesus wasn't actually all that "nice," come to think of it. He walked around challenging the deeply held religious beliefs of the most devout people in His country, mocking them as hypocrites, intentionally flouting their rules, and claiming divine authority for doing so. If anyone tried to "imitate Christ" in this sense, he'd quickly find himself either shunned as a pathological narcissist or elected to public office. One of the barriers I've encountered in reading the Gospels for inspiration has always been my gut reaction: "This guy had better be God, or else he's the biggest egomaniac in history."

43. Oh, that old argument of C. S. Lewis's: He was either a madman, a monster, or God.

Lewis knew better than to try to do original theology. (There's a word for that: *heresy*.) He was citing an argument that goes back at least to St. Thomas Aquinas. But

it's something that must have occurred to the apostles, don't you think? The Pharisees certainly argued that Jesus "cast out devils" using the power of the devil. As each of the apostles—except for St. John, and Judas of course—suffered persecution, imprisonment, torture, and finally violent death, you'd imagine that this is precisely the doubt that must have gone through their mind. "Am I going through all

---

[22] CCC, 406

this for the sake of a really persuasive charlatan?" Since they all could have saved their lives by simply admitting as much, each of them must have had a fairly overwhelming, first-hand experience proving that such doubts just couldn't be true. Something strong enough to counterbalance the powerfully moving argument of some Minor Asian soldier with pincers ready to skin him alive (St. Bartholomew), or a bunch of inquisitorial Jews ready to toss him off the roof of the Temple (St. James the Lesser).

44. I can't imagine anything that would steel me against that kind of treatment.

Me either. I'd tell them whatever they wanted to hear, skip town, then issue a press release claiming I'd been coerced. These men were made of sterner stuff, which is why God let them be tested. (That's a good argument, come to think of it, for never letting one's stuff get too much sterner, lest you tempt God to make a saint out of you.) But imagine for a moment that we weren't both modern wimps, used to Novocain in the dentist's chair and iPods on the subway to block out the conversations of teenage girls. Even if we were used to day-to-day suffering, the prospect of torture or death for the sake of a religious conviction would cause us suddenly to acquire a much more rigorous epistemological standard of certitude. Some really potent, perhaps even creepy experience like . . . seeing the rabbi we had followed made most definitely dead (whipped till He lost His skin, nailed to a cross, then stuck through the heart and buried) only to run into Him a few days later walking, talking, eating fish, and passing through walls—still with the nail prints in His hands. If I and a dozen other guys had all seen something like that, and we'd had a chance to compare notes so we became convinced we weren't hallucinating, it just might do the trick.

45. OK, what was that third option you were talking about?

It's a more recent way of interpreting Jesus's suffering, another lens through which to see it. It's something the Jesuits wrote about in the seventeenth century as they developed the devotion to the Sacred Heart—trying to win people away from the Jansenist heresy, which pictured God as a stern, remorseless Judge Who saved people or damned them as He pleased, regardless of their merits, including unbaptized babies. (They borrowed this god from the Calvinists, who seem to me to be sharing him with the Muslims. That's what Pope Benedict XVI said at Regensburg that got him in so much trouble.)

Here goes: You don't deny that Christ suffered in our stead to purge our sins (the Jimmy Stewart option). In fact, you insist on that, but you go on to say something else as well. God in His eternity, in the crystalline changeless perfection that we can come up with by reason alone, is incapable of suffering. He is perfectly happy in Himself, and He cannot be grieved when we sin, or even when one of us rejects Him completely and buggers off to hell. How heartbroken would you be if one of the ants escaped from your ant farm to drown itself in a puddle of spilled Mountain Dew? But what if you could shrink down and become one of those ants, like them in every conceivable way (except for their taste for sugar and caffeine), and live in their midst? Without losing access to your human consciousness, you would acquire a kind of empathy for them. Your ant nature, in hypostatic union with your human nature, conjoined but not intermixed in a single person.

46. If your goal here is to make Christianity seem more reasonable, you've got a funny way of going about it.

OK, squash the ants. Christ emptied Himself of the dignities of divinity, became first a helpless infant in stinky, nondisposable first-century diapers, then a manual laborer who belonged to a defeated and occupied nation that had been despoiled by the Romans of all their toilet paper. And their deodorant. He got sweaty and sick, got the runs, was afraid, felt lonely, felt tempted to sin. He suffered excruciatingly at the hands not of God—He wasn't crushed by a falling meteorite—but of the best that mankind had to offer: the purest religion, and the greatest civilization on earth. Both faith and reason colluded to destroy Him, but from the cross He didn't say what you and I would have: "I'll see you in hell!" Instead, He prayed, "Father forgive them, for they know not what they do." Christ learned first hand, in a human nature that was subject to suffering and loss, all the heights and depths of human experience.

He learned most of all what innocent suffering feels like, and in those long minutes on the cross when He felt abandoned by His Father, he changed the very nature of that kind of suffering, the kind Job endured. From that moment forward, every innocent who suffers partakes—whether or not he knows it, whether or not he's a Jew being persecuted by Christians—in the sacred mystery of the Messiah.[23] Even more convenient for, er, careful people like us who will never stand still long enough to be persecuted, He gives us a way to recycle all the day-to-day moments of solitude, sadness, boredom, frustration, and canker sores. If we make the tiny effort of will required to ask God for the strength, we can unite our sufferings to Christ's. Since each of our sins helped press one of the thorns into His scalp . . .

47. OK, now it's all coming out. You sound like one of those Jesuits who scared James Joyce into apostasy and unintelligibility.

Every Lent I try to read *Ulysses*, as a penance. On Holy Saturday, I burn a page to light the Paschal candle.

But bear with me. Since by choosing sin we made Christ suffer—and in some sense He stands out of time, always on the cross, but also always rising from the dead—we can take our own sufferings and use them to comfort Him, on the cross. We can offer Him a sponge full of good wine, not vinegar. Every time we repent a sin or suffer for someone else's sake, we pull a nail from the crown of thorns. Christ's human nature is the living bridge between us and that abstract, self-sufficient god whom Aristotle saw no point in praying to.

48. So the Christian God is a weird hybrid of icy, mathematical perfection and a suffering Jewish carpenter? How do those two things even relate?

Now you sound like one of those eminently reasonable Greek and Roman philosophers who reacted to Christianity as if it were the cult of the monkey fish. But here's where it gets really interesting. It isn't that God has changed, that He used to be a solitary, austic monad floating in eternity, Who after a while decided it was time to grow a human limb. God was never a monad in the first place. The doctrine of the Trinity, which Christians had to develop to make some sense of what Jesus had said, shows us that there has always been a relationship written in God's own eternal nature—a love relationship, one that entails self-giving, even self-emptying. By sending Jesus into the world, God didn't alter His nature but revealed it. When God emptied Himself to become a slave, then that slave emptied Himself for us—in short, He showed us what He'd been up to all along. God took off His mask, if you will, or split the veil.

---

23 CCC, 1521

49. I thought you were about to say that He mooned us.

No. Oddly enough, I wasn't. There's nothing funny about Christ's redemptive suffering on the cross, and if you'd care to step outside and discuss it . . .

50. OK, cool it. Put down that shillelagh. I was just kidding. You don't think God has a sense of humor?

Clearly He does. In creating man and woman, for instance, as natural enemies doomed to mate. Why didn't he make cobras and mongooses such that they had to breed together to make more cobras and mongooses?

When a man wants a brown belt, he buys one—then leaves the store. We watch a single channel at a time, and we don't know how to multitask. I've never heard of a woman crashing her car just because she was trying to put on makeup, talk on the phone, and steer through rush-hour traffic at 75 mph—while I've known guys to rear-end vehicles while pushing a radio preset button. Women crash cars when they're paying full attention—just enough to lapse into deadly indecision. "Will he think I'm a bitch if I try to merge . . . ?" *Kaboom.*

51. Hey, we were talking dogmatic theology . . .

The male mind is a small, solid-fuel incendiary with no moving parts. We're bottle rockets. It's hilarious to overhear women in restaurants speculating about the motives of their men. "When he tells me, 'I'm sick of casseroles,' what do you think that *means*?" They come up with elaborate theories, and all the gals at the table jump in with gusto, taking turns pretending to listen. Women imagining men's complex emotions sound like cat ladies insisting that their tabbies are doing algebra. "He just doesn't know how to articulate it."

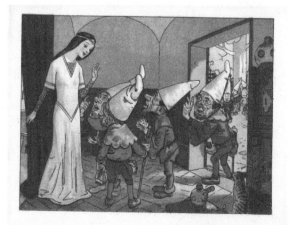

52. . . . but I guess we aren't anymore.

I've offered this helpful suggestion to female friends: "If you're wondering, really wondering, why one of us does or says something—if you're a psychology minor and self-help books don't answer the question, try this instead: Imagine you're Snow White, then pick a dwarf: Sleepy, Happy, Grumpy, Lazy, Dopey, Bashful, or Horny. It's pretty much one of those."

But as you'll discover, if you ever learn natural family planning or watch the Oprah Winfrey Network, women are cuckoo clocks. Body and mind, they're like those baroque timepieces artists used to make for European royals. They have gears and flywheels and pulleys, chains and ratchets and dials. They register fine distinctions, and react to the slightest change of pressure. That's why they can find in a simple male grunt all the subtleties of a chess problem. When we sneeze, they can read our minds. On the other hand, if we get everything perfect, if we study the mechanism and handle it with gentleness and precision, they'll respond to us as the Watchmaker meant them to. Cuckoo! Cuckoo! Regular as clockwork.

53. So that's the whole story of divine revelation?

Yes, I think we can end it there.

The Father

1. OK, so we've worked our way through the uncounted millennia between the emergence of man and the first glimmers of revelation, then the six-thousand-something years it took God to gradually tease out what he had in mind for mankind. On the face of it, the whole thing seems suspicious. Why go through all these fits and starts? Why feed us a series of tantalizing hints, to spice up a steady diet of red herrings and dead ends? Why—if God is so simple, perfect, and benevolent—did he reveal himself to mankind through a series of clues it would take Sherlock Holmes to figure out? Or, if it pleases you, Father Brown?

Elementary, my dear godson. What we've derived so far from considering revelation is (a) that God is in Himself a perfect unity, but also (b) that His essence is in some sense refracted, as if one ray of light were passing through three distinct lenses, each of which is a Person.[1] That tells us that the primitive rational insight into God's unity was true but incomplete. Likewise the original revelation of the One God to the Israelites. Within the very essence of God is a nexus of relationships, which He revealed is one of love between a Father, a Son, and a Spirit Who "proceeds" from their interaction. Already, then, there's something embedded in the very essence of things that tests our brains till they bleed. Add in the intellectual jiu-jitsu required to account for Christ's divine and human natures—a doctrine that'll tackle us later—and it almost seems as if God's purpose all along in revealing Himself to man was to provoke complex heresies, interminable Church councils, and impenetrable tomes in Greek and Latin devoted to explaining the inexplicable.[2]

No wonder so many different sects emerged over the centuries, each devoted to seizing one piece of each of these mysteries and making sure it wasn't forgotten—at the cost of denying something else

---

[1] CCC, 65
[2] Note to self: Was it?

of equal importance. Remember the joke about the blind men describing the elephant? One grabs the trunk and declares it a snake, the next the leg and calls it a tree, et cetera? That joke was first told at the Council of Chalcedon by Bishop Pachasinus of Lilybaeum to Anatolius, patriarch of Constantinople.

2. Really?

Strictly speaking, no. That story probably goes back to ancient India. But it was applied to specifically Christian religious disputes by the poet John Godfrey Saxe, who wrote:

> So oft in theologic wars,
> The disputants, I ween,
> Rail on in utter ignorance
> Of what each other mean,
> And prate about an Elephant
> Not one of them has seen!

3. So you're admitting that the Church has spent centuries tussling over a tangle of logical contradictions in search of a plausible story?

If only it had. Then maybe we'd have one. My life would be a lot easier, and this book would only need to be a pamphlet. Like modern physicists who wrangle with the equally persuasive but mutually irreconcilable claims of relativity and quantum mechanics, the Church was presented with evidence that was devilishly difficult to understand all at once, much less to reconcile. Our theologians used the best tool at hand, Greek philosophy,[3] to tease out the real-world implications of what God had told us about Himself, to figure out how we should pray and to whom. If what we had been trying to craft was a cogent fable, we certainly would have lopped off one manageable piece of that enormous, intractable elephant and held it up as the whole: "Behold the trunk of God!" Heresies have always been simpler and more persuasive than nuanced orthodox answers. Orthodoxy, like reality, is tediously complex when you try to account for all the details. Like math, it's hard. Like surgery, it's work, and lazy, clever people who breezed through high school and aced the SATs are tempted to turn instead to magic. Marlowe's Dr. Faustus grew weary of ancient inconclusive books and tedious experiments, so he sold his soul to gain technological power on the cheap. Heresy, magic, and pragmatism alike skim over reality lightly and read the Spark Notes instead.

Aside from plastic tanning beds and the self-reproducing nanorobots that someday (some hope) will smother the earth in "grey goo," there's nothing new under the sun. The heretical temptation goes all the way back to Adam, nibbling at Satan's sour apple in search of easy answers. When Alexander the Great faced the impossibly complex Gordian Knot—whose legend foretold that the man who untied it would rule over all Asia—the king forgot his Aristotelian training,[4] pulled out his sword, and cut through the knot. With a single stroke, he became the first great heretic in the West. He did conquer Asia, most of which his feuding heirs—devoid of any rationale for why they should rule—would promptly lose. Now, all of us who watched Indiana Jones take the pith out of a showoff Saracen swordsman with a single shot

will sympathize with Alexander. There's a reason for that: You and I are moderns and grew up with a gut admiration for crudely pragmatic answers. Since Francis Bacon and Rene Descartes, like General Sherman and P. T. Barnum, we believe that what's true is "what works." Anything else seems un-American.

Heresy works. It gets things done, damn the consequences. (Dam the river, and damn the fish.) It's easier to rally a band of Visigoths, Arabs, or Ivy Leaguers with a streamlined creed that fits neatly on a banner. In politics as well, coherent political philosophy frequently loses out in the short run to ideology—that is, to a half-baked idea holding a fully loaded pistol. Marxism, fascism, and anarchism are each better suited to pamphlets than are the worldviews of Edmund

---

[3] CCC, 39
[4] That lucky king was actually home-schooled at the great philosopher's knee.

Burke, Russell Kirk, or G. K. Chesterton. Orthodoxy, by contrast, can seem pedantic and plodding. It always amounts to statements like "Wholly (a) but also wholly (b), without confusion or distinction."

It shouldn't surprise us that orthodoxy is complicated, in the same way that science is puzzling. We start off with a God Whose internal relationships are by their nature beyond anything our neurons are wired to savvy. Let's imagine, to make it easier, that He exists in more than three dimensions. If we lived in Flatland, with only two dimensions, and encountered a sphere, we could never perceive the whole thing at once. We couldn't even imagine it. As it passed through our plane, we'd see first a point, then a series of curves that expanded for a while, then contracted until they turned again into a point. Our theologians would tear out their hair and each other's beards attempting to explain the thing, and the best they would come up with would be profoundly unsatisfying formulas—none of which did justice to the felt experience of those who had seen the mysterious passage of the sphere through Flatland. By which I mean, the apostles. To them it was a miracle that demanded to be announced throughout the world. They could hardly contain themselves and were literally on fire (see Pentecost) to share with others its power to transform their lives. But to offer an account that will make sense to other Flatlanders, they would need to do more than enthuse, safely handle poisonous snakes, or even speak in tongues. They would need to learn geometry.

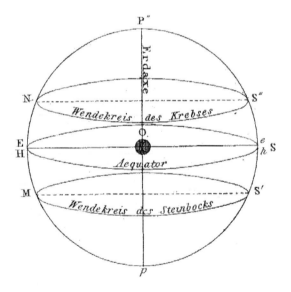

That's the best way to conceive of philosophy, as the two-dimensional science of space we use to account for the way things work in our world. Theology is the discipline that tries to account for the third dimension, despite the fact that all its practitioners still live solidly just in two. Before the Christian phase of revelation, there was no real need for theology; in the Greek and Roman world, the philosophers and the priests had nothing to talk about and would eye each other suspiciously in the street. Among the Jews, a few like Philo attempted to account for the God of Sinai in language drawn from Plato, more to help the Hellenized Jews in places like Alexandria avoid intellectual embarrassment than to convince more Hellenes to be circumcised (which anyway was, as St. Paul would point out, a very hard sell). Without the third dimension that blasted its way into the world with Jesus, philosophy must remain a fairly tepid enterprise: an attempt to show men how to live wisely within their limits, avoid self-destructive vice, and treat each other justly before their souls disappear like pet fish down the toilet.[5] Without the stern discipline of philosophy, religious enthusiasms must end as they always had before: at best in the rigid rectitude of the Temple and the Law; more often in secret, Dionysian rites designed to "save" the few by whispering shibboleths whose meanings were long forgotten; in orgiastic frenzies, which like Woodstock are much less fun than they sound; or in the fanatical life-denying practices of gnostic cults, whose "sacraments" included suicide and abortion.

Now add in the fact that man is fallen, and our reason functions like a 1980s-vintage American car—in fits and starts. (If you doubt this fact, go sit sometime in a faculty lounge and listen to the academics speak past each other, cover their asses, run down each other's research, and squabble over parking spots.) We've already agreed that man's religious sense is every bit as prone to go astray as his erotic urges—even when he doesn't somehow confuse the two and dirty up heaven with a string of myths that reflect his unexamined fantasies of incest and cannibalism.

These facts, the irreducible complexity of what God has to say for Himself, man's limited rational faculty, and the power of our passions to cloud how we think, could account all by themselves for the fact that God's revelation to man would most likely happen not all at once but instead through a series of stages mediated by human history. But there's another reason that occurs to me.

4. Feeling prophetic, are we? Is this a new stage of revelation I'm witnessing right now?

Prophets typically fast and pray. What I do is think fast, and pray that what I write makes some kind of sense. That's a critical difference. Besides, all public revelation ended with the death of St. John the Apostle. That's when God stopped adding to the great ball of yarn and left it to the Church to untangle and knit into a sweater.

5. How far along are you?

By my reckoning, we've just about finished one sleeve. I have friends who are wistful millenarians, who see in every Church crisis, ecological catastrophe, or

---

[5] My older sisters always dried my tears with the theory that, when they reached the ocean, those guppies would rise again, but I suspect that their hypothesis was somehow imbued with a Christian bias.

innovative social perversion solid evidence that we're in the "end of days," when the final persecution of the Church will give way to the Second Coming. To which I say, "You wish." I reckon that we have ahead of us thousands and thousands more years of mediocrity and muddling through. (Which is just as well—there are still so many old episodes of *The Dog Whisperer* left to watch.) You think things are bad today, that they couldn't get much worse? Think again. Use your imagination, or better yet, drink a dozen cans of Red Bull mixed with vodka, then sit down to watch the director's cut of *Blade Runner*.

6. I'm sure that your counsel consoles them.

It silences them, at least. Now, back to my private theory of why divine revelation has passed through human history like a rabbit through a snake: because God is an artist, and slow, organic development seems to be essential to His style. All that we've learned from geology about the antiquity of the earth, from biology about the slow development of animal species, and from physics about the mind-numbing spaces and times encompassed by the universe, points to a Craftsman Who works not in action painting but scrimshaw.[6] Such information, which upsets biblical literalists so badly, in fact seems to echo the text of Genesis, which lays out "days" of unspecified length—St. Augustine in the fourth century opined that they might be eons—and breaks out the act of creation into slow, incremental steps that culminate in man. We could say the same of the fact that animal species evolved from one another in increasing orders of complexity right up to very high primates that seem to have been the "dust" from which man was made. The question most often contended between the advocates of mechanistic evolution and those who see God's hand behind the paintbrush is typically stated this way: Can we believe that

blind and random mutations of DNA—which in organisms more complicated than fruit flies more often result in cancer or deformities than new and "adaptive" traits—gave rise to all the exquisite complexity of life? But the real gut revulsion we theists feel when atheists insist that life is random centers on man himself. We might, just might, be able to wrap our minds around the idea that nothing but blind chance lay behind the different tail markings on subspecies of skunks. But is that also the origin of our minds?

PUNCH'S ALMANACK FOR 1882.

MAN·IS·BVT·A·WORM·

[6] CCC, 337

7. If that's what science tells us . . .

The reason we trust the answers science gives us more than we do pseudonymous e-mails from the Philippines offering "herbal" treatments to regrow amputated limbs is *the power of experiment*. The root of scientific certainty is the sheer predictive and explanatory power of lab experiments, where we limit the variables and repeat the same process a thousand times to figure out which factors were the critical ones. Until we develop a time machine, there is absolutely no way for us to test what will happen randomly over millions of years—which means that the kind of science that claims to explain past events that can't be repeated or tested is radically different from experimental chemistry. It's really a species of philosophy—which oddly enough is what they used to call subjects like biology and geology: they were subsets of "natural philosophy." And given that we aren't contesting lab results, philosophical arguments start to matter. We have switched the remote control from *CSI: Staten Island* to *Law and Order: SVU*, and expert witnesses are going to have to take the stand.

There's a basic problem with the theory that our minds are merely the latest tumor that grew because of imperfectly replicating chromosomes: It seems that our minds are a reliable guide to truth. Not just to the kind of thing that animal brains are good at perceiving—for instance, when my beagles Franz Josef and Susie spot a skateboarder, then follow my training and attack. No, our minds produce unique things that generate abstractions, like language, that other human beings can understand and act upon. They can use those abstractions to figure out not just what is useful for survival but also what is true, what is really out there in the world. Among those assertions is the theory that . . . our brains are the mere result of random evolution, and our very thoughts are likewise accidents of electricity. I remember sitting in a hotel in Baltimore listening to an unrepentant social Darwinist "break some bad news to the theists in the room." With a sardonic smile he explained in a plummy British accent, "Within ten years or so, neurologists will have proved that all human thoughts are determined not by free will or conscious intention, but by the random firing of neurons across our brain's synapses. I'm terribly sorry, but there it is."

Ever the peacemaker, I leaped up in the question period to ask whether every single human thought was the by-product of bioelectric sparks in the grey meat between our temples. "Absolutely," he said.

"Including that one?" I asked. "Is your perception that these scientists are reliable equally random? How about the thoughts that are in their minds when they read the PET scans and write up scientific papers interpreting them? Either their assertions are not random brain farts but reliable guides to truth, in which case their theory is wrong—or if their theory is right, then they can't possibly know what is true or not, because their very thoughts are random, meaningless events like a rock rolling down a hill."

The speaker frowned. "I don't understand your question."

"No," I concluded genially. "You don't."

8. All right, enough of your private theories and victory anecdotes. I'll admit for the moment that the sheer size and awkward shape of the "rabbit" that God meant to reveal required a very long snake that stretched out for centuries. But what exactly emerged at the end? What are we meant to know about God after all?

OK, we've already brushed up against the mystery Christians call the Holy Trinity. The notion is that God is at once perfectly unitary—as He had revealed Himself to Abraham and Moses—and yet His unity is composed of three equal, coeternal persons with distinctive attributes: the Father, the Son, and the Holy Spirit.[7]

9. Did the Father create the Son?

No.

10. Is the Holy Spirit the only one who's a holy? Or a spirit?

No, and no.

10. So how helpful exactly are these terms? Why don't you people pick something more descriptive?

Because we didn't pick these terms, and we didn't think any of this up. Believe me, if this were a merely human invention, it would make a lot more apparent sense. But like a team of puzzled scientists who happen upon what appears to be an alien ship that has landed in Central Park, Jesus's followers had to deal with the evidence they were given: the things Jesus said about

---

[7] CCC, 253

Himself and this intangible Holy Spirit, and then the things they had seen that confirmed those statements. For example, Jesus claimed to be co-eternal with the Father . . . and to prove it, He rose from the dead and disappeared into the sky: *Check!* Jesus promised that the Holy Spirit would come and abide with the apostles . . . and right on schedule, tongues of fire appeared over their heads and taught them to preach the gospel in dozens of alien languages: *Check!*

The apostles, who handed on their understanding of what Christ said, some of which ended up in the four Gospels, weren't trying to create a new mystery religion with secret rituals that conveyed some intangible, numinous gestalt that was ultimately obscure. In fact, they didn't have much use at first for the pork-eating, uncircumcised, statue-worshiping, naked all-male wrestling fans they met in places like Athens and Alexandria. Their core audience for the message that Jesus was the Messiah was the people who actually knew what a Messiah was and had hoped for one—the Jews. And that was one group of people who had learned the hard way (through exiles, invasions, plagues, you name it) to shun every form of idolatry and stick to straight-ahead monotheism. If there had been any way to spin what Jesus had said about Himself that would have made it less offensive—for instance, if the apostles could have asserted that He was just an angel or a prophet—they would have done so. It would have made their mission not just easier but also safer. There would have been no reason for inquisitors like Saul of Tarsus to come along and stone men like St. Stephen to death.

But thanks to the puzzling words of Christ, and the bizarre events that confirmed them, they didn't have the option of being tactful. Instead, St. Peter was moved to share with his fellow Jews what they surely considered "too much information":

> "Men of Israel, hear these words: Jesus of Nazareth, a Man attested by God to you by miracles, wonders, and signs which God did through Him in your midst, as you yourselves also know—Him, being delivered by the determined purpose and foreknowledge of God, you have taken by lawless hands, have crucified, and put to death; whom God raised up, having loosed the pains of death, because it was not possible that He should be held by it." (Acts 2:22–24)

11. So the Trinity is the best theory you people could come up with to account for the data?

You could put it that way. And yes, it's strange and paradoxical, but so is string theory—which even its leading advocates admit they can't explain.

12. Do you understand string theory?

No, but neither do they. That's basically how theologians feel about the Trinity. If you come up with an explanation that goes much deeper than "It's kind of like a shamrock," congratulations! You have happened upon a heresy. It reminds me of French; if you don't sound like you're coughing up a lung, you aren't pronouncing it right. And Parisians will pretend not to understand you—as if you were trying to explain the Holy Trinity.

13. So it all comes round right in the end?

The last end. In the next life, we're told, we'll have a better *feel* for the Trinity, but we still won't comprehend it. But by then, we really won't care.

14. Hah! We nonbelievers already don't care.

To paraphrase that old gangster Leon "Icepick" Trotsky, *You may not care about eschatology, but it cares about you.* Pascal wagered that it was worth at least attempting to believe, in case it might all be true. There is presumably no atheist after-world where those who were foolish enough to believe will live to regret it.

15. So your argument boils down to just that—a threat? When logic won't heat up that gumbo of oddball assertions you've thrown together, whip out your Bic and apply a little hellfire to the brew?

Not us. Remember that Pascal was a Jansenist, who thought unbaptized children (along with all non-Catholics, and most Catholics, too) were damned. The Church teaches that honest unbelievers, who have plumbed the deep questions and somehow come up empty, may be in for a very pleasant surprise. But there's still some value in what that mystical mathematician said: If you come across plausible arguments that life *might* have a purpose, underwritten by a Person who wishes you well and wants to infuse your existence with meaning, how much sense does it make to dismiss the possibility—to assume the worst, in effect, because it makes life seem a little easier? That's a typically modern solution, like dosing the water supply with Soma.

16. Soma?

You know—Prozac? Soma is the generic version they make in England. It's put out by Huxley-Aldous LLP.

17. Well, well. Look who was doing all the reading . . . in ninth grade.

Actually, I was jumping back and forth between reading Jacques Maritain and listening to heavy metal bands practice in guys' garages, but yes . . . I did end up finishing *Brave New World* back then. High school freshmen really are the wrong audience for a book that warns against a future society based on sloth, rampant sex, and technological hedonism—at the price of giving up Shakespeare, Milton, and the character virtues one gains by enduring suffering. Like everyone else at Mater Christi Catholic High in Queens, all I wanted to know was, "Where do I sign up?" Much better to read that novel once you've turned thirty or so and burned your fingers a few times on the electrified cookie jar called "Life."

18. And who was it that rigged it with electrodes in the first place?

At last our considerations bring us to speak of God the Father. Not that He wired us that way in the beginning. In many respects, our brains and bodies retain the healthy connection we see in animals between what we want to do and what we should. Man was constructed such that his strongest pleasures—eating, having sex, asserting dominance—were linked to things that serve each one of us and our species. But Original Sin got into our mental computers like a virus, so now we want those good things at the wrong time, in the wrong way, or in vastly greater quantities than is good for us.[8] We've got all these pop-up windows we don't know how to block that direct us to sites like *Thyneighborswife.xxx* and *Allbaconallthetime.com*. You know those experiments where they rigged up rats so they had to choose between cocaine and food? The poor buggers just sat there with their paws on the lever for "blow" like senior citizens at Atlantic City slot machines, till they finally starved to death. That remains my enduring image for fallen human nature.

[8] CCC, 407

19. Well, to banish that mental picture, why don't we talk about God the Father. Why does the Church insist on continuing to use that exclusionist, patriarchal title for God? Aren't feminists right to complain about that?

On balance, I'm unlikely to admit that feminists outside Saudi Arabia or polygamous Mormon compounds are ever right to complain. Feminism[9] is to women what Marxism was to workers: a paint-by-numbers guide on how to screw the group you'd intended to help. Look at every society that has adopted feminist tenets and applied them to the relations between the sexes, and what do you see? Plummeting rates of marriage and more divorces, more abortions, more single mothers rearing kids in poverty, but plummeting birth rates .... Let me turn the question around on you: If feminism were a scheme invented by covetous dolphins to wipe out the human race so they could inhabit our empty cities, *how would it look any different?*

20. Wow, that was inclusive. But for the moment, let's leave aside women who are angry they can't be priests. Couldn't some earnest, faithful Catholic woman feel excluded by the fact that whenever any member of the Holy Trinity is mentioned, the male pronoun is used?

Yes, that could certainly happen.

21. Then what is wrong with updating the language of prayer and theology a bit—maybe using gender-neutral words and pronouns?

You mean like *parent* and *it*? Let's see, "Our Parent, which art in Heaven, hallowed be Thy pseudonym."

22. OK, that doesn't sound very personal or welcoming, but you get the idea.

I do, and it's a dreadful one. The effort of the American bishops in the 1990s to neuter the language of the Bible for Sunday readings resulted in texts so robotic that Rome

---

[9] By this term I mean the ideology that emerged in the mid-twentieth century with Simone de Beauvoir, whose countless, infinitesimally different variants dominate women's studies departments and emptying convents across the country. Those Christian women who wish to call themselves "pro-life feminists" or "new feminists" will get no argument from me. I hope that each one of them meets a nice "anarcho-monarchist" and settles down in the suburbs.

stepped in to stop them. In more recent news, in 2010 the Holy See intervened and imposed on the English-speaking world a version of the Roman Rite whose text had been rendered in our tongue by the weirdly old-fashioned process of *taking the words in Latin* and *translating them into English*. Of course, all the liturgists were appalled.

23. But what if the traditional language confuses or offends people?

What if people decided to grow up? Or at least grew thicker skins? The reality of a fallen world offends me all the time—should I demand that the Church transform it into the magical realm of Equestria so I can live with My Little Pony? It's long past time to replace sensitivity training with Callousness Training^{sm}, where we rub people the wrong way with sandpaper till their tender membranes turn into tortoise shells. Come to think of it, that's the hidden agenda in all my books.

One more thing: It's not as if the sexual imagery inscribed in Christianity is uniquely designed to freak out feminists. Each of us is called to a tender, intimate love relationship with an all-powerful masculine God, in which the human takes the role of a surrendered, receptive bride. As a street-fighting, straight guy from Queens, how do you think that makes me feel? If anything, traditional language concerning the divine (or "God-talk," as some have crassly thought it clever to say) seems suited to assuage women's emotional needs, not mine. I got over it. So can you.

People who get all sniffy about sexed language in prayer and scripture are really offended by sex itself—the messy, fertile, dangerous, infectious fleshy business that's dripping with hierarchy, power struggles, conquest, and surrender. None of that scary stuff fits their Kantian fantasies of themselves as packets of rational data trailing behind them infinite gossamer strands of individual rights. I'll offer you proof: The almanac I edit while wearing my other (non-Tyrolean) hat, *Choosing the Right College*, has documented that at one of America's elite universities, that dreary hedonism compound still called for some reason Wesleyan University, the Student Assembly:

> is constantly pressing the administration to implement gender-neutral housing for all students. A WSA resolution states that since "gender and biological sex are separate and distinct concepts" and "the historical rationale for same-sex roommate assignments is based upon antiquated heterosexist assumptions and obsolete concerns," incoming freshmen should not be excluded from the right "to define their own gender and make housing decisions, irrespective of that definition."

Just to prove they mean it, a student organization, the Wesleyan Trans / Gender Group, sent out a memo to every student, teacher, and staffer at the school insisting that students replace he / she / him / her with "ze (subjective) and hir (objective and possessive). For example, 'I was talking to my friend Kris earlier. Ze told me that hir paper was due tomorrow, and it was stressing hir out.' Some students prefer to be referred to with gender neutral pronouns, and many students prefer to use gender neutral pronouns in papers instead of the universal he."

Which inspires me . . .

24. No. Please don't.

. . . to offer a less-offensive version of some key lines from the Song of Songs:

> [3]As the apple-tree among the trees of the wood, So is my beloved among the offspring. I sat down under hir shadow with great delight, And hir fruit was sweet to my taste. [4]Ze brought me to the banqueting-house, And hir banner over me was love.
>
> [5]Stay ye me with raisins, refresh me with apples; For I am sick from love. [6]Hir left hand is under my head, And hir right hand doth embrace me.
>
> [7]I adjure you, O daughters of Jerusalem, By the roes, or by the hinds of the field, That ye stir not up, nor awake my love, Until ze please.

Works for me. Let's try it with the rest of the Bible!

25. So your reason for rejecting nonsexist language is aesthetic? My, aren't we persnickety. Are you one of those forty-something, Latin Mass–acolyte "daughters of Trent" with a fetish for lace?

Beauty ain't everything, but it's not nothing. How else can we explain why people show up to hear what Angelina Jolie has to say about Sudan? On a deeper level, beauty points to truth, and ugliness celebrates error. Compare the buildings of Catholic Habsburg Vienna to the Stalinist monstrosities of Moscow, or the ritual of a papal Mass to North Korean gymnastics exhibitions. I really could go on all day.

26. I have no doubt of that. So what is this "truth" you're talking about?

The history, psychology, and theology behind the title God "the Father." First of all, we call God "Father" because that's the title He gave us to use.[10] God describes

---

[10] CCC, 270

Himself in the Old Testament as overwhelmingly paternal rather than maternal, and other places—Hosea, for instance—depict God as a husband who mourns while patiently waiting out his wife's adulterous "walk on the wild side." In fact, one of the most profound metaphors in all of Jewish theology is that of Israel as the Bride and God as the Bridegroom. The Church took that up, and we call the Church (among other things) the Bride of Christ.

27. Shouldn't we see that language as the fruit of the patriarchal culture in which the Jewish revelation took place? The expressions of religious devotion that arose in such a context would naturally be distorted, even constrained, by what the people were willing to accept.

Whereas our culture is free of distortions, so what we come up with will be more truthful than the phrases a bunch of dusty old Jews used in the desert? Our computers and our dentists are better than Moses's, so our prayers must be better, too? C. S. Lewis called that attitude "chronological snobbery," and it reminds me of an old saw—"The Past is another country." If it is, then we are the Ugly Americans, swaggering through the chapel taking flash pictures and knocking over the statues, complaining about the humidity and the lingering "peasant smell."

There's a wistful feminist theory[11] out there, popular among people with M.A.s in Jungian psychology who run conferences like "Women Who S***t with the Bears," that human culture began with a primeval, egalitarian matriarchy, then "fell" into patriarchy and capitalism. Despite the complete absence of evidence, let's for the sake of argument say that's true. Then God had plenty of other options for peoples to choose beside the *muy macho* Hebrews. "She" could have revealed Herself to one of them. Or if no matriarchies existed, "She" could have created one. That's one of the perks that come with omnipotence.

Then of course you have the fact that Jesus Himself called God "Father" rather than "Mother." That's the kind of argument from authority that isn't terribly popular nowadays, so let me reconfigure it in a way that appeals to modern man. Imagine if the U.S. Supreme Court had dictated, in a 7-to-2 decision (with only Ginsberg and Sotomayor dissenting), that we should call God "Our Father." That would make it

---

[11] Which they took from Marx's collaborator Friedrich Engels, in case that grants it even more credibility.

part of the law of the land, a settled decision, an integral part of our "living Constitution." So let's just pretend that's what happened and move the argument along.

28. So you're hinting that God intentionally chose a patriarchal people, and used masculine language on purpose, to make some deeper point about Himself and His relation to the created universe?

I never hint. That's for people from a higher social class. I'm flat out *saying* it. There is something much deeper entailed in the Fatherhood of God than the side effects of social repression in early Semitic culture. In fact, if I thought that the way we imagine God and the very name we use for Him had been so distorted by crassly human sexual politics that we were obliged—in the light of all we've learned from Gloria Steinem—to change it all, I'd develop grave doubts about the whole enterprise of divine revelation. If it's not the tree of life but merely some rubber tree plant that our forefathers twisted all out of shape so that it's our job to set it straight . . . well maybe we ought to pull it up root and branch and put a nice artificial ficus there instead. I could be won over to the cult of Progress, or Humanity, or even the Flying Spaghetti Monster—the last of which would at least explain why we're all so addicted to carbs . . .

29. And this deeper meaning of the Fatherhood of God amounts to . . . ?

OK, I'll need to introduce a little philosophical jargon here, so you might want to fire up your Keurig.

Now, the two words we'll need to make sense of in this profoundly important question are *transcendence* and *immanence*.[12] To transcend something means to rise above it, not be in any way dependent on it, to look down on it like a diver on a swimming pool. To be immanent means you are intertwined with it, engaged with it, either dependent on it or at least vulnerable to it. We are immanent in the market economy, in the country of which we're a citizen, in the city where we live, in the

---

[12] CCC, 1028

airport where we're taking off our belts and shoes. Now, looking at the God described by the philosophers and revealed in the Old Testament, would you say that this God fundamentally transcends the universe or is immanent in His relation to it?

30. Well, a watchmaker doesn't live inside the watch, and even an architect who designs his own home can leave it. If the first cause is itself uncaused, then its link to the rest of the Chain of Being seems kind of tenuous.

Not tenuous but voluntary. In other words, God chose to create a world separate from Himself. He didn't give birth to it, but planted it. He made it, and by choice He is present throughout it. His creation of man was a free choice, like my decision to write this book—not an inexorable necessity, an emanation from God's being that simply had to come out, as a baby must someday emerge from a pregnant woman or else both of them will die. A transcendent God can choose to take dips into immanence, to whatever degree and in whatever way He wants. A God who was immanent in the universe would not be free to transcend it from time to time, any more than I can "opt out" of the human condition. Such a God would be more like the pantheistic deity some ecologists choose to believe in, less a personal God than a nebulous force like Gaia—a name for the sum of all forces in the universe. No wonder the very feminist theologians who want to see women ordained, and like to call God "goddess," also subscribe to a smushy pantheism. Instead of strictly delineated sacraments, they want to find "the sacred" in stones and shrubberies, in manatees and stagnant pools full of algae.

31. So you're saying that motherhood is too intimate a bond to describe God's connection to the world?

Almost. Fatherhood can be tender and intimate. But men don't carry babies inside their bodies, they cannot nurse, and they can always pick up and leave. As so many dads do nowadays.

32. So fatherly love is less instinctual?

For better and worse. Once he has dropped his batter on the griddle, a man can walk away from the process of reproduction in a way that women (whose bodies *are* the griddle) really can't—and that's precisely what pro-choice feminists have been trying to change by giving women a spatula, so they'd have the same "freedom" to opt out that men have always had, and too often have used.

The point of all this is that God's love for us is free, His involvement with us is not hardwired into His nature, and He would go on existing even if the universe winked into nothingness. Meditate on that for a while, and you might start to feel some old-fashioned sentiments like "awe" and "the fear of God." Keep at it, and you'll start to experience gratitude, dependence, and docility. Those are the feelings that God made it clear He expects out of us.

33. God wants us to be "docile"? I don't like that much . . .

You know who else didn't? Adam, Eve, Cain, Noah, Abram, and every other fallen human being in history. I'm sure that sinners have always chafed at the idea of God as a masterful Father, prone to mercy but capable of wrath. No wonder we have found so many creative ways to reimagine the divine in some other form that's more appealing to our rebellious natures: a thundering, flummoxed adulterer who's a "player" on earth but gets henpecked at home; a dim and distant watchmaker who wound us all up and forgot us; or a hot fertility goddess whom we can commune with through pious visits to temple prostitutes. And sometimes, instead of wishful thinking or wanker fantasy, man's religious imagination instead fell into despair. Looking at the endless rounds of births and deaths, and the savagery of nature, men projected into heaven not their hopes but their darkest suspicions. That's how we invented the bloodthirsty gods of the Aztecs, the child-consuming fertility god Moloch, and the hideous, many-headed Norse Frost Giants who would someday consume the world and even the gods. Those are the kinds of deities we invent all on our own—gods who embody the various genres of movie offered by Netflix: Action (Thor), Adult (Ishtar), Gay / Lesbian (Apollo), Romantic Comedy (Zeus), and Science Fiction (Gaia).

Compared to the prospect of trying to believe in and placate one of *them*, I'd say that learning how to be docile before a loving Father really isn't half bad.

The Son

1. Transcendence, immanence, and docility to an omnipotent Being who's at once transcendent and immanent—somebody save me!

Perhaps Someone did. At least that's what we contend concerning the next Person of the Trinity, Whose career on earth was the occasion for all the complexity of which you've been complaining. Of course, there were any number of theories concerning who and what Jesus was, both among His contemporaries and those who claimed to have followed Him. Perhaps, since Christ breached in a unique way the wall between God and man, eternity and time, spirit and flesh, we shouldn't go at this question from the top down but the bottom up.

2. Since you're saying that the ineffable God now *had* a bottom—one his mother had to wipe—that seems fair enough.

You might be attempting irreverence, but try again. The Church made a huge point of insisting on this herself. During the Renaissance, in fact, Christian artists baptized the new upsurge of humanism by laying a heavy emphasis on the fact of the Incarnation. The Word became flesh, real flesh, and God became man—not mankind in general, but one male child in particular. To press home this point, they did a whole series of Madonnas-with-child where Our Lady is pulling back the drapery to reveal that her Son is a healthy, completely human and clearly Jewish human male. As Our Lady would surely have testified, Jesus had dirty diapers,[1] while Satan prowls the earth, a pristine spirit, seeking whom he may devour.

3. Let's move on to something more spiritual, like the nature of Christ.

We can't. We have to stick with the sticky, sweat-and-blood flesh of Jesus and Mary for the moment.

4. Why, for heaven's sake? I thought that what we were talking about was religion.

Precisely. We humans can't get to the spiritual without going through the fleshly—that just isn't how we were made. The story of God's descent into the immanence

---

[1] The Greeks have a recipe for these, which they call *Diples*, that does not, alas, call for chocolate.

of the world, and his expansion of the plan of salvation from a single tribe to every human soul, begins with a virgin birth. Or so the Church has believed since the beginning—that Mary was a virgin when she conceived and remained so for the rest of her life.[2] Those two points were taught infallibly at councils several centuries later, but they are based on Gospel accounts that were written while eyewitnesses and gossipy neighbors were still around who could have contradicted them. Some Jews, appalled at Christian "idolatry," came to write in the Talmud that Mary was impregnated by a Roman soldier. But they put that story out several hundred years later. Think of it as damage control.

5. Why is this issue so important such that you people never even mention Mary's name without appending "the Virgin," as if it were her academic title? Not that there's anything wrong with being a virgin, I guess. But why treat it as such an honor—one you seem to equate with Mary's also being sinless, unless your church secretly regards not being a virgin, and thus sex itself, as somehow evil? Or at least imperfect . . .

You aren't as wrong as you sound.

6. Uh, thanks.

By which I mean that there *are* key truths that stand or fall on the historical fact of Mary's lifelong virginity, which I'll explain in a minute. But there is also a strain of Gnostic contempt for the body that pre-existed Christianity, which the Church couldn't quite wipe out, that comes to the surface in the strangest ways, sometimes centered on Mary. It doesn't poison the Church's real teachings, of course, but appears in popular superstitions and heretical filigrees that well-meaning prigs have added on to her story. For instance, there was a widespread belief in the Middle

---

[2] CCC, 499

Ages that Mary hadn't just been conceived without sin, but also without sex. According to the story—which some[3] find uplifting but that turns sane people's stomachs—the hitherto barren, aged St. Anne miraculously conceived the Virgin Mary after a chaste kiss from her husband. This notion came from a noncanonical book, the so-called Gospel of James (or Protoevangelium), which was written around 145 and seems to have been a grab bag of third-hand knowledge and pious fancies. As often happens, the Holy See was eventually forced to be the buzzkill and sift out which traditions had roots in apostolic times and which were simply invented to make for a better story. In 1677, even as he approved the then-theory that Mary had been conceived without Original Sin, Pope Benedict XIV condemned the "chaste kiss" story as historically baseless and "kind of creepy." This Church decision reinforced the fact that sexuality was neither a result nor the cause of Original Sin. Of course, since the sex act (when done right) generates new people complete with—you guessed it—Original Sin, it's easy to see how the ideas got confused in the popular mind. Of course, if this theory were true, then test-tube babies would be free of sin. In much the same way, many Catholics used to think priests were automatically holier than laymen[4] simply because they were celibate.

7. Wow. Thanks for getting us past all the earthy stuff.

The point of the Incarnation is that we'll never get completely past it. God made the material universe (as He judged it) "good" in the first place, and made our bodies as they are—except that they weren't constantly falling apart from age or getting gnawed to pieces by tigers. Original Sin didn't transform us from perfect spheres (as some Neoplatonist heretics held) into hairless apes. All it really did was take away our antioxidants and our Kevlar.[5] Then Christ came into the flesh, which made it not simply "good" but sacred, and when He rose from the dead He brought the first flesh into heaven. Our Lady went to join Him at her Assumption—but they were just the king and queen. At the general resurrection, God will gather in all of us rooks and pawns and knights as well. He wants a complete set, you see. Till then, till the world ends and is made new again at

---

[3] I.e., people with obsessive-compulsive disorder or contamination phobias.

[4] Yes, Virginia, people used to think that, instead of (sadly) the contrary.

[5] This bulletproofing material is not to be confused with *lekvar*, which is a Slavic sort of jam that is meant to fill *kolaches*, pastries served at Czech and Slovak weddings. The mistake is easy to make, but it leads inexorably to dead cops and inedible cookies.

the Second Coming, the souls of the dead (damned and saved) are bereft of their bodies and incomplete—the equivalent of the pieces in blindfold chess, which you play in your head.[6]

By making the fleshly sacred, Christ also raised the stakes and made fleshly signs like virginity and marital love *more important* than they had been before. Now marital sex was not simply a mitzvah (a double mitzvah on the Sabbath) but also the ordinary means of sanctifying grace in one of the seven sacraments. Likewise, virginity went from being merely a biological signal ("sealed for your protection") to a way of showing unique dedication to God. Christ's own virginity, which was very unsettling in a rabbi, echoed His

Image courtesy Wikipedia Commons.

mother's—and vows of celibacy were a way for Christians to make their entire lives into a witness of faith in the afterlife. Because otherwise—who would bother?[7]

So it isn't that we rejected a Jewish conception that sex is good for a Christian theory that it's evil. That's a primitive misunderstanding, held by the uninformed,

whose model of a faithful Jew is Gina Gershon or Larry David. The Old Testament wasn't written down by people who practiced the faith of Abraham by eating bagels and voting for Democrats but by fierce monotheists who fought off the vile fertility cults that surrounded them by refusing to eat with, talk to, or even touch the tainted Philistines. Adultery and sodomy were punishable by death—along with a long list of other things, including witchcraft. I'm glad the Hillel at Bryn Mawr doesn't try to revive that particular stricture; it would plunge that Wicca-friendly campus into civil war.

No, the Christian difference is that after the virgin birth sex became *more* sacred—which means that it had greater power for both good and evil. [8]

---

[6] If you're an obnoxious showoff.
[7] CCC, 922
[8] CCC, 2362

8. So why insist on the virgin birth?

Well, most obviously because (and I don't mean to sound like a Hardshell Baptist here), *it's in the frickin' Bible*. Plain as day. There's a long narrative explaining in painful detail how an angel appeared to Mary and told her something impossible would happen, and how her fiancée Joseph reacted—by nodding at her and smiling as he slowly backed out of the room. Can't you hear him saying to himself, "Boy, did I dodge *that* bullet," as he logged on to Jdate.com? It took another angel (appearing in a dream) to convince him otherwise—that this was the child not of man but of God.

Christ's existence began with a miracle that wedded God to a woman. She represented the whole human race from that moment, and her "fiat" to the angel (rendered by the New American Bible as "OK, whatever you want") was the inversion of Eve's decision to obey the snake.

So Mary was mystically wedded to the creator of the universe, and Joseph saw her, needless to say, in a very different light. This was not your average marriage. For that very reason, I've always been confused by priests who held up the Holy Family to ordinary couples as a model of behavior. What can a regular Joe Schmo Catholic husband really gain from imagining that his wife is a sinless virgin and his kid is the adopted son of God? What *part* of that is supposed to be helpful?

9. Can you tell me why on earth it matters whether Mary remained a virgin, instead of having subsequent children with Joseph?

OK, whatever you want: Because God's union with Mary was a marriage and not some (Zeus-like) one-night stand, it was sacramental and indissoluble. Mary wasn't simply some useful, dispensable vessel, but a "type" of redeemed mankind, united again with its creator. Her single-minded devotion to Him, and to her Son, is the model for every Christian life. The fact that she could have told the angel "No" marks Christianity off in a radical way from pagan accounts of gods consorting with human women. It also connects to the Church's insistence that man's will is free and God's grace can be resisted. Adam and Eve were free not to fall, and Mary was free not to help pick us up again. Ironically, while Jesus would be tempted, He could not have sinned; the Virgin Mary could have. She simply didn't. In one way, that's more impressive. [9]

10. So that is why Catholics and Orthodox make so much out of Mary?

That and the fact that she keeps appearing to us and giving us messages from heaven. Which also makes a strong impression.

I'm tempted to leave it at that, but there's actually a truth we haven't touched on that is much more important than apparitions or even virginity: the fact that the Virgin Mary was conceived without Original Sin. This has been believed far and wide since the early Church, but there were always plenty who dissented. The Immaculate Conception really stuck in the craw of important theologians—like St. Thomas Aquinas, and with him the whole Dominican order. This question provoked fierce arguments among Catholics well into the eighteenth century, remaining one of the deal breakers dividing Catholics and Orthodox. And Protestants want no part of it, since it goes against their emphasis on the "total depravity of man" (the Calvinist Synod of Dort) and seems on the face of it to say that Mary didn't need to be redeemed by Christ. So, pious as it sounds, maybe this teaching is more trouble than it's worth.

But the Bl. Pope Pius IX considered the Immaculate Conception so essential that he proclaimed it solemnly in 1854, then sixteen years later called the First Vatican Council to define the infallibility of the pope (we'll get into that in chapter 5). Of all the things that very emphatic pope ever said, the only one he pointed to as infallible was his declaration that Mary was sinless from the moment of her conception.

Our Lady seemed to agree. Her 1858 apparition at Lourdes centered on what she told the shepherdess St. Bernadette: "I am the Immaculate Conception." Bernadette had no idea what she was talking about—not being quite up to date on the theological literature of her day. (Rural French academic libraries still aren't up to snuff, by the way, but that's a horse of a different feather.) But Bernadette faithfully repeated to the bishop what must have seemed to her incomprehensible jargon, and the phenomenon of Lourdes helped convince those Catholics who still had their doubts.

Let me anticipate your objection here: We can all agree that Jesus's mother was a heroically virtuous woman. St. Thomas and his allies would even stipulate that Mary never committed a personal sin. So what difference does it make whether we attribute Original Sin to a bunch of replicating cells inside a uterus? Couldn't we say

---

[9] CCC, 973–975

that Jesus wiped that guilt away from her on the Cross and leave it at that? And that is, in a sense, exactly what we do say: *That Mary needed Jesus's sacrifice just like everyone else.*[10] Without it, even she couldn't enter heaven. But there's more going on here than meets the eye, something so subtle but significant that we have every reason to look over Our Lady's ultrasound.

The Church sees Jesus as the new Adam who reverses our tragic ancestor's rebellion through His obedience. Both His human and His divine natures accepted the Father's will and rebuilt the bridge between earth and heaven. If Jesus had been solely divine, his sacrifice wouldn't have helped us. If He had been merely human, it wouldn't have been enough. Because both things were true, His sacrifice more than sufficed—in fact, it poured forth enough grace to save the human race many times over, (the only proviso, sadly, is that we must say "Yes" when it is offered). But looking at Christ as our role model has its problems: For one thing, we cannot possibly conceive what it was like to possess both a human and a divine nature. For another, we know that Christ was incapable of sin. Christ's mission impossible, which He chose to accept, and in fact accomplished, is one extended divine initiative from start to finish.

The only thing the human race contributed to the process came from Mary: She gave Jesus human flesh, and she did that by consenting to the Incarnation, by freely saying "Yes" to the angel—even though he conveyed to her (tradition teaches) the full extent of what her decision entailed, all the suffering she would watch her Son endure. Could an ordinary daughter of Eve, weighed down by Original Sin, have freely made this kind of decision before the source of sanctifying grace had even opened its spigot? Isn't it more plausible to think that when the angel called her "full of grace," he meant it—that she was in fact as spiritually pure as Adam and Eve had been to start with? That would make her the first human being to know this kind of freedom since the Fall. It would also resolve the question of how Mary could have given Jesus His sinless flesh if her own was already tainted. Since sin (for St. Paul) is passed along in the blood, we clearly needed a miracle here. But when did the miracle happen? Was Jesus mysteriously immune to the sin that remained in His mother's flesh, or did "full of grace" imply that she was herself made without the fatal flaw our first parents introduced into our DNA? That was what Pius IX taught, that the grace of the Cross didn't so much heal the Virgin Mary as vaccinate her (although he didn't put it quite that way). In fact, I wonder if Pius IX even approved of newfangled practices like vaccination. But he never condemned them ex cathedra, so it really doesn't matter.[11]

---

[10] CCC, 491–492

[11] In fact, it is Pius's predecessor Leo XII whom historians credit as banning vaccinations in the Papal States—except that they are fibbing. Anticlerical gossip that found its way into anti-Catholic textbooks attributed this law to Leo, but there is no evidence of it in law books, or anywhere else—as Rev. Daniel O'Keefe, S.J., documents in the *Fellowship of Catholic Scholars Newsletter*, September 1986, where he exposes the use of this imaginary vaccination ban by Catholic supporters of contraception, artificial insemination, and the use of extraterrestrial DNA in cloning experiments.

Why does any of this matter? Because of the way the Church has, from East to West, universally up to Luther, viewed the function of divine grace as restorative: God pours His blessings on us through Christ to repair in us the effects of Adam's sins and our own, and then to infuse us with His own nature:[12] hence the ancient (and at first a mite disturbing) maxim *God became man so man might become God.* The tortured, scrupulous Luther couldn't see what effect all his fervent, sincere devotions and penances were having on his bad habits (whatever they were), so in order to stave off despair, he invented an entirely novel theory of justification: The sacraments, prayer, even the most lavish outpouring of grace by whatever means, do nothing to alter man's profoundly corrupt and tainted nature. Not even God can (seemingly) redeem that. No, what Christ does is

take our place at the judgment seat and offer His own seamless garment in exchange for our filthy rags. Christ's sacrifice doesn't gradually or even suddenly transform our corruption, but instead He covers it up like (in Luther's words) a fall of snow on a pile of dung. In regard to the Immaculate Conception, then, we'd be saying, in essence, that Christ took His sinless flesh from a snowy, white pile of . . . shite.

Instead, the Church believes in the promise that Christ came to renew mankind—to rehabilitate and restore him, not simply to issue a pardon to an unregenerate criminal. The figure of Mary, granted by a special favor the same clean slate as Adam and Eve, serves if you will as the fertilized cell, the embryonic start of the new human race.

11. Are you sure she isn't a goddess? The way some of you people like to pray to her instead of to God would suggest that not everybody got the memo.

That objection is typically raised by Protestants, not pagans. The latter don't typically care if we worship tree stumps carved into gnomes so long as we aren't praying to the God of Abraham, Isaac, and Jacob, and the typical West Village atheist is a lot more comfortable with Santeria than sanctity.

But it's kind of you to bring the issue up. If you're wondering why Christians got into the habit of asking the Virgin Mary to add her prayers to our own, there are several causal explanations of how it may have happened—which isn't the same thing as an explanation of why it makes sense. Too many apologists for religion hear the first question but

---

[12] CCC, 1999–2005.

answer the second, which makes us seem to you all as if we're blowing nice halo-shaped smoke rings up your skirts. Which isn't the sort of thing I'd ever do, if only out of fear of an explosion. Let's start with the factors that likely gave rise to Marian devotion:

- Judaism's conception of God is starkly transcendent and hence masculine, for the reasons we laid out in chapter 2. But . . .
- there are qualities of excellence that are specifically feminine that God must possess—such as tenderness, nurturance, and an intimate concern with the particular. We see little glimpses of this side of God in what Gerard Manley Hopkins called the "dappled things" of nature ("skies of couple-colour as a brinded cow . . . fresh-firecoal chestnut-falls; finches' wings . . . all things counter, original, spare, strange"). This level of love for detail can suggest a Divine artisan, of course—but sometimes, when nature seems especially welcoming and wonderful, as on a crisp New Hampshire October morning, it also evokes an infinitely gracious hostess who thought of absolutely *everything*. And He does think of everything, and everyone, all the time, with infinite tenderness. So . . .
- we yearn for a way to picture these qualities in the divine economy, without blurring or distorting God's transcendence (as feminine images of divinity historically have, and it seems psychologically must). Happily . . .
- while we don't have a mother goddess, we *do* have the Mother of God—by which I mean the early Church had her, still tooling around the planet for years and years after Jesus ascended to heaven. She was even present at Pentecost. While there isn't any record of her trying to boss around the apostles, we can be sure that she gave them advice—reminding them what her Son had really said, explaining what he'd meant, and when they got things wrong, gently kvetching until they corrected it. Then something very strange happened, namely . . .
- her life ended, as everyone else's has since the Fall. But when the apostles looked into her tomb, it was mysteriously empty.[13] Having witnessed her Son raised from the dead and ascended into heaven, they concluded that she'd been assumed. This belief dates back to the earliest days of the Church;[14] there is no record anywhere of anyone claiming to have her remains—though any ambitious bishop would have been strongly motivated to say so, given that it would have turned his cathedral into the greatest pilgrimage center on earth. Can you imagine how many Filipinos, and Univision media vans, would be lined up around the block of such a shrine? Given how comparatively minor saints like Francis Xavier found their incorrupt bodies pulled to pieces by holy collectors, and Italian towns have fought bloody wars over the ownership of really *primo*

---

[13] CCC, 966

[14] The dogma of the Assumption was only declared infallibly in 1950 by Pius XII, but he was simply ratifying a belief that we see recorded in prayers and icons dating from the ancient world. He was moved to affirm this ancient teaching, some say, by rumors of the Sputnik program and the need to beat the atheistic communists into space. See *The Bad Catholic's Guide to Good Living* (2005) for how to throw a NASA-themed Assumption party to mark the Vatican Space Program.

relics, the fact that nothing like this ever happened concerning Our Lady is literally a miracle. That's the least implausible explanation.

Since the Middle Ages, theologians with lots of extra time on their hands have speculated that what happened to the Blessed Virgin suggests how Adam and Eve might have left the earth if they hadn't sinned: a painless, seamless trip up into heaven, to make room for all the fruit that they'd gotten busy multiplying.

So, given her decisive role in the salvation of the human race, the fact that her body was assumed into heaven, and the widespread belief from apostolic times that she had lived free from sin, it was only natural that Christians focus their prayers on Mary.[15] Instead of worshiping an incestuous fertility goddess like Isis, Christians asked for prayers to the one God from the Blessed Virgin Mother—a simple Jewish girl whose power came from obedience, whose grandeur was woven out of humility. Given that she was purely and simply human, but free from sin, she makes a much more plausible model for imitation than Christ—for those of us, that is, who aren't here to work miracles or preach a bold new gospel.

Now, for any Protestants who are still reading at this point, I'd like to point to a firmly biblical precedent for asking Mary to intercede with Christ: His very first miracle, at the Wedding of Cana, took place because His mother noticed that the wine casks were running dry. Christ's public ministry dates from this festive event—and if you remember the story, when Mary asks for something, Jesus brings out the best.

12. OK, so that may be *how* Marian devotion developed. Now why do you think it makes any sense? If Christ came as the bridge between God and man, why do we need an additional intermediary? Is Mary the on-ramp?

After five years of trying to merge onto highways and bridges in the teeth of autistic, Hobbesian New England drivers, that metaphor doesn't make me feel warm and fuzzy, but it isn't bad. What Mary accomplished once through biology, she continues in theology. But there's much more to it than that. If the regeneration of man could take place only by the unimpeded choice of a human being to cooperate with grace, that says something profound about what God wants to accomplish. He wants to rebuild our species from living bricks, to center the new covenant like the old on man's free response to the offer of love. That's the only way it makes sense to say that each of us chooses his own

---

[15] CCC, 969

fate for eternity. Otherwise, God would be on the hook where Calvin hung Him, arbitrarily choosing whom to save and whom to damn—a deity no more admirable than any number of pagan gods. Instead, we have the God-man giving men the chance to take part in His divinity. Tragically, for some, He will take "No" for an answer.

CRITICAL CRITICAL CRITICAL CRITICAL CRITICAL CRITICAL CRITICAL CRITICAL CRITICAL CRITICAL CRITICAL CRITICAL CRITICAL

FAQs from Your Stoner Neighbor #3
What if Jesus was really a benevolent space alien from an advanced civilization who came to teach the human race how to live more peacefully before our species developed advanced weapons and became a threat to the rest of this sector of the Galactic Federation?

Yes, I saw that movie too: *The Day the Earth Stood Still*. There are probably half a dozen episodes of *Star Trek* (in various avatars) that play with the same idea, and I've heard this hypothesis argued with deadpan sincerity by an ex-Catholic schoolboy living in Hollywood who wanted to justify his lifestyle of hooking up with aspiring actresses.[16] And if that's the extent of your interest in the question of Jesus's nature and mission, it's as good a rationale as any—better, surely, than the standard post-Christian answer (believed by the kind of people with "Coexist" bumper stickers on their Priuses), which says essentially that Jesus was someone with

- deep Rogerian insights into the wounded "inner child" each of us carries within us;
- advanced, tolerant views on religious pluralism;
- enlightened ideas about sexuality and self-expression;
- a passion for income redistribution through progressive taxation and social welfare programs;
- a plan for resolving the Arab-Israeli conflict amicably; and
- a really cool, authentic Peruvian *chullo* handwoven in the Andes by members of a self-sustaining, nonprofit co-op, just like the one I bought at the Unitarian church.

History and scripture suggest that Jesus had none of these things.

---

[16] He also claimed to have been at one time a high-ranking CIA agent—recruited so young he had to drop out of tenth grade—with consequent access to gray-market sources from which could smuggle into the country high-powered, highly profitable "natural magnets," if only I would supply him with the start-up capital . . . .

Nor is there any direct evidence that He arrived via spacecraft, used advanced technology to perform any of His miracles, showed any interest in reforming the political system He found prevalent in the Earth civilization where He found Himself, or warned the Romans against pursuing research on nuclear fission. Indeed, it seems clear from His few recorded statements concerning politics ("My kingdom is not of this world," "Render unto Caesar what is Caesar's") that Jesus was primarily concerned with asserting His special intimacy with the God of the Israelites, demanding that Jews look to the spiritual essence of their rituals and laws, and deflating the self-righteousness of pious frauds—all by way of preparing to serve as a perfect sacrifice for sin. Indeed, the only event in the Gospels that could even benefit from being filmed by Steven Spielberg would be Christ's ascension into heaven.[17] That part, at least, seems to fit your E.T. theory—but fails to explain why the friendly alien would bother going through with the charade of a crucifixion and a resurrection. Why not simply beam up a message to the mother ship right after Judas kissed Him on the cheek? And if Jesus really was a brilliant alien visitor with advanced scientific knowledge and a mission to spread peace on Earth, why didn't He give His followers a few more tangibly useful pieces of information—like the secret to avoiding outbreaks of cholera? Or a really solid warning to the Jews not to keep on rebelling against the Romans? In that case, His last words on earth would not have been "Follow me" (John 21:22) but rather "Resistance is futile!"

Of course, the other-worldly nature of what Jesus came to do—make reparation for sin and set up a sacramental system for men to commune with God—had many this-worldly effects, most of them salutary. While Jesus did not hand His followers a textbook in basic science, the Christian worldview as it developed did in fact convince philosophers that the material world was important (since God had not only made it but also come to dwell in it) and intelligible to reason (since Christ was the Logos). That broke them of the Platonist and Gnostic contempt for matter and laid the groundwork for medieval scientists like Hildegard of Bingen and Albert the Great to begin empirical science, conducting experiments with a daring and dedication unknown to the greatest thinkers of antiquity.

Likewise, while Jesus did not preach pacifism, His admonitions against vainglory and vengeance offered a starkly different model from that of classical heroes like Achilles and Alexander. Had Christians not been forced to struggle with hard sayings like "turn the other cheek," it's doubtful the world would ever have known the "just war" theory that now prevails (in name at least) through most of the world—which St. Augustine first articulated. [18]

Again, the first world civilization ever to think there was something wrong with slavery and strive to abolish it was Christian Europe—though thanks to Original Sin, we took our sweet time getting around to it.

---

[17] OK, and the Book of Revelation. That just cries out for *Raiders of the Lost Ark* treatment, and full-on IMAX 3-D. Too bad that when somebody finally gets around to filming it, the movie will star Kirk Cameron as Jesus and have a special effects budget of maybe $30,000.

[18] CCC, 2309

For that matter, the status of women rose higher in the Christian world than it had ever stood in the West. The Church was the first religious institution to insist that marriage must be consensual, divorce was sinful, and polygamy was evil. Those who'd like to attribute these advances to some mysterious force of inexorable "progress" should explain why the next world religion to come on the scene, Islam, accepted none of these innovations.

All of which is to say that Jesus was not in fact the monolith planted by aliens in the midst of howling apes in *2001: A Space Odyssey*. Sorry, man.

CR⅏CR⅏CR⅏CR⅏CR⅏CR⅏CR⅏CR⅏CR⅏CR⅏CR⅏CR⅏CR⅏CR⅏CR⅏CR⅏CR

13. Well, if he wasn't a benevolent space visitor, who was Jesus anyway? I can't make sense of any of this.

Welcome to the welter of enthusiastic confusion historians charitably call "the early Church." When bishops and theologians plunged the intellectual world into hundreds of years of controversy, heresy, and celibacy, they weren't just logic chopping or working toward theories that offered intellectuals some deniable plausibility. No, they were trying to account for *events as they had unfolded*. The apostles did not transmit an ancient myth (like that of Orpheus) or weave a web of speculation (like the Stoics), but reflected on recent current events. Imagine them as veterans, returned from a war, gathering to tell their stories. With Bill Moyers on PBS.

So in order to gain some understanding about the nature(s) of Christ, let's start with the different responses people had to Him while He was alive. These broke into just a few categories, namely those who thought Jesus was:

(a) Some earlier prophet, such as Elias or John the Baptist, come back from the dead. Since there was no broadly accepted Jewish idea of reincarnation, this was a real nonstarter.

(b) The Messiah the Jews had expected, come to throw out the Romans and lead Israel to military dominance over the world, from which God's people would impose a reign of peace and justice, shining as a "light unto the Gentiles." This theory—which in retrospect we might call the neocon heresy—seems to have peaked in Jerusalem on Palm Sunday and taken a major nose dive sometime on the night of Holy Thursday, when Jesus told Peter to sheathe his sword.

(c) A demon who cast out devils because he was himself the lord of devils. The Pharisees who condemned Jesus to death for blasphemy told themselves that this was what they believed—though that raises the question of why they believed a diabolical spirit was something the Romans could kill with a cross. Did they think He was a vampire?

(d) The anointed of God, Whose mission and nature were turning out to be something quite different than anyone had looked for. He had, apparently, come to announce His divinity and to die, and to somehow offer His body and blood to His followers so they could live forever. This was the incomplete account Simon Peter had pieced together from what Jesus had said in the course of three years—all of which seemed to fall to bits on the night Christ was arrested, to the point that the first pope denied Him three times. These were the first of many noninfallible pronouncements.

With the shocking turnabout of the Resurrection and the gifts of the Holy Spirit at Pentecost, the apostles were able at last to agree on, and start preaching, theory (d): They came to believe at once that Christ was the human Messiah promised to the Jews, and the "Logos"—a Greek term St. John's Gospel used for Christ, which is so rich with meanings one could spend an entire book unpacking them. Translated roughly as "the Word," Logos also refers to reason itself, to meaning, and indeed the very principle of intelligibility in the universe.[19]

Of course, this apostolic account was the most unlikely and unsatisfying of the four, introducing as it did apparently endless logical obstacles. Sadly, it was the only one that fit the facts, so the Church was compelled to stick with it. Not every Christian in subsequent centuries would prove so deferential to the evidence. Later attempts to prune the truth down to a streamlined travel size would result in what historians call the Christological heresies. To highlight how central these issues are to every form of orthodox Christianity, I'll cite as my source for them not one of our old warhorses like Hilaire Belloc but a modern Protestant scholar, Millard Erickson of Baylor University. In his phone-book-sized tome *Christian Theology*, Erickson taxonomizes the heresies according to the aspects of Christ's Incarnation they deny or get all muddled:

• The **Ebionites**. According to the *Catholic Encyclopedia*, there may have been Ebionites without an Ebion; the term comes from the Aramaic and means the "poor men." This epithet appears in the works of Church Father Origen, who wrote of these dissenters, "Those poor men! *Bless their hearts.*" But the term may go back further and indicate that this group clung to the austerities practiced by John the Baptist. The Ebionites were Jews who accepted Jesus as a messiah and moral teacher but not as the Son of God. These people disappeared in Palestine by the fourth century, only to rise again in nineteenth-century New England as prosperous Unitarians who took over Harvard.

[19] CCC, 438–445

- The **Arians**. There was an Arius, and he was a brilliant, highly educated priest. A classic academic, he insisted on the primacy of theory over evidence.[20] In theory, God the Father's oneness could not admit of other Persons or a Trinity, so no matter what Christ in fact had said about Himself ("Before Abraham was, I am"), it could not mean He was fully divine. An infinite gap divides the transcendent deity and the fleshly world of men, and Jesus was a sort of demigod, a theological centaur who offers us pony rides to the Father. Arius's ideas dispensed with several pesky mysteries, simplifying theology in much the way Pol Pot would someday streamline urban planning. Soon crowds were fighting this theological controversy out in the streets, attacking bishops and driving them into exile, until the still half-pagan emperor Constantine was so alarmed that he called the Council of Nicaea to resolve the question. Imagine a U.S. president locking up the U.S. bishops until they finally decided if limbo existed and you have some idea how well this turned out; controversies continued for centuries, as variants like semi-Arianism emerged, and Arian missionaries took their slimmed-down, simplified creed and sold it to invading armies of Goths.

These black-clad, mascara-eyed hordes of Germanic EMOs would soon be persecuting orthodox Christians in France and Italy. Still, we got the Nicene Creed out of that council, which also featured Santa Claus (St. Nicholas, bishop of Myra) slapping Arius in the face.[21]

- The **Docetists**. This group dates all the way back to the time of the apostles and consists of those who were quite convinced that Jesus was divine—and therefore not human at all. The fishermen who claimed that they'd seen Him, eaten with Him, and like Him made use of reeking first-century restrooms had been looking at an illusion—a Jesus suit that God had worn in order to talk to the miserable earthlings. Hence the name of this heresy, which translates as "Illusionists." Christ, as the greatest magician of all, had pulled off the slickest act in history—even pretending to be crucified. How did He do it? Come on, magicians never reveal their tricks! (Though some claimed that Simon Magus, the possibly legendary founder claimed by the group, had been nailed up in Jesus's stead, while Christ sat behind a tree cackling.) The Docetists weren't motivated so much by the awkwardness of reconciling divinity with humanity; they didn't get that far. Convinced by the Gnosticism that permeated the Mediterranean world,[22] which believed the flesh was itself intrinsically evil—the creation,

---

[20] CCC, 465

[21] Reports of St. Nicholas's filling Arius's stockings with coal appear to be apocryphal.

[22] Contempt for the body and hence the material world, unsurprisingly, is perennial in sweaty climates where people eat spicy, gassy foods.

in fact, of a bumbling or evil Demiurge from whom the higher God wished to save us—the Docetists refused to believe that the Creator of the spiritual world would taint himself by inhabiting human meat. Starting with this premise, many Docetists came to agree with another group, the Marcionites, who held that the God of the Old Testament was in fact the evil Demiurge and that the Jews were his despicable servants, from whom Jesus came to rescue us. (Others who'd claim that mankind needed rescue from the Jews would in the 1930s try to rehabilitate Marcion as a father of the Church, casting Christ as an Aryan sent by Odin.[23]) The Gnostic impulse never quite went away but instead crept underground, eventually bubbling up like a sulfurous spring in France with the Albigensians[24] and poisoning the sex lives of married Irish Catholics well into the 1970s—when they began to ape the rest of the West in flipping the Gnostic pancake to the "funner" side, where sex is not condemned, merely procreation.[25]

- The **Apollinarians**,[26] named for the bishop Apollinaris, who was once the friend and follower of Athanasius—the greatest enemy of the Arians. Eager to prove them wrong, but like them unable to leave well enough alone, Apollinaris determined to square the Incarnation's circle by insisting that Jesus was fully divine but only partly human. He had a human body and emotions, Apollinaris allowed, but lacked a rational human mind. That part was helpfully supplied by—you guessed it—the Logos, which was essentially operating Jesus of Nazareth as a sock puppet. This heresy was quickly condemned by all Apollinaris's old friends, but it also makes its appearance among us again in curious ways—for instance, among theological

---

[23] Or something. The toxic, murderous fantasies cooked up by the neopagans and pedophiles who pioneered Nazi ideology are hard to disentangle. Roy Schoeman does a yeoman's job in his recent *Salvation Is from the Jews*.

[24] A similar heresy arose in medieval Bulgaria with the Bogomils (also known as the Buggerites), who preached the sort of sex that didn't (ahem) generate more fleshy humans. The next time you tell someone to "bug off," keep in mind what you're asking him to do.

[25] CCC, 285

[26] CCC, 471

conservatives so eager to fight off modernist doubts about Christ's divinity that they imagine Jesus omniscient in the cradle, even the womb. It's impossible to conceive of such a Jesus ever really experiencing childhood, growing in age and wisdom, ever feeling surprised or afraid—in short, being really human.

- The **Nestorians**,[27] who also went astray through misplaced zeal, fighting off one error by inventing yet another. Nestorius started off as a heresy hunter, celebrating his consecration as patriarch of Constantinople by ordering an Arian chapel torn down. (At least he didn't renovate it, replace the altar with an ice cream table from the Marble Slab, and fill it with gruesome modern art; as I said, he had good intentions.) But Nestorius hailed from Antioch, whose theological tradition was so committed to countering Arianism that it made too sharp a division between Christ's divine and human natures. To emphasize the fact that Christ was truly God, Nestorius began to preach against the most beloved epithet for the Virgin Mary: *Theotokos*, or God-bearer. Mary, he insisted, was the mother only of Jesus's human nature, which Nestorius thought was somehow stapled, but not really glued, to His divinity. This position did more than wall off the danger of Jesus as Arian Superman; it suggested something more like *The Man with Two Brains*. Or at any rate two identities, only one of which we should worship as God. In his intellectualist attempt to whittle the mystery down to size, Nestorius seems to have quipped, "No one can bring forth a son older than herself." The one thing you should avoid in Christological controversies is cleverness—especially concerning a title like *Theotokos* that pops up throughout the very liturgy it's your job to lead each Sunday. It's a little like having a U.S. president who chuckles sarcastically every time he uses the word "democracy." It leaves a bad impression—

or at least it did to the churchmen of Constantinople, who already hated Nestorius because he was a foreigner from Syria.[28] Local clergy who'd vied for Nestorius's job complained to the pope, who read Nestorius's statements and condemned them. Attempting damage control, Nestorius pressured the Byzantine emperor to summon a council at which he could vindicate himself—but instead it denounced him. Still convinced he had been misunderstood, Nestorius rejected the council's authority. Deposed from the second most powerful diocese in the Church, he was driven like first baseman Bill Buckner from the community, to die in exile in the desert. His theories went on to be popular in

Goat

goat. 2.

person who tends

---

[27] CCC, 465

[28] If you're not middle-aged and from New England, you should read Philip Lawler's account in *The Faithful Departed* of the persecution Humberto Cardinal Medeiros suffered in Boston for the sin of not being Irish. At least Medeiros had the good sense not to mock what his flock held sacred: the Red Sox.

precisely those Christian communities surrounded by hordes of hostile pagans—for instance, Iran and India—again showing an eerie historical parallel with the fate of the Boston Red Sox: However hard the Nestorians played, there would always be the Yankees.

•   The **Monophysites,**[29] who went on to prove that if squaring a circle does nobody any good, neither does trying to circle the square. Reacting against the Nestorians (you'd think people would have learned to stop zigging and zagging by this point), the Monophysites denied the idea that Christ had two radically incommensurate natures—one human, one divine—yoked together unequally, like an (admittedly sinless) suckerfish and a shark. In place of that Nestorian notion, the Monophysites imagined Our Lord as something more like a genetically modified tomato, with a single firefly chromosome added so that any pizzas made with its sauce would glow in the dark. Like the bug's DNA, Christ's human nature still existed, but it was swallowed up in His divinity, to the point where it made little difference. When this kind of image proved disconcerting to people, other Monophysite writers attempted still more elaborate theories intended to keep alive some tiny sense of Christ's humanity, without in any way impairing His divinity. There were the tritheists, who resolved the mystery of the Trinity by saying, simply, that it was a kind of coalition of three different Gods, as well as subtler theologians like Bishop Severus of Antioch, who celebrated his baptism by refusing ever to bathe again—even when doctors demanded he do so to save his life—and marked his accession as bishop by demolishing the baths inside the episcopal palace.

A young Monophysite Christian receiving his first Holy Communion.

---

[29] CCC, 467

14. Hold on. This is getting weirder. Precisely why did the Monophysites favor dirty bishops?

The *Catholic Encyclopedia* explains his motivations better than I can:

> Severus intended to practise [monasticism] in his own country, but he first visited . . . the head of St. John Baptist at Emea, and then the holy places of Jerusalem, with the result that he joined Evagrius who was already a monk at Maïuma; the great austerities there did not suffice for Severus, and he preferred the life of a solitary in the desert of Eleutheropolis. Having reduced himself to great weakness he was obliged to pass some time in the monastery founded by Romanus, after which he returned to the laura of the port of Gaza, in which was the convent of Peter the Iberian. Here he spent what his charities had left of his patrimony in building a monastery for the ascetics who wished to live under his direction. His quiet was rudely disturbed by Nephalius, a former leader of the Acephali, who was said to have once had 30,000 monks ready to march on Alexandria when, at the end of 482, Peter Mongus accepted the Henoticon and became patriarch. . . .

15. Wait, wait! Nephalius and the Acephali? Peter Mongus and the Henoticon? Is this Church history or *The Hitchhiker's Guide to the Galaxy*? Or the Book of Mormon?

At times, I will admit, such distinctions blur.

16. OK, I give up. Enough with the alternative theories and theorists. What did the "orthodox" bishops with adequate standards of personal hygiene finally decide was true about Christ?

Finally, after centuries of fierce debate, competing creeds, and theological lynch mobs, the Church pronounced at the Council of Chalcedon (451)[30] that Christ was at once divine and human, that His two natures existed in what we call a "hypostatic union." That's distinct from "hypodermic," which goes only skin deep. But the union of Christ's two natures went all the way down to the bone; without either one of them dissolving into a kind of half-divine or half-human soup, both natures existed in the single person of Christ—without either conflict or confusion. He was fully God and fully man, and if you think you can offer a metaphor that makes common sense of that mystery, you have just invented another heresy. In which case, would you like to hear about the Henoticon?

---

[30] CCC, 467

17. No! But thank you. Really. So Jesus was human exactly like everyone else?

No.

18. How did I know you were going to say that?

You must have been paying attention. He was like us in all things except for sin—and sin's results. That means He was conceived without Original Sin, and in fact was incapable of sin[31] (as we said before), since that would have introduced a conflict into the Second Person of the Blessed Trinity.

19. Would that have been like matter meeting antimatter, resulting in the destruction of the entire universe?

Theologians differ.

20. Really?

No. It simply couldn't happen, any more than a polynomial equation could turn into a fruit bat and eat the Monophysites' tomato. Nevertheless, Our Lord voluntarily suffered the pains of temptation. Likewise, He wasn't by nature subject to the penalties for sin, such as physical death, but He willingly accepted them on our behalf. No sacrifice we could offer was perfectly free of sin; our motives are never perfectly pure, as a few moments' honest introspection will tell you. So Jesus offered Himself as a sacrifice for sin to His Father, becoming the spotless Lamb that was slain.

21. Isn't all this pharisaical logic-chopping about the nature of Christ and the internal structure of the Trinity completely alien to the mission and message of Jesus?

It is if you believe that Jesus was a guru out of a book by Hermann Hesse or Khalil Gibran whose mission was to inspire people through random acts of kindness and whose message was the same as Rodney King's in the wake of the L.A. riots: "Can't we all just get along?"

It's a fuzzy, uplifting theory, which satisfies the kind of people who proudly (so proudly!) describe themselves on eHarmony and to the passengers trapped next to

---

[31] CCC, 827

them on airplanes as "spiritual, not religious." It doesn't appeal to me much, but then I'm not spiritual, just religious.

On the other hand, all these fine distinctions really were necessary if Jesus's mission was:[32]

- to fulfill (in a starkly surprising way) the messianic promise to the Jews;
- reform monotheism;
- reveal the Trinity;
- replace the Temple sacrifice with His own death on the cross;
- reconcile fallen mankind to its Creator by making perfect reparation for all sins of the past, present, and future;
- conquer death by death, and to those in the grave bestow life;
- revise the exclusive covenant with the Jews, offering one that invited the whole human race;
- establish a spiritual family, the Church, which would be the New Israel;
- lay the groundwork for an institution that would preach His message first to the Jews, then to the rest of the world,
- offer redemptive meaning to all human suffering, so long as we unite our own daily crosses with His.

Likewise, if His message was:

- Before Abraham was, I am.
- No one comes to the Father save through me.
- After me, a Spirit will come and abide with you.
- The gates of hell will not prevail against my Church.
- Thou art Rocky (i.e., Peter), and on this rock I will found my Church.
- Father, forgive them, for they know not what they do.
- I will make you fishers of men.
- As the Father sent me, even so send I you. Receive the Holy Spirit: Whose soever sins you forgive, they are forgiven; whose soever sins you retain, they are retained.
- If you do not eat my body and drink my blood you will have no life within you.

Those are the really distinctive messages of Jesus—not His empathy for the poor and

[32] CCC, 512–570

unfairly marginalized, which while morally crucial was hardly unprecedented. The Gracchus brothers were tribunes in ancient Rome; they sided with the poor against the rich and were killed for it. But I don't see millions of Baptists, black and white, getting gussied up in suits and fancy hats on Sunday mornings to go worship the Gracchi. But then I've never traveled through the Florida panhandle, and they say nearly anything goes down there.

22. But wasn't it unseemly, even absurd, for Christians to divide themselves and turn against each other over these abstruse theological points? You mentioned mobs of enraged "heretics" and "orthodox" led by monks, fighting these controversies out in the streets. Was that really the Christian thing to do? What about the Crusades?

Self-defense, and defense of the innocent against aggression, is perfectly Christian. We don't worship Gandhi. If Christ had (like Gandhi) forbidden us to use force to stop a rapist or a murderer, He would have proved Himself a fraud, and Pontius Pilate would have done the world a favor. But I'll grant you that the spectacle of roving bands of laymen led by wild-eyed hermits to sack episcopal palaces is disconcerting—though that might have been just what was called for during the sex-abuse crisis. The use of force to coerce people to act against their conscience is wrong, as the Church admitted at Vatican II.[33]

23. In 1965. What were you waiting for—the results of the Warren Commission?

We needed some time to think the matter over, OK? In the early Church, all Christians asked for was religious freedom. Then Emperor Constantine adopted Christianity as the rallying cry to reunite the Roman world. Suddenly, the security of the state depended on religious unity—and the emperors pressured our bishops to settle their quarrels for the sake of social peace. And the emperors kindly offered to send in the cops to help. It was an offer we couldn't refuse. The young St. Augustine defended religious liberty—then in his cranky old age, frustrated with armed bands of aggressive heretics, he changed his mind and called on the state to "compel them to come in." That policy was adopted by various popes over the centuries, but it was never taught infallibly—which left us free at Vatican II, in the wake of the Holocaust and the

---

[33] CCC, 2108

absence of Catholic emperors, to go back to the Church's original teaching. Which, when you think about it, fits in much better with the whole idea of man having free will in the first place. If He lets us choose heaven or hell (or much more frequently, purgatory), who are we to stop people from choosing Mormonism? Or mullets?

24. Now you're just being snobbish.

Bingo.

25. Let's leave the sacraments till later, OK? Even aside from violence, didn't these doctrinal controversies needlessly divide Christians and weaken the Church?

I'm not sure it was needless, any more than doctors in Joseph Lister's time were "needlessly" divided about whether they should wash their hands after cutting up cadavers before they went upstairs to deliver babies. Ideas have consequences, especially false ones. If you believe that Jesus was not God but a superman, you will pray differently, think differently, and therefore act differently.[34] That doesn't mean we shouldn't have peaceful dialogue with people whose beliefs differ from ours—so long as they're peaceful too. As that greatest of Protestants, Ronald Reagan, once said: "Trust, but verify."

Courtesy of Wikipedia Commons.

---

[34] For instance, the monk Pelagius who denied Original Sin and the need for grace. He said that Jesus didn't come to redeem us but to set a really good example, which each of us was perfectly capable of following unaided. This sounds really optimistic and upbeat until you realize what it entails: Each of us is called to absolute moral perfection and expected to accomplish it on our own. This theory made Pelagius into a ferocious, moralistic scold and drove his followers to crazy, self-punishing acts of asceticism. By contrast, an Augustinian realism about the weakness of human will is completely at home eating *zeppoles* with small-time mafiosi at the Feast of San Gennaro.

26. So you're comparing alternative theories to "orthodox" Christology to the pathogens conveyed on dirty fingers from carcasses?

Well, yes.

27. That means they were deadly. So following your own metaphor, you think Monophysites and Arians and Nestorians were "killed" by them spiritually or damned to hell, don't you?

No. There's a key distinction here between objective fault and subjective blame. We can say that an action is evil (that is, that it's less than it should be, since evil is nothing more than a lesser good) without pretending to know how culpable the person was who committed it. That's between him and God. That doesn't make his ideas any less false, however. To make this distinction clearer, the Church doesn't use the term "heretic" for people born into a false belief, reserving that label for those who invented a heresy or left the Church as grown-ups. Not that we even know how blameworthy those people are, of course.[35] If Arius (or Khalil Gibran or even Gandhi) acted in perfectly good faith, and was genuinely deluded, he might not have been blameworthy at all.

28. So it's hate the heresy, love the heretic?

You got it. Not that we've always practiced what we've preached. The Bl. Pope John Paul II had a long list of sins committed by Catholics for which he atoned on the Church's behalf, and prominent among them was the persecution of heretics. Reading about the cruelties inflicted in defense of doctrinal truths is almost enough to make you want to throw them all out as moot, if only to keep the peace.

---

[35] CCC, 817–818

29. Yeah, why don't we?

For one thing, because they're true. But leave that aside. Men don't need fine points of doctrine as pretexts to slaughter each other. In a pinch, anything will do. In 1914, Europe launched a war that killed more than twenty million people over the question of who would govern Bosnia.[36] Josef Stalin's various purges were aimed at perfectly "orthodox" Marxists, just as Mao's Cultural Revolution targeted loyal Communist Party members. Most of the members of "Monophysite" or "anti-Arian" mobs were probably settling private scores, or else just joined up for the chance to commit some mayhem. Barring a strong reason not to attack their fellow man, people will pretty much do it. Have you ever been to a Cubs game?

30. Your family's from the former Yugoslavia, isn't it?

And Ireland.

31. So you speak with some authority.

Though not as part of the ordinary magisterium, I'll hasten to add. But I'm not done making my point. Modern secular liberalism really is one long, extended, hysterical overreaction to the violent doctrinal conflicts that once afflicted Christendom. If we were living in France after its religious civil wars, or Germany after the Thirty Years War, such an attitude might be understandable. But it has been hundreds of years since the last major intra-Christian religious violence. Given that in the past hundred years, some 169.2 million civilians were killed during peacetime by militantly secular governments, maybe it's time to stop seeing faith as the gravest threat to social peace.

Just as we said with heresy, errors tend to lie at the extremes of any paradox—which describes most of the key questions in life. Truth, like virtue, resides in the Golden Mean. If we equate sinners with sins, or mistakes with the mistaken, we will harden ourselves into persecutors. If we decide that religious Truth is like plutonium, too dangerous to touch, we'll melt into relativists—who can't offer decent

---

[36] As if anyone ever could. To whoever's trying to by the time you read this: lots of luck!

arguments against bold, "consistent" ideas like fascism, eugenics, or modernist architecture. So what the Church advocates today is a fierce commitment to truth, human freedom, and the dignity of the person. I like to call it "dogmatism on Xanax."

Courtesy of Wikipedia Commons.

ໃໝ່ໃໝ່ໃໝ່ໃໝ່ໃໝ່ໃໝ່ໃໝ່ໃໝ່ໃໝ່ໃໝ່ໃໝ່ໃໝ່ໃໝ່ໃໝ່ໃໝ່ໃໝ່ໃໝ່ໃໝ່ໃໝ່

**FAQs from Your Stoner Neighbor #4
What would Jesus do?**

How on earth should I know? More to the point, how would anyone—and why would you trust somebody who claimed he did? Indeed, if you read the Gospels in the same spirit you would a Shakespeare play or a Chekhov story,[37] the first word you'd probably come up with would be "unpredictable." In this scene, the protagonist is tenderly saving an adulteress from a stoning that by Mosaic law she'd merited; in the next, He is taunting the most pious members of his own oppressed religion for hypocrisy and blindness. In one town, He heals lepers and raises the dead while swearing the beneficiaries to secrecy. In the hamlet just down the road, He flamboyantly violates the Sabbath and claims the right to forgive men's sins. His parables, which He admits are intended to leave most people puzzled, alternate between a loving concern for lost sheep and prodigal sons—and warnings about the hellfire that awaits foolish virgins and underdressed wedding guests. He eschews the trappings of wealth and refuses the

---

[37] Not that I recommend that.

fawning of crowds—then marches straight up to the walls of the Jewish Vatican and promises to tear the place down then rebuild it Himself in a weekend. At one point He tells the apostles to preach only to the Jews; at another, He warns that the Gentiles are fated to take their place. When He isn't shocking pious monotheistic Jews by claiming to be divine, He is meekly allowing Roman soldiers to spit in His face and scourge Him. In a single scene, He goes from lauding "eunuchs for the Kingdom of heaven" to praising the one thing eunuchs cannot produce, which is children. One really could go on all day. The Jesus we meet in the Gospels is end-lessly puzzling and provocative—and if He were a mere mortal claiming to be God, He would not be much more likable than Prince Hamlet as played by Mel Gibson, and His story would be as uplifting as Kafka's "The Metamorphosis." Given what he said about Himself, was the historical person Jesus of Nazareth:

(a) a great moral teacher, whose followers got carried away and started worship-ping him, then conducted symbolically cannibalistic meals at which he was the main course? Where on earth would pious, blockheaded Jewish fisher-men like Simon Peter have come up with these ideas? Even the wildest false messiahs (like Sabbatai Zevi) knew better than to make such *verkakte* claims.

(b) a prophet whose sole mission was to cut through the convoluted letter of the Law to reveal its spirit—which, boiled down, is simply solidarity with the poor and the marginalized? If all Jesus wanted to do was to found a Reformed synagogue with a Democratic club, He needn't have died on a cross. The Sadducees would gladly have worked with Him, as long as He could deliver the Jewish vote in return for babka and circuses.

(c) a kind of Hebrew Socrates, whose incessant skeptical questioning annoyed the ruling elites to the point where they settled on killing him? Now, every college graduate knows how irritating the "Socratic" method is and has day-dreamed about nailing up a professor who used it incessantly. ("On what continent is the European Union? Anyone?") But how much of a threat was Jesus, really, to the Romans? The Pharisees didn't like Him, but they were too scared of His palm-frond-waving supporters to arrest Him during the daytime. If He didn't in fact march to Jerusalem at Passover to become the Lamb that was slain, it's hard to see why things had to end so unhappily.

(d) A proto-existentialist "seeker," such as Dostoevsky's Jesus in the "The Grand Inquisitor," who died as a witness to spiritual independence, scorn-ing such tools as "miracle, mystery, and authority." In fact, Jesus per-formed a series of stunning miracles precisely to prove His divine authority to preach . . . a long string of mysteries. So scratch that theory.

No, the only honest response to the Gospels is to conclude, with C. S. Lewis and Thomas Aquinas, that Jesus was either *possessed*, *insane*, or *divine*. If either the first or the second, who cares what He would do? It's clearly a bad idea. We can go back to our old role models, like Ayn Rand, Julius Caesar, Robespierre, and Thor.

If He was divine, then He had powers and privileges we don't share—so following His example would be at once presumptuous and impossible. What is more, few share His mission to reform the one true religion, reveal ourselves as divine, and die for the sins of mankind. Given all these subtle (but key) distinctions between Christ's life path and our own, we probably ought not to use our private interpretations of scripture as roadmaps; instead, we can each look at our vocation, state of life, and station in life to discern in the light of two thousand years of Christian moral reflection and authoritative Church teaching, with wise counsel from a pastor, what is the prudent, Christian course of action. Of course, that takes a long time and involves either obeying orders or taking advice, so what the heck? Why not go ahead and try to do what you guess Jesus would:

THE WOMAN TAKEN IN ADULTERY.

- When you meet a blind person, restore his sight.
- While you're at it, absolve his sins.
- At a heavy metal concert, hop onstage to drive the demons out of the band and into the roadies, who will hurl themselves into the sea.
- Drop by a stranger's wake, tell the widow "He's only sleeping," then help the corpse out of the coffin and give him something to eat.
- For a family picnic, serve up loaves and fish for five thousand. Your kids can distribute the leftovers to the homeless.
- Take your local scout troop hiking, and when you reach the top, proclaim your own beatitudes. ("Blessed are the blistered, for they shall be bandaged.")
- The next time you blunder into a LifeTeen Mass, use a bicycle chain to clear the rock band out of the sanctuary. Dump the collection all over the floor.
- When you disagree with a priest or bishop about religion, make arguments like "The Church says 'X,' but I say unto thee . . ."
- Die. Rise from the dead.

32. If Jesus was such a puzzling, enigmatic figure, and His teachings were so opaque, why follow Him in the first place? You just admitted that you feel kind of ambivalent about Him.

Hold on there, Smokey. The catalogue of cavils I rattled off was aimed not at Christ but at you, and the post-Protestant picture you tried to paint of Jesus as some itinerant philosopher who died tragically young—before He could even publish an article—as a victim of religious intolerance. It's a very tempting theory for people who don't want to wrap their minds around Christian dogmas, or their lives around Christian morals, but who still feel attached in a cultural sense to things like Christmas trees and candy canes, human rights and soup kitchens. Those are consequences of Christian faith, the branches if you will, and if you cut the roots they will sooner or later turn brown and drop little dead needles all over your carpet. But the nice folks who attend a United Methodist church twice a year don't like to admit that. What they want is Christianity in homeopathic doses. They want to "revere" a Jesus who never existed, and apply His words and deeds in ways He never intended.

What I'm saying here, I'll admit, is stark and potentially shocking, but I think the mental experiment is necessary in order to lay out the stakes we're playing for. So here's some homework—read through one of the Gospels some time (it takes only an hour), assuming:

(a) that Jesus really said everything attributed to Him (taking the statements that make you queasy and pretending that "Church authorities" added them later is cheating—and it's not how we treat any other historical document), and

(b) that Jesus was not divine.

And you'll come to the conclusion:

(c) that Jesus was a crackpot, exactly as Willem Dafoe played Him in *The Last Temptation of Christ*. Sure, He made some worthy ethical points, but he also handed out a lot of really bad advice ("Sell all you have and give it to the poor"), made empty threats of hellfire, undermined the Jewish national resistance to the Romans, and suffered from delusions of grandeur that wouldn't be equaled until Caligula declared himself a god.

That's the Jesus whom they revere in those tasteful Unitarian churches. Thanks, but I'll take Barabbas.

33. So if He was merely man, Jesus was not an especially good one.

Good men don't claim to be God. They also don't presume to read the hearts and souls of apparently earnest religious authorities such as the Pharisees and denounce them as scheming hypocrites. Nor do they revise the contents of divinely revealed religions on their own authority and support their claims with miracles (which on this theory must have been magic tricks). They don't get their followers so whipped up that they steal their bodies from the tomb to fake their resurrection from the dead—then run off to preach that "resurrection" till all but one of them get themselves killed. Such a man would not be the equal of Buddha or Socrates—or even Muhammad. He would be more like a first-century prototype of modern founders of cults, like L. Ron Hubbard or Jerry Garcia.

34. So doesn't this mean you reject Christian ethics?

No, it means I believe in them because I accept Christian metaphysics. Most of Jesus's arguments in the Gospels are arguments from authority—and His personal authority at that. If we see Him as a philosopher, He's one who is overly fond of logical fallacies, like the Sophists.

Now, on the other hand, consider what it means if He was in fact who He said He was: the coeternal Word of God through whom the entire universe was created. Somehow in the mysterious commerce between His human knowledge (which grew over time) and the divine omniscience that saw things from the perspective of eternity—and I don't pretend that I can explain this—He knew (for instance) that divorce was not an option in the Garden of Eden, not because He'd read about it, but because He *remembered* it. Jesus knew which of the Pharisees were sincere and which were hypocrites, because He *could read their souls*—something He'd later teach Padre Pio how to do. When He spoke to the young rich man and told him to sell all he had and give it to the poor, Jesus wasn't giving commands to the whole human race—which if we followed it would abolish private property and quickly lead to mass starvation. He was telling that one man what *he in particular* needed to hear—that he had what we would now call a religious vocation. When He told the apostles to leave their fishing and their wives to follow Him and preach the Gospel, He wasn't giving commands to the whole human race but calling particular people to a way of life—as the first bishops of the Church.

It's only by taking with absolute seriousness the idea that Christ was God, and that He intimately knew the souls of everyone He met, that we can make sense of what Jesus said to people and reconcile Christian faith with civilized life and the survival of the species. That's where the Church comes in—to sift out which sayings of Christ are universal commands and which are particular counsels, or advice to individuals He met that apply to some of us but not all of us, depending on our vocations.[38]

35. This is all sounding like rather a downer. Why spend so much time insisting what Jesus's nature *wasn't*, what He didn't really say, or what His words didn't mean?

Because the key to understanding orthodox, creed-based Christianity if you're outside it is not to start with Jesus the human being, pretend that He was a political philosopher or revolutionary, then cherry-pick which parts of what He said fit in with what you already believe or what seems like a neat idea. First of all, that approach is totally ahistorical. It makes the Gospels one of the Great Books assigned to you freshman year, to be treated just like Plato's dialogues and Machiavelli's *The Prince*. The New Testament is much more like a meteorite that hit the planet, changed our climate, wiped out the dinosaurs, and seeded some weird new species of trees. The Church represents the people who saw this event as a blessing and started eating the fruit that fell from those trees. Nonbelievers are still nostalgic for the *Tyrannosaurus rex*, and they insist that the fruit is poison. But please don't pretend that the meteorite was just a hailstone and that the trees had been there all along.

36. So now we're back to the extraterrestrial theory . . .

Very funny. My point is that the words and deeds of Jesus only really make sense if you take the imaginative leap to interpret them as they were obviously intended. Accept them, reject them, but don't edit them down and arrange them into "Deep Thoughts" or bawdy limericks. The reason I mentioned the meteorite is that you need to look at Christ from the right point of view, from the top down, not the bottom up. So start with the Second Person of the Blessed Trinity, the Logos Who preexisted the universe and embodies the very principle of intelligibility and reason. That Person, we claim, was sent by His Father to take on a real human nature, to rebuild for all mankind the bridge that our inbred sinfulness blew up and couldn't rebuild. He spent only three years teaching and never bothered to write a

---

[38] CCC, 587-594

book. The Gospels are memoirs by people who knew Him, compiled (we claim) with divine assistance, but if that were all Christ left behind, it would be little more than a curiosity, like Stonehenge.[39] Christ appointed stewards of His legacy, who organized a Church that would offer a constant source of contact between Jesus and the subsequent generations in the form of the sacraments—which we'll cover in chapter 6.

Accept this at least for the sake of argument, and go read the Gospels now. You'll see a figure Who first strives to prove to anyone who will listen that He has something radically new to say, a stark reinterpretation of the Jewish covenant with God. He goes out of His way to show that He holds Himself above the letter of the Law by healing people on the Sabbath and driving the moneychangers out of the Temple. He debates and rebukes the orthodox authorities on the Law, goading them until they realize the nature of His claims. Then they start scheming to kill Him—and it's only at that point that Jesus begins to display the meekness, mildness, and humility that is all we really like to remember. The same man who argued His points like a world-class canon lawyer when confronted in the Temple doesn't even try to wriggle out of the death penalty. He proclaims His divinity to the whole robe-tearing Sanhedrin, is silent before King Herod, and resigned to His fate at the hands of Pontius Pilate. His whole demeanor changes from the Lion of Judah to a lamb meekly led to the slaughter. If we want to use Hebrew figures, imagine Moses climbing down from Mount Sinai only to turn into Isaac following Abraham up the mountain to be sacrificed.

The whole point of His mission, as He makes clear over the perfectly human objections of Simon Peter, was not the preaching—that was all a prologue. Of course, we get what's distinctive about Christian ethics from what He said. But Christ's birth into the flesh was intended to end in death, a death more innocent than anyone's (even Abel's), which He would turn on its head by raising Himself from the grave.[40] Because the grim fact of human death became the nightmare it was—with no hope of meaning or happy afterlife—through human sin, God would reverse it by the very same means: by becoming a man and turning death into life. It's heady stuff, and not everyone can accept it, of course. But it is a fundamental answer to mankind's most basic question, which is why it has sustained so many billions of souls through the grim millennia before ibuprofen, Lexipro, and Novocain.

Now, when we see Christ as a cosmic deity who willingly signed up as our scapegoat, Who climbed down into the darkest hells our species creates for itself so He could take our hands and pull us out, we can make more sense of His injunctions to detach ourselves from earthly goods, care for the sick and poor, and accept an occasional slap in the face instead of launching a vendetta. Christ, having viewed the human condition from the perspective of eternity, and knowing

---

[39] CCC, 126
[40] CCC, 616.

what He would have to endure for each of our sakes, had the knowledge and the moral authority to reach into the tangled human soul and show us how to straighten it. The effort of following His instructions is typically pretty painful; with the Fall, man lost his exemption from disordered animal instincts—and in fact, they mixed with the craftiness and cruelty that only a rational creature could devise. You know how cats like to play with mice? Men like to play that way with entire nations, enslaving whole populations (as the Mongols did to the Slavs, and the whites did to the blacks), driving them into the desert to die (as the Turks did to the Armenians), and so on. On a much smaller scale, think of the bitterest breakup, inheritance lawsuit, or divorce you know about. Can you imagine chimpanzees or turtles acting like that? That creature, the inventor of prison camps and computer viruses, identity theft and sex slavery, is what Jesus came down to save.[41] He climbed into our skins, announced Himself, and left Himself to our tender mercies. Then when we were finished showing our inborn response to Goodness personified, and threw Him in a cave like a broken piñata, He shrugged it off and reappeared to the apostles to eat some fish. That's the fellow we're talking about.

Maybe He speaks with authority such that we ought to be paying attention.

37. OK, I'm impressed. But even viewed from this "cosmic" perspective, some of the things Jesus said were pretty weird and hard to jibe with reason, common sense, or the survival of the species.

Agreed. We even have a name for those kinds of statements: the "hard sayings" of Jesus. Their difficulty is another reason why He left behind a Church—beyond preaching the gospel and offering grace through the sacraments, she would control, clarify, and

[41] CCC, 402-409

codify how we're to understand what He said. Remember, He typically spoke in the mode of a Hebrew prophet, not a legal philosopher or a psychologist—so there was a fair amount of poetic imagery, even hyperbole, in what He said. It was the Church's job to make a day-to-day life plan out of these somewhat puzzling injunctions. In that task, she was guided by the oral traditions He'd passed along to the apostles, the Holy Spirit (we'll get to Him later), and the Greco-Roman love of reason and order that God's Providence had planted throughout the Mediterranean world.

38. Wait, wait. Are you saying that Plato and Aristotle, Roman law and aqueducts, were an essential part of God's plan?

Every bit, I am tempted to say, as much as Abraham and Moses. But that might amount to heresy. So I won't go quite that far. I'll just say that I'm very glad that the bishops who interpreted statements like "If your eye causes you to sin, pluck it out" had been intellectually formed by the Greeks and not the Mongols. I don't think that was an accident. The Incarnation had been in the planning stages for a very long time—some billions of years at least—so God had the chance to get all such ducks in a row.

39. Fine. Now let's go through some of those "hard sayings" and see how the Church has wrestled with them through the centuries.
From Mark 7:

> From there He arose and went to the region of Tyre and Sidon. And He entered a house and wanted no one to know it, but He could not be hidden. For a woman whose young daughter had an unclean spirit heard about Him, and she came and fell at His feet. The woman was a Greek, a Syro-Phoenician by birth, and she kept asking Him to cast the demon out of her daughter. But Jesus said to her, "Let the children be filled first, for it is not good to take the children's bread and throw it to the little dogs."
>
> And she answered and said to Him, "Yes, Lord, yet even the little dogs under the table eat from the children's crumbs."
>
> Then He said to her, "For this saying go your way; the demon has gone out of your daughter."
>
> And when she had come to her house, she found the demon gone out, and her daughter lying on the bed. (24-30)

What a nice guy. Didn't He create this Gentile woman, same as any Jew? Why talk to her so contemptuously?

What's wrong with "little dogs" anyway? Unlike you and me, they don't have Original Sin. Indeed, Aquinas teaches that every animal by simply existing is doing the will of God and pleasing Him. That's more than I can say for most people.

Still, I'll admit that this passage presents Christ at His seemingly least lovable. His words embody the stern sense of superiority that the Jewish people needed to keep their self-respect under foreign occupation and persecution, and their mono-theism clear of the infant-sacrificing fertility cults that were all around them. But with Jesus, actions spoke louder than words: On the one hand, He insists that the Jews are the first audience for His message—the rightful heirs, if you will. But notice what He did: He snuck into the house of a Gentile (where pious Jews wouldn't normally go) to seek out this woman who had no apparent connection to Judaism at all—and hence no true faith in God. His very presence overwhelmed her, and she begged Him to banish the devil from her daughter. He tested her humility and sincerity, making her admit in essence that salvation comes from the Jews, then granted the daughter an instant healing. A Pharisee wouldn't even have entered the house. A Stoic might have offered the woman some maxims about how suffering was irrelevant. Jesus reminded her of the sacred status of Judaism, then healed her daughter anyway. Remember also that by the time this Gospel was written down, it was clear that the Gentiles were already beginning to outnumber the Jews among the Christians.[42] Mark may have chosen to include this story rather than others precisely to remind the newcomers to whom they owed salvation. Most of us have managed to ignore the point, energetically, over the centuries.

---

[42] CCC, 781

40. OK, now this one, sticking to the Gospel of Mark for the moment. From Chapter 8:

> When He had called the people to Himself, with His disciples also, He said to them, "Whoever desires to come after Me, let him deny himself, and take up his cross, and follow Me. For whoever desires to save his life will lose it, but whoever loses his life for My sake and the gospel's will save it. For what will it profit a man if he gains the whole world, and loses his own soul? Or what will a man give in exchange for his soul? For whoever is ashamed of Me and My words in this adulterous and sinful generation, of him the Son of Man also will be ashamed when He comes in the glory of His Father with the holy angels." (34-38)

Isn't He saying here that we should all seek out martyrdom, the same way He did?

No, though numerous monks and even some saints seem to have misread the Gospel in just that way. An entire heresy—Donatism—arose to advocate that position. It was Donatists whose self-destructive tenacity drove St. Augustine to toss out religious liberty and seek the emperor's help in squelching them.

You'll note that in the passage you quoted, He said "take up" your cross—that is, carry it, not die on it. Martyrdom is a hideous evil, which we're meant to prefer only over something worse—like betraying our faith, committing a grievous sin, or failing to preach the gospel. We're absolutely forbidden to seek this evil out on purpose, just as we may not court opportunities of being raped—if for no other reason than that it enables someone else to commit a grievous sin. It's true that the apostles (like thousands of missionaries over subsequent centuries) *risked* death for the sake of spreading the Faith. But they weren't kamikazes. Death was a possible, unwanted side effect, as it is for soldiers, firemen, and cops. Christ—and Christ alone—was born to offer Himself as a sacrifice for sin. He climbed the tree of the cross to die for us all; He didn't come down to nail the rest of us up.[43]

---

[43] CCC, 2473

41. At the very least, isn't He condemning the self-preservation instinct that He (presumably) implanted in mankind when He created us?

No. If he were, then Christianity would be a suicide cult, and the Romans would have been right to try to snuff it out: a process that ironically produced our earliest martyrs. But the self-preservation instinct in most of us—apart from those crushed by addiction, depression, or anorexia—is plenty strong, as God designed it to be.[44] Here Jesus is trying to say that there is something even more important: the love of God. We ought to be as devoted to our maker as a mother is to her children, or as Jesus is to us.

42. Continuing with the Gospel of Mark, what about this one, from Chapter 9:

> And He said to them, "Assuredly, I say to you that there are some standing here who will not taste death till they see the kingdom of God present with power." (1)

So the Second Coming was supposed to happen while at least one of the apostles was still alive. As sorority girls like to say: "Whoopsies!"

Yes, this line was the source of significant confusion in the early Church—though people might have gotten the hint when St. John, the last of the apostles, died peacefully in his bed. Like those early millenarians, you seem to have overlooked the very next lines in chapter 9:

> Now after six days Jesus took Peter, James, and John, and led them up on a high mountain apart by themselves; and He was transfigured before them. His clothes became shining, exceedingly white, like snow, such as no launderer on earth can whiten them. And Elijah appeared to them with Moses, and they were talking with Jesus. Then Peter answered and said to Jesus, "Rabbi, it is good for us to be here; and let us make three tabernacles: one for You, one for Moses, and one for Elijah"—because he did not know what to say, for they were greatly afraid.
>
> And a cloud came and overshadowed them; and a voice came out of the cloud, saying, "This is My beloved Son. Hear Him!" Suddenly, when they had looked around, they saw no one anymore, but only Jesus with themselves.
>
> Now as they came down from the mountain, He commanded them that they should tell no one the things they had seen, till the Son of Man had risen from the dead. So they kept this word to themselves, questioning what the rising from the dead meant. (2-10)

---

[44] CCC, 2281

Apparently, what Our Lord was predicting was the very next thing that happened: His Transfiguration, which was a vision of the "Kingdom of God present with power." But the apostles didn't get it, any more than they "got" what He meant by "the rising from the dead."[45] I've no doubt that early Christians were disappointed when they figured this out; end-of-the-worlders are such irrepressible optimists. They're always eager to find some hint that the Antichrist is coming soon. I'm not sure why. Christ Himself said of the End Times:

> So when you see the "abomination of desolation," spoken of by Daniel the prophet, standing where it ought not (let the reader understand), then let those who are in Judea flee to the mountains. Let him who is on the housetop not go down into the house, nor enter to take anything out of his house. And let him who is in the field not go back to get his clothes. But woe to those who are pregnant and to those who are nursing babies in those days! And pray that your flight may not be in winter. For in those days there will be tribulation, such as has not been since the beginning of the creation which God created until this

45 CCC, 555

time, nor ever shall be. And unless the Lord had shortened those days, no flesh would be saved; but for the elect's sake, whom He chose, He shortened the days. (Mark 13: 14-20)

Which part of that, exactly, are we supposed to be looking forward to? Me, I'm happy to wait. I have no powers of prophecy, but I expect we Christians have whole millennia of mediocrity lying before us before God decides to announce "last call." Though I will confess that I did briefly wonder if it was a sign of the End Times when NBC canceled *Law and Order*.

43. How about this masterpiece of holistic living, from Mark, chapter 9:

And if your foot causes you to sin, cut it off. It is better for you to enter life lame, rather than having two feet, to be cast into hell, into the fire that shall never be quenched—where *"The worm does not die And the fire is not quenched."* (43-48)

This seems all of a piece with the blithe willingness of Christians to wreck their earthly lives in pursuit of a promised "pie in the sky when you die" for which there is no conclusive evidence. You have to take it on faith; that's fine when faith affirms your stable, happy heterosexual marriage in a peaceful society. But when faith demands that you throw everything away for the sake of uncertain promises, I start to recalculate the odds on Pascal's bet.
Sorry, was there a question in there?

44. Fine. Do you really think people whose deepest natural drives can only be satisfied by violating Church rules should "pluck out" or "cut off" those drives? I believe the old Catholic term that used to be beaten into schoolboys was "mortify." As in the call to "mortify" the flesh.

That term was used. More common was "custody," as in "keep custody" of your eyes or your mind so they didn't wander off on paths that would lead you into trouble. But as to your main question: It depends entirely on what those "natural drives" are goading someone to do. Maybe they're urging a man to cheat on his wife who's sick in the hospital. Or a stepfather to dally with his buxom, sixteen-year-old stepdaughter. Perhaps a professor to use his charms on that strapping freshman coed. Let's dig a little deeper into the darker side of desire: What about middle-aged men with a "thing" for adolescent (or younger) boys? Were the American bishops who covered up for sex abusers right when they didn't insist on mortifying the desires of a small, sick segment of priests who "naturally" had this drive? It's interesting—and probably no coincidence—that the plague of sex abuse coincided with the disappearance of physical mortifications among the clergy. I think even you would agree it's better for such a man to sleep with a hair shirt than with a twelve-year-old.[46]

You look like you're about to barf on the carpet. So you're willing to agree that some "deep natural drives" need to be mortified—cut off or plucked out, if possible. You might disagree with the Bible (and hence the Church) about how many drives and which ones require this kind of treatment, but we can get into details another time. You've granted my major premise. So let's move on.

45. Absolutely. I find it curious that your Church solemnly condemns socialism,[47] since Jesus seems to endorse it. See Mark, chapter 10:

> Now as He was going out on the road, one came running, knelt be-
> fore Him, and asked Him, "Good Teacher, what shall I do that I may
> inherit eternal life?"
>
> So Jesus said to him, "Why do you call Me good? No one is good
> but One, that is, God. You know the commandments: 'Do not commit
> adultery,' 'Do not murder,' 'Do not steal,' 'Do not bear false witness,'
> 'Do not defraud,' 'Honor your father and your mother.' "
>
> And he answered and said to Him, "Teacher, all these things I have
> kept from my youth."

---

[46] CCC, 2015

[47] Leo XIII, *Quod Apostolici Muneris:* "They leave nothing untouched or whole which by both human and divine laws has been wisely decreed for the health and beauty of life. . . . Lured, in fine, by the greed of present goods, which is 'the root of all evils which some coveting have erred from the faith,' they assail the right of property sanctioned by natural law; and by a scheme of horrible wickedness, while they seem desirous of caring for the needs and satisfying the desires of all men, they strive to seize and hold in common whatever has been acquired either by title of lawful inheritance, or by labor of brain and hands, or by thrift in one's mode of life. These are the startling theories they utter in their meetings, set forth in their pamphlets, and scatter abroad in a cloud of journals and tracts. . . . For, indeed, although the social-ists, stealing the very Gospel itself with a view to deceive more easily the unwary, have been accustomed to distort it so as to suit their own purposes, nevertheless so great is the difference between their depraved teachings and the most pure doctrine of Christ that none greater could exist: 'for what participation hath justice with injustice or what fellowship hath light with darkness?' "

Then Jesus, looking at him, loved him, and said to him, "One thing you lack: Go your way, sell whatever you have and give to the poor, and you will have treasure in heaven; and come, take up the cross, and follow Me."

But he was sad at this word, and went away sorrowful, for he had great possessions.

Then Jesus looked around and said to His disciples, "How hard it is for those who have riches to enter the kingdom of God!" And the disciples were astonished at His words. But Jesus answered again and said to them, "Children, how hard it is for those who trust in riches to enter the kingdom of God! It is easier for a camel to go through the eye of a needle than for a rich man to enter the kingdom of God."

And they were greatly astonished, saying among themselves, "Who then can be saved?"

But Jesus looked at them and said, "With men it is impossible, but not with God; for with God all things are possible." (17-27)

What do you have to say to that?

That question is such a farrago of illogic that it's hard to know where to start. First of all, socialism means the forcible confiscation of private property by the state. Perhaps I missed the part of the story where Jesus calls a Roman soldier over and has him take away all the rich man's property, then hand it out to the poor in return for their votes.

I'll assume you meant that Jesus endorses the voluntary renunciation of private property—which is not socialism but monasticism. And I'll agree that He does, at least in the case of this rich young man, who clearly is already living justly and in a manner pleasing to God. But this fellow wants something more; he has approached God Himself, and pestered Him for direction in how to delve deeper. This young man has been called to something higher, to "follow" Christ as one of the apostles, the men whom Jesus would very soon commission as the first bishops of the Church. In other words, he has what we now call a religious vocation. Of those with such vocations, Christ at several points in the Gospels makes greater demands—for instance, to become "eunuchs for the kingdom of heaven," embracing celibacy. In later centuries, when monastic orders began to emerge, their founders added another stern requirement needful for life in community: obedience. A monk, friar, or nun agrees to treat the will of his superior as the voice of God and obey it in everything except sin.

Why bother to single out a creative minority among Christians to carry such a burden? I'm tempted to say, "Ask God!" But in fact there is an answer: God planted as the three most powerful drives in man acquisition, reproduction, and self-assertion. The Fall seeded cancer in each, producing tumors like theft, rape, and tyranny that stain every page of human history. By proving through their example that it is possible through God's grace to renounce these drives altogether, these Christians bear witness against the abuses and "walk the talk" that proves they believe in immortality. (Why else give up so much of what makes earthly life worth living?) Think of them as athletes in the Paralympics, racing in wheelchairs or on artificial limbs to shame the rest of us—as (heh, heh) Lance Armstrong shames Vince Vaughn in *Dodgeball*.[48]

The Church came to call the three vows that monastics take—poverty, chastity, and obedience—the Counsels of Perfection. There is a particular form of perfection in this world that can be attained by imitating the apostles, and the results of the small elite whom God calls to do that (in a wide variety of ways) have been enormously fruitful for the human race. Here's just a tiny, representative sample:

- The Benedictines, who formed little islands of order and learning during the barbarian invasions, and patiently recopied virtually all the Greek and Roman literature we still have. They also offered the first advanced schooling to women in Western history.
- The Cistercians, who developed more rational methods of farming that helped feed Europe for centuries.
- The Dominicans, who educated ordinary people in the Faith and formed the backbone of Europe's great universities.
- The Franciscans, who tended lepers and beggars—and lived among them—when no one else would, and who also pioneered the art techniques that led to the great works of the Renaissance.
- The Jesuits, who helped lift the Church from corruption when the Renaissance got overripe, who fought for the rights of native peoples against the Conquistadors, creating new industries and political safe havens for the dispossessed.
- The Ursuline nuns, who opened hospitals for the Indians who were dying of European diseases, and who ran schools that reached from the bayous of Louisiana to the icy hills of Quebec.

None of this could have been accomplished by individualists, through the profit motive, or by men or women with families to support. Married couples couldn't have traveled (as St. Francis Xavier did) to China and Japan to plant the Church among pagans. Indeed, the Western Church still insists on celibacy even for nonmonastic priests, largely to prevent the priesthood from becoming a profession, or parishes the inherited "property" of pastors. The men and women whom God calls to live the Counsels of Perfection have always served the doughy mass of ordinary Christians as a kind of yeast.

---

[48] CCC, 1974

But you can't eat yeast—though the English still are trying (see Marmite Yeast Extract, which has been ruining perfectly good slices of bread since 1902). Nor could the great mass of people ever live by the Counsels of Perfection. What would happen if they tried? The answer comes alike from simple logic and the dismal history of utopian movements and cults that have emerged over the centuries.

• **Poverty**. St. Thomas Aquinas taught that private property would have existed even in the Garden of Eden; it was even more desperately necessary in the context of the Fall, when to healthy self-interest was added the taint of ruthless acquisitiveness. Property rights are the bright line that separates what I have worked for and what is mine from what you've worked for that I can steal—especially if you or your group is smaller or weaker.[49] Deprive men of the right to the fruits of their labors and you make them slaves—and lazy slaves at that, who absent the profit motive can be motivated only by the lash or the threat of a labor camp. Josef Stalin tried to remake Ukraine on the model of a monastery, in the process starving up to twelve million peasants to death. Mao Zedong and Pol Pot were even more ambitious . . . but I think you get the idea.

• **Obedience**. The idea has been unpopular since 1789, and almost incomprehensible since 1968, but we each have certain duties that are inseparable from our rights; like Siamese twins, they share a hip and a liver. We owe *fidelity* to spouses, *stability* to children, and (within limits) *obedience* to employers and to policemen. Our best attempts to act our entire lives like spoiled teenagers have yielded predictable outcomes: broken homes, bankrupt countries, and crime-haunted public squares sprayed with urine and graffiti. Liberty clearly can grow only in the well-tilled soil of order. But that doesn't mean it's a plant we can live without; within the clear limits of respecting each other's rights and human dignity, we are meant to be free, and any government that pretends it can treat adults like children, or laymen like monks, is intrinsically evil and ought to be overthrown. The entire nightmarish experiment of totalitarianism could be seen as the attempt to impose monastic obedience on the laity, forcibly ordering free men and women's lives as if they were all locked in a convent and the bureaucrats who ruled them spoke with the voice of God.

• **Chastity**. This one is easy. Monastic chastity is celibacy, and if universally imposed would solve all mankind's problems in seventy years. Clearly, Jesus doesn't want all of us to be "eunuchs for the kingdom of heaven." If that had been what He meant, He would have been the enemy of mankind. But some groups arose that believed precisely this: the Manicheans of Augustine's age, and the Albigensians who revived their ideas in medieval France, regarded the flesh as evil, a prison for immortal spirits that used sex and marriage as the cheese that baited the rat trap. These sects promoted universal celibacy but were willing to settle for sodomy, contraception, and abortion—anything, really, except reproductive intercourse. Their notions sound at once bizarre and eerily modern, echoed as they are by both ecologists and pornographers.[50]

---

[49] CCC, 2409
[50] CCC, 2360

46. How about this passage from Mark, chapter 16:

Later He appeared to the eleven as they sat at the table; and He rebuked their unbelief and hardness of heart, because they did not believe those who had seen Him after He had risen. And He said to them, "Go into all the world and preach the gospel to every creature.

"He who believes and is baptized will be saved; but he who does not believe will be condemned. And these signs will follow those who believe: In My name they will cast out demons; they will speak with new tongues; they will take up serpents; and if they drink anything deadly, it will by no means hurt them; they will lay hands on the sick, and they will recover." (14-18)

That Bible snippet has caused countless emergency room admissions in Appalachia over the decades.

My first instinct is to point to the context: Jesus had spotted signs of skepticism among a group of men to whom He was appearing *after He had risen from the dead.* They'd apparently tried not to accept His Resurrection, dismissing the women who'd first seen the risen Jesus as a band of hysterical yentas. Even now, with Him standing there, complete with the crucifixion marks on His hands and feet, they weren't entirely confident. (From a modern perspective, given all that they'd been through[51] since Gethsemane, we might diagnose the apostles with PTSFD[51] and cut them some slack.) So even as Christ delivers to them what theologians have called "the great commission" to preach "to every creature" throughout the world, He uses Jewish hyperbole to bolster their confidence. Now some of what He said would prove to be literally true: Missionaries like St. Boniface would indeed drive out demons, especially those disguised as bloodthirsty pagan gods; the Jesuits in India, China, Japan, and North America would master dozens of alien tongues, the better to spread the Word; and countless sick, poor pagans, slaves, and peasants around the world would find their only treatment at the hands of disciples of Christ—the Church still runs the world's largest private, nonprofit health care network on earth. That leaves us with the snakes and the deadly drinks, which are admittedly hard to account for in literal terms—though St. John's story contains them both: While he was the only apostle to die of natural causes, we have to give his enemies an "A" for effort. The legend of St. John reports that someone tried to poison his wine, but

---

[51] Post-Theophanic Sangfroid Deficiency

when he picked it up to drink it, a little serpent leapt out of the cup to warn him, then crawled away. John blessed it and drank it anyway. He wasn't harmed, and to mark this miracle, we still bless wine on St. John's Feast Day (December 27), which also happens to be my birthday.

47. What do you mean "we"? Have you got a frog in your pocket?

I mean my friends and I. It's not clear if we are friends yet. But I see that I haven't fully explained the literal sense of those verses—which I can only gloss as Our Lord's version of the Darwin Award; he put these lines in the Bible to keep the IQ of his disciples good and high. Only those with the good sense to interpret this passage allegorically would live long enough to preach.

48. You're making God sound kind of cold and ruthless, aren't you?

No, but who was it that came up with natural selection in the first place? Or with critters like tapeworms, crab lice, and the candiru—that's the parasitical river fish that swim up men's urethras. They've got hundreds of long, spiny bones that dig into—

49. Enough already! Sheesh . . .

What hath God wrought, eh?

50. OK, smart guy. Aren't there any Bible verses that you find troubling? Or do you just thumb through the New Testament at airports with a chuckleheaded smile saying, "Yup, yup! Hunky-dory!"

Sure. There are a couple that make me shudder and say to myself, "Thank God there's a Church to tell me that this doesn't mean what it *seems* to." But I'll focus on the one that, in my experience, most troubles honest seekers, from Matthew, chapter 5:

"You have heard that it was said, 'An eye for an eye and a tooth for a tooth.' But I tell you not to resist an evil person. But whoever slaps you on your right cheek, turn the other to him also. If anyone wants to sue you and take away your tunic, let him have your cloak also. And whoever compels you to go one mile, go with him two. Give to him who asks you, and from him who wants to borrow from you do not turn away.

"You have heard that it was said, 'You shall love your neighbor and hate your enemy.' But I say to you, love your enemies, bless those who curse you, do good to those who hate you, and pray for those who spitefully use you and persecute you, that you may be sons of your Father in heaven; for He makes His sun rise on the evil and on the good, and sends rain on the just and on the unjust." (38-45)

Stomach wrenching, right? For most of my life, I just skimmed over this passage as I would the Bible's tedious genealogies, or injunctions like the following, from Ezekiel, Chapter 38:

"Son of man, set your face against Gog, of the land of Magog, the prince of Rosh, Meshech, and Tubal, and prophesy against him, and say, Thus says the Lord GOD: Behold, I am against you, O Gog, the prince of Rosh, Meshech, and Tubal. I will turn you around, put hooks into your jaws, and lead you out, with all your army, horses, and horsemen, all splendidly clothed, a great company with bucklers and shields, all of them handling swords. Persia, Ethiopia, and Libya are with them, all of them with shield and helmet; Gomer and all its troops; the house of Togarmah from the far north and all its troops—many people are with you." (2-6)

The Ezekiel passage contained, as far as I could see, the quotient of useful advice as the Matthew. So I let both of them slide.

But over time, I began to observe that far more people distilled what they thought was the "essence" of Christianity from the Matthew passage than from Ezekiel's promise to put hooks in the jaws of Gog, so I needed to face it squarely.

51. Er, you are aware that this is *not* the part of the Bible to which most people object?

Not openly. Your average postmodern person will pull out instead the condemnation of a trendy sexual sin, or some miracle that seems to him unlikely (which is, you know, the point of miracles, but never mind), and treat this cheek-turning, enemy-blessing business as a sweet, uplifting idea, the kind of thing the Dalai Lama might whisper to Richard Gere at Sundance. Not that anyone really intends to put it into practice; the only conceivable reason to really try something so outrageous would be if you believed in Christ's divine authority, as affirmed by those irritating miracles and expressed in those laws about sex. But people like to think that they'd like to turn the other cheek; that's just the kind of person that they aspire to pretend to hope to be.

Not me. If I didn't believe in the divinity of Christ precisely as laid out in the Council of Chalcedon, my choice for personal lord and savior would fall instead on Achilles. Over four decades of life,[52] it has seemed to me that no good deeds go unpunished, few lambs escape the slaughter, and the only earth that the meek inherit is the potting soil they push around in wheelbarrows as they groom the lawns of the haughty. This is every bit as true among self-professed Christians as pagans, though at least the latter are sometimes more honest about it. The best of them don't even pretend to be self-effacing, so you can speak to them man to man. Since my heroes have always been warlords, my reading of Catholic history has tended to dwell on Catholic emperors and crusaders, guerrilla fighters in the Cristero rebellion or the Vendée, St. Joan of Arc and Don John of Austria. I'm probably not the only person who chokes down the Beatitudes for the sake of Charlemagne and Chartres. I'm just one of the few who admit it.

St. Francis, in his youth, had a particular loathing of lepers. When he experienced his dramatic conversion and fell in love with Lady Poverty, Francis forced himself to confront what he feared and despised, to look it in the face and engage it day to day: He started tending and bathing lepers, even kissing (gargh) their sores. It is in that spirit that I've tried to look at the meekness preached and practiced by Christ,[53] to discern what others see in it, envision the situations where we are meant to practice it. Of course, one could accept this injunction simply on authority, to avoid damnation, but think of what that would imply: *You'd be trying to be as meek and mild as Christ for fear that, if you didn't, He would plunge you for all eternity into a lake of fire.* My mind isn't limber enough for that kind of mental gymnastics, so I needed to think through the tangible, earthly outcomes of particular instances of meekness and nonresistance to evil, to see which ones make sense.

---

[52] Much of it, admittedly, in shockingly Hobbesian environments: a blue-collar nuclear family, David Dinkins's New York City, secular academia, and the Catholic traditionalist movement.

[53] One excellent source is Fr. Lawrence Lovasik's *The Hidden Power of Kindness* (Manchester, NH: Sophia Institute Press, 1999). Another is the forgotten classic *The Good God*, by L. Garriguet (St. Meinrad, IN: Abbey Press, 1959).

Conveniently enough, the Church has taken the exact same approach over the centuries. In reflecting on the question of how to deal with aggressive evil, theologians came to see three potential types of response: sinful Wrath, holy Patience, or cringing Servility.[54]

- The deadly sin of Wrath uses the evil that one has suffered as a pretext for launching outsized retaliation—gleefully (given man's fallen will) taking not just an eye for an eye but a nose as well, and perhaps an ear for good measure. Indeed, our all-too-human faith in our own immaculate hearts and irreproachable motives will tend to magnify in our own minds any offense committed against us, writing "Vendetta" in the clouds, and shrink down to puny amoebic scale whatever we might have done to provoke it. If you don't believe me, pick up the newspaper and turn to a story (any story) about events (any events) anywhere in the Middle East.[55]

- The virtue of Patience, which accepts trivial slights against one's dignity like a slap on the cheek as (perhaps) God's punishment for an unrepented sin, or suffering you can unite with Christ's for the sake of the souls in Purgatory. Patience modeled on Christ's endurance of the Passion has been the greatest help to the helpless—the billions of people who throughout the centuries have lived without power, weapons, wealth, or the liberty to acquire these good things. When one is subject to a chronic, irreparable injustice, or has striven mightily to overturn evil and failed, the spirituality of the Cross makes it possible to *recycle* this residue of inescapable suffering into supernatural grace, a radiant force with a much longer half-life than fleeting secular supremacy. The blood of the martyrs really can be the seed of the Church. Certainly, the example of Christians who were willing to die in the Colosseum rather than worship the emperor made a profound impression on the jaded citizens of decadent Rome.

- The neurosis of Servility, which combines aspects of cowardice and self-congratulation to mold the kind of person who could stand by and watch his children be abducted, his wife be raped, or his country conquered and colonized without putting up any resistance. This is the disease Nietzsche diagnosed in modern liberal Christians, which now expresses itself in a form much darker than even he could have imagined: the voluntary self-gelding of European peoples and their lazy willingness

---

[54] See *The Bad Catholic's Guide to the Seven Deadly Sins* (Crossroad, 2010), chapters 3 (Wrath) and 4 (Patience).

[55] CCC, 2302

to import wholesale an alien civilization to mow their lawns and mop their toilets—in return for inheriting their countries. This closeout sale of Western man's birthright for a maggoty mess of pottage is the melancholy history of contemporary Europe.[56]

So in the midst of all this, can we come up with an ethic to live by? We can. We ought to disregard assaults against our trivial personal dignity, shrugging them off as the fruit of our enemy's weakness and desperation—provided we aren't thereby enabling and encouraging his sinful habits. Such lofty magnanimity breathed forth from enormous souls like St. Edmund Campion, who earnestly prayed for his Anglican torturers from the scaffold; St. Maria Goretti, who forgave her murderer (and would-be rapist) with her dying breath; St. "Padre" Pio, who patiently endured campaigns of slander[57] that led to his suspension from the public exercise of the priesthood; and Aleksandr Solzhenitsyn, whose long years in labor camps led him to conversion, and to novels in which he treated even communist kapos with compassion. Compared to such spiritual grandeur, the thin-skinned vanity of Achilles and the transgressive glee of Machiavelli seem petty and adolescent. The pre-Christian "honor" ethos that led so many noblemen to kill or die in duels was not in fact "tougher" or more realistic than the Christian code of humility and patience. Genghis Khan may have left behind more descendants than did St. Francis of Assisi, but which one left a better taste in history's mouth? The pagan love of "glory" that Jesus deconstructed both by word and example gave way to something much more powerfully enduring: a love of the Good for its own sake, despite the hungry urgings of man's insatiable ego.

That said, there is never the slightest excuse for rewarding evil with success. The moment that bowing one's head to the oppressor betrays one's duty to protect an innocent third party, Christian meekness vanishes into the cracks in the ground, replaced by a Servility befitting the herd of Gadarene swine. That is why pacifists who refuse to defend their neighbors from either tyranny or anarchy deserve no deference for their high-mindedness and idealism, but instead holy contempt for their criminally irresponsible posturing. It is sinful to accede to evil whenever and wherever it might encourage the doing of further evil; you have no more excuse to surrender to someone else's Wrath than you do to his Lust, and your reward will be the same.

Nor, the Church has solemnly taught, can we let our enemy drag us down to his level; whatever cruelties a country's army commits, they never justify targeting its civilians.[58] Incinerating women and kids to spare your own soldiers a battle is pure and simple

---

[56] CCC, 2265

[57] John Allen wrote in the *National Catholic Reporter* (Dec. 28. 2001): "This is a man who was investigated by the Holy Office, the forerunner of the Congregation for the Doctrine of the Faith, somewhere between 12 and 25 times, depending on how you count. He was forbidden from saying Mass in public, from publishing, from receiving visitors, even from talking to women alone. . . . The whispered consensus on Padre Pio in the halls of the Vatican was that he was at best a naïve hysteric, at worst a con man."

[58] Here's a quick and easy rule: Soldiers can't ever kill civilians on purpose; leaders have a solemn duty to minimize civilian casualties while pursing legitimate military targets. So we can't nuke an entire city just to kill a terrorist leader; doing things like that makes you . . . a terrorist.

murder. While massive bombing of enemy cities might indeed shorten a war—and thus in theory (you can't see the future) save lives—there is a very big difference between targeting soldiers (even draftees) and civilians (even those whose work might contribute to the war effort). The first is a sad necessity in a fallen world; the second is a grave sin. Part of the "yoke" that Christ laid on us is that we may not fight like the pagan Romans, who flattened cities and killed or enslaved the conquered. We must be willing to risk higher casualties among our troops rather than wipe out unarmed women and children.[59]

The basic rule, if I may put it bluntly, is "Try not to act like Hitler." Along with launching murderous wars he claimed were acts of preemptive self-defense, and fire-bombing enemy cities, that dictator's greatest crime was his attempt to exterminate the Jews. He justified the Holocaust with the claim that Jews had been responsible for sparking the First World War and conniving at Germany's defeat, then launching communist revolutions all across Europe. He asserted in *Mein Kampf* and other writings that if Germany had wiped out its six hundred thousand Jews in 1913, millions of German soldiers' lives would have been spared. In fact, wiping out the Jews was the key to future world peace. Of course, such claims were empirically false. But is that the only objection we can raise against them? If we embrace the theory that it's moral to kill civilians to save soldiers' lives, that's all we are really able to say—that Hitler was . . . *mistaken*. Likewise Stalin and Mao, who promised a worldly paradise in return for a just a few decades of hell on earth. Without rigid rules that prevent us from taking tempting moral shortcuts to get what we want, we are all reduced to the relativism and pragmatism that marked modern dictators, social engineers, and eugenicists. If Christians can do no better than that, we might as well throw in our Shroud.

---

[59] CCC, 2314

 *The Holy Spirit*

1. On that cheerful note, perhaps we can move on to the Trinity's "silent partner," the Holy Spirit.

Give me a Christian rock band and a double-wide converted into a storefront church, and I'll throw back my head and let Him speak for Himself. As the Spirit once said via Little Richard: "A wop bop a loo bop. She bop bam boom."

2. Very funny. I gather you aren't a fan of the charismatic renewal in the Church?

I am the eggman. / You are the eggmen. / I am the Walrus. / Goo-go o-g'joob.

3. OK, then.

As long as we're clear about that . . .

The theology of the Holy Spirit is far less fully developed than that of the Father or the Son, for an obvious reason: the whole of the Old Testament spoke directly of God the Father, with subtle intimations of both the Son and the Spirit; the New Testament shows us Jesus in the flesh and offers attractive promises of the Paraclete, whom we meet only indirectly in the form of His interactions with Jesus and the apostles. This comparative silence and shadow are at once a powerful stimulus to mysticism and prayer—and a grave temptation for those who crave something "more" out of Revelation than God saw fit to tell us. But tempting as it is to start by skewering heresies, in this case it's better to focus on what we do know about the Holy Spirit from scripture and Church tradition. Why not go in chronological order?

Throughout the Old Testament, there are countless passages where God is said to reside among His people—not in the sense of His appearance in the burning bush to Moses, or the special, localized sacredness of the Ark of the Covenant, but rather as a spirit that comes to dwell with the Israelites. The word that Jews came to use for this sense of divine presence was the *Shekinah*, which has connotations of "dwelling" or even "nest." Mystics even speculated that the Hebrews, infused with this divine presence, in some sense *constituted* the earthly shadow cast by God. Remembering all that we said in chapter 2 about the transcendence of God as Father and creator, when we come to the Holy Spirit, what we see instead is the person of God most entailed in immanence. God the Father revealed Himself through a few stark interactions with men like Abraham and Moses; Christ came to earth at a specific time and place in history, remaining with us mainly now in the elements of the Eucharist; but the Holy Spirit has been engaged directly in interaction with man through the whole of salvation history. Jews believe that the *Shekinah* rested upon each of its prophets, psalmists, and indeed the transcribers of the Torah; in Catholic terms, these men were infused with the Holy Spirit.[1]

The face of God the Father is too much for man to look on and live; Jesus's presence, as the Gospels record, often provoked perplexity; but the Spirit working inwardly is the source of creativity, confidence, and joy (a theme the later Jewish mystical work *The Zohar* explores in extensive, eccentric depth). Hence Jesus promised before the Ascension that He would be followed by a spirit He called the "Comforter" (John 14:26). As the apostles celebrated the traditional Jewish feast of Pentecost—commemorating the day Moses gave the Torah to their assembled ancestors at the foot of Mt. Sinai—the expected Spirit appeared in "a mighty rushing wind" and "tongues, as of fire" (Acts 2:1, 3), giving these previously timid men the courage to preach the risen Christ to the community that had rejected Him only forty days before. The snarkiest of the assembled Jews thought the apostles must be drunk on new wine, but few were able to explain these evangelists' power to *speak in tongues*.

Now, this incident in the New Testament has surprisingly little to do with aluminum buildings full of overexcited Christian laymen wailing incoherently at each other. Indeed, the actual events in Acts are less reminiscent of a late-night Texas TV preacher nattering at the camera while selling magic prayer cloths than they are of the *Star Trek* reruns playing on the very next cable channel: On this occasion, the Holy Spirit kick-started the Church's mission to every nation by loaning the

---

[1] CCC, 687–688

first pope and his bishops the automatic translator that let Captain Kirk explain the Noninterference Doctrine to the Romulans and get busy with green-haired chicks like Shahna of Triskelion:

> And there were dwelling in Jerusalem Jews, devout men, from every nation under heaven. And when this sound occurred, the multitude came together, and were confused, because everyone heard them speak in his own language. Then they were all amazed and marveled, saying to one another, "Look, are not all these who speak Galileans? And how is it that we hear, each in our own language in which we were born? Parthians and Medes and Elamites, those dwelling in Mesopotamia, Judea and Cappadocia, Pontus and Asia, Phrygia and Pamphylia, Egypt and the parts of Libya adjoining Cyrene, visitors from Rome, both Jews and proselytes, Cretans and Arabs—we hear them speaking in our own tongues the wonderful works of God." So they were all amazed and perplexed, saying to one another, "Whatever could this mean?" (Acts 2:5–12)

Naturally, this joyous display of supernatural power was enormously popular, and Christians in subsequent decades spent considerable energies pestering God for an encore—and when He wouldn't oblige, they sometimes made do with emotive outbursts of jabbering. This seems almost the opposite of what took place at Pentecost; instead of coherent, persuasive sermons that foreign Jews could understand, these believers come out with random phonemes not even Christians can make sense of. It's almost as if Christians eager to replicate the raising of Lazarus were to run about knocking people over the head and stuffing them into caves. Unwilling to be a buzzkill, St. Paul did not dismiss the supernatural provenance of such gibberish; he merely rolled his eyes[2] (1 Corinthians 14:23) and set what seems a simple enough condition: "If anyone speaks in a tongue, let there be two or at the most three, each in turn, and let one

---

[2] "Therefore if the whole church comes together in one place, and all speak with tongues, and there come in those who are uninformed or unbelievers, will they not say that you are out of your mind?" (1 Cor. 14:23)

interpret. But if there is no interpreter, let him keep silent in church, and let him speak to himself and to God."

That doesn't seem like too much to ask. And in certain modern Pentecostalist churches, whenever someone starts speaking "in tongues," some dutiful soul appears to interpret them. Results here can vary. A friend of mine who converted from an evangelical church recalls how a fellow congregant rushed up beside a visitor who appeared to be speaking in tongues. The parishioner rattled off a long and edifying interpretation, which provoked a chorus of gratified whispers: "Praise Jesus!" Then the visitor turned on him, shaking his head, and explained in broken English that he had been asking directions to the gas station—in Arabic.

Those who believe that the "gift of tongues" is the mark that the Holy Spirit is working within you, something "real" Christians have enjoyed since the beginning, must reckon with the fact that *glossolalia* seems to have disappeared with the first generation of Christians, only popping up in eccentric, heretical corners like the Quaker and Shaker movements and the early Mormons. The practice would resurface (where else?) in California, at a Los Angeles awakening called the Azusa Street Revival—whose tent stood highly pitched for an amazing nine years (1906–15). That event was led by followers of the Pentecostal preacher Charles Parham, who taught among other curious things (like the importance of speaking in tongues) the theory of "British Israel"—that is, that the Anglo-Saxons were not merely the most successful band of Teutons to invade Roman Britain, but were in fact one of the "lost" tribes of Israel (the tribe of Dan, to be specific) and that the English royal family were the descendants of (you guessed it) King David.[3] The Irish were Gentile Canaanites whom God wished to see suppressed, and the pope was (of course) the Antichrist.

---

[3] This theory boosted both the political career of Benjamin Disraeli and the cause of imperialists who hoped that Britain would seize Palestine from the Ottoman Empire. One offshoot of this movement, Christian Identity, came to believe that the British were the only true descendants of ancient Israel, while others claiming Jewish identity (that is, Jews) were diabolical imposters. For more, see Michael Barkun, *Religion and the Racist Right* (Charlotte: University of North Carolina Press, 1996).

At the Azusa Street Revival the fervent Parhamite preacher William Seymour would regularly whip up participants into a spiritual tizzy until some would erupt into tongues. Convinced that they had experienced Pentecost all over again, some left the revival determined to use this apostolic power to preach the gospel—in India, China, and Japan. History has not recorded the reaction of the natives.[4] But at least the missionaries weren't martyred, which suggests that the Pentecostalist approach is safer than the Jesuit method, which entailed actually learning difficult foreign languages and preaching the dangerous gospel.

I wish I could report that this quixotic endeavor snuffed out the Pentecostalist movement, extinguishing it with a cringe. But any ecclesial body that sees as proof of God's special favor grown men and woman rushing around waving their hands and vocalizing, clearly lacks the chromosome for shame. So despite its *Life of Brian* beginnings ("Blessed are the cheesemakers!"), Pentecostalism quickly spread in the past century—until it forms now, according to John L. Allen's *The Future Church*,[5] the single most powerful religious movement in Asia, Africa, and Latin America. Allen notes that millions of poorly catechized Catholics have abandoned their parishes for newly built chapels where self-taught pastors (funded by money from south of the Mason-Dixon line) offer laying-on of hands, miraculous "cures," and self-help lessons in the "gospel of success." As Allen notes, the Catholics in such areas are now incorporating "charismatic" elements into their worship in a desperate attempt to compete. On the positive side, these churches have a better track record of sobering up alcoholics and goading people into starting their own small businesses—and many of the "apostate" Catholics who make them up had never really been taught their old faith in the first place, which means that for them these churches offer the deepest Christian experiences of their lives. Less encouraging is the heavy "burnout" factor Allen identifies, as members of these sects grow weary or jaded by the incessant religious hysteria—how many of us can live like Jimmy

---

[4] D. William Faupel, "Glossolalia as Foreign Language: An Investigation of the Early Twentieth-Century Pentecostal Claim," *The Wesleyan Theological Journal* 31, no. 1 (1996): 95–109.
[5] John L. Allen, *The Future* Church (New York: Doubleday, 2009), 375–413.

Swaggart all through our lives?—and drift away from the practice of any religion whatsoever. The fragility of frenzy-based spirituality was best documented by Msgr. Ronald Knox in his phlegmatic *Enthusiasm*, where he traces the poignant trajectory of groups such as the Quakers—who began as wild-eyed, quivering revolutionaries who would rush about naked in public "for a sign," and ended up as respectable post-Unitarians whose religious services consist of very well-dressed WASPs sitting in silent circles in empty rooms, waiting for the "voice of the spirit" to speak through one of them. But it seems He's too embarrassed, so after a while they just grab their Abercrombie jackets and shuffle on home.

Another key doctrine Parham taught, and the one that still prevails among most Pentecostalist Protestants, asserts that charismatic "baptism in the Holy Spirit"—as demonstrated by marvels such as speaking in tongues or being "slain in the spirit"—is of equal or greater importance to the water baptism that Christians have regarded since the early Church as a sacrament. There's a reason traditional Christians have thought water baptism is a sacrament: Jesus said so (Matthew 28:19).[6] Indeed, the practice of baptizing new Christians with water can be traced all the way back to the time of the apostles, whose authority presumably can be trusted. From St. Paul we have evidence that infants were baptized from the earliest days of the Church: In Colossians 2 he says that baptism is the replacement for circumcision (a rite for infants—who were too young to say, "Hell, no!"), and elsewhere (1 Corinthians 1:16) he speaks of baptizing entire households. Since these were hardy, fertile Jews, not self-sterilized Québécois French, it is certain that such households included young children. Yes, that very event which in the "best parts" of town entails ordering silver rattles from Tiffany's was begun by Jesus Christ around the year 30 A.D. Speaking in tongues seems to have died out shortly after St. Paul did, and not resumed again till 1906. If it had been an essential part of Christianity, something tells me that God would have noticed.

The new Pentecostalist doctrine treats as sterile, empty rituals the sacraments that the apostles learned from Christ. Instead, the Pentecostalists offer sensational, apparently miraculous "happenings" that erupt for public consumption during jacked-up emotional outbursts akin to rock concerts or hockey fights. A friend who grew up among Pentecostalists recounted to me how "when they ran out of tongues or people stopped passing out, the preacher would set a TV on fire or draw a picture of the devil for everyone to stomp on." I personally have seen a "charismatic" Catholic priest interrupt the Eucharistic prayer to lapse into "tongues" (none of which included Latin) and attempt to "lay hands" on me during confession. When I didn't pass out, he started babbling. Torn between morbid curiosity and the silent thought "Bless his heart!" I waited the good priest out until at last he gave me absolution. I ran outside with a saving word on my lips: "Taxi!"

---

[6] CCC, 1253–1260

Image courtesy Wikipedia Commons

4. So you don't believe that the Holy Spirit manifests Himself?

Don't even kid about that; if He didn't, we'd all be doomed. You know that super-natural, "actual" grace that allows us to overcome the world, the flesh, and the devil and perform any good action whatsoever? [7]

5. Not really.

Well, that comes from the Holy Spirit. Indeed, the Church believes that the Holy Spirit is the active, ongoing factor in each of our lives that leads us closer to God. The Father remains transcendent; the Son comes to us primarily through the Eucharist; but the Holy Spirit moves through all the sacraments. Furthermore, He pervades the ups and downs of ordinary life, gently attracting us to goodness and repelling us from evil. He serves as the "still small voice" of conscience, and the return address for all the consolations that make life meaningful or even barely tolerable. The Church has identified the "gifts" that come from the Holy Spirit that bring us closer to God: [8]

• **Wisdom.** Solomon was famous among Jewish kings for this quality— though one hopes that the Holy Ghost nowadays warns Christians against acquiring seventy wives and three hundred concubines.

• **Understanding.** If you have slogged with me this far through the thickets of Trinitarian and Christological heresies, you've probably been getting a little extra supernatural help.

• **Counsel.** This is a form of supernatural prudence that helps a soul judge what practical course of action will speed his journey to heaven. It can be distinguished from natural prudence, which typically aims at keeping us alive and healthy on earth.

• **Fortitude.** Ever wonder how those martyrs could keep their cool while Indians were skinning them, or as they hung face down for days in Japanese trenches full of dead animals and excrement? This is the gift of the Spirit that kept those

---

[7] CCC, 2000
[8] CCC, 1831

brave souls from doing what you or I would in the circumstances—checking whatever box on whichever form was required to apostasize, then fleeing the country to hold a press conference.

- **Knowledge.** This gift helps us see the truth when we might otherwise willfully miss it; everyone Jesus preached to was granted the grace to know He was telling the truth. Otherwise, He wouldn't have blamed them for disputing His extraordinary claims or accused some of blaspheming not Him but the Holy Spirit (Mark 3:28–30).

- **Piety.** This word means many more (and much better) things than most of us tend to think of when we hear it nowadays—especially when it's paired with modifiers like "cloying." Piety is much more than the act of a little old lady dropping in a quarter to light an electric candle. (Not that there's anything wrong with that.) It's the virtue of *staying loyal to something greater than yourself*, especially something that came before you and to which you feel a debt of gratitude. No surprise, it's a rare commodity in modern times, since we all know we created ourselves ex nihilo and the universe owes us a living. Piety was what drove Aeneas to rescue his family's household gods from burning Troy, and Paul Comtois (then the highest public official in Canada), who first saved his wife and children, then rushed into a burning chapel in 1966 and burned to death attempting to rescue the Eucharist.

- **Fear.** Now this one doesn't sound like much of a gift at first, until you consider my beagle, Susie. At twelve years old and only forty pounds, she is known for making kamikaze attacks against much larger, stronger dogs—and once broke through my wooden picket fence to jump off a four-foot stone wall and pounce on a German shepherd. (Don't worry, the German shepherd wasn't hurt—and I reinforced the entire fence with steel.) Susie could use a little holy fear. So could most of us, who even when we deign to consider that God exists, imagine Him as a doting grandma wrapped in a doily who'll welcome us regardless of our unrepented sins, thanks to her advanced case of dementia. She's just delighted that we dropped by! Think of holy fear as the 375 feet of chicken wire that keeps us in the yard.

Yet another blurry photo of one of the author's dogs.

6. So is the Holy Spirit something like a demon that possesses you— except in a really good way?

No, no, no. By which I mean: emphatically not. None of the gifts above annul a believer's free will, displace his consciousness, or enable his head to spin around. A much better model to use is a medical one: Imagine that our species suffers from a kind of spiritual depression. Thanks to the Fall, while living in the world and the flesh, we find it devilishly hard not to sin. We tend to ignore the voice of conscience—which also speaks to us via the Holy Spirit. So He comes to us (when we ask Him to) and reinvigorates our resolve—like a much-needed dose of serotonin.[9]

7. So the Spirit's gifts work something like psychiatric meds?

As I said, it's a metaphor. But yes—insofar as He doesn't alter our minds or decrease our freedom but instead simply helps us follow our best intentions and be the best free person each of us can.[10] In fact, there is another set of benefits the Holy Spirit can grant us, which was enumerated by St. Paul (Galatians 5:22–23) and best explicated by Aquinas.[11]

These "fruits" of the Holy Spirit are actions that, without His help, we might not be able to manage at all—but with Him, we do them with ease, good cheer, and peace of soul. There are twelve different varieties of this fruit, which I like to imagine arranged in bright, shimmering rows at Trader Joe's:

Love. Not in the sense of the Beatles' song, where it's "all you need," or Lady Gaga's "Bad Romance" ("I want your love / and I want your revenge . . . I don't wanna be friends"), but in the sense of Christ's otherwise impossible command to "love your enemies." When martyrs like St. Isaac Jogues prayed sincerely for the

---

[9] CCC, 406
[10] CCC, 798
[11] CCC, 1832

howling pagans who were torturing them, there was clearly something supernatural at work.

Joy. This is something distinct from cheerfulness or even the happiness that philosophers tell us is the proper goal of every man. When the Bl. Mother Teresa endured four decades of spiritual "dryness," all through which she felt like God was absent, there was a mysterious level on which at the same time she experienced Joy (as her journals report). I would explore this issue further, if I had any earthly idea what it entailed. If I had been Mother Teresa's spiritual adviser and had known what she was going through, I would have yanked her out of Calcutta and sent her to Canyon Ranch with a big fat bottle of happy pills and a copy of *Eat. Pray. Love.* Which may explain why no one comes to me for spiritual advice.

Peace. We don't mean the peace the hippies and yippies were seeking at Woodstock—which ended, as you history buffs will remember, with communist victories and the killing fields. Nor the Middle East "peace process," though there, again, we're discussing something that's humanly impossible. This Peace, which surpasses all understanding, is what can pervade the soul of someone unjustly imprisoned and disarm the hostility of his guards. It filled third-century martyr St. Felicity, a slave arrested for her Christian faith when she was nine months pregnant—who thanks to a weirdly pro-life Roman law could not be executed until she gave birth. As she endured the horrors of natural childbirth[12] in a squalid prison, jeered at by Roman guards about her upcoming torture, she answered them calmly: "I suffer now, but [when I am executed] another will be in me Who will suffer for me, because I suffer for Him." Creeped out, they backed away, and her healthy newborn daughter was adopted by a very nice Christian couple who sent her to private school.

Patience. This is a quality enforced on those of us dwelling in major cities who must placidly wait in line for train tickets, bus tokens, elevators—and even in our off-hours for our Organic Soy Pumpkin Frappes—behind long streams of odd-looking, off-smelling strangers. Conversely, those who live in suburbs must wait long months, and sometimes years, for anything interesting to happen. But it isn't the Holy Spirit that keeps us tapping our toes and rolling our eyes instead of exploding in hateful epithets and hacking our way through the mob with a machete. (More likely, it's the fear of all those neo-Nazis you'd meet in prison.) No, the Patience that comes as a fruit of the Holy Spirit imparts a placidity of soul that will allow a man of action like St. Maximilian Kolbe—once a cranky, partisan right-wing Catholic journalist—to keep his cool in a prison camp and calmly minister to his fellow prisoners. Kolbe finally offered his life in place of a family man and spent weeks slowly starving to death without complaint.

---

[12] If men gave birth, there would be no discussion of breathing exercises but instead swift and certain general anesthesia, every time.

Image courtesy of Wikipedia Commons

Kindness. This quality is often conflated with namby-pamby niceness, of the sort practiced selectively by NPR junkies driving Volvos at 10 mph below the speed limit in front of us. Tempting as it might be to dismiss the idea altogether (and key their cars), we should instead remember that Kindness is one of the virtues most often attributed to Mary, the Mother of God. From her weary pregnant pilgrimage to visit her cousin Elizabeth to her thoughtful intervention to keep the wine flowing at Cana, Our Lady went on to live in the midst of the early Church without arrogating authority—which surely would have been granted her—and in successive centuries she has appeared to the humblest Christians, offering them special blessings and messages of mercy. All those piled up "thank you" plaques at Marian shrines around the world marking healings that she helped obtain show us the real shape that Kindness takes.

Goodness. It's easy to get confused: We aren't here speaking of the absolute Goodness proper to God—nor of "good" as something inferior to "better" and "best," as in "It's *good* that Navy Seals killed Osama Bin Laden. It would have been *better* if they had gravely wounded him and he had died nice and sl-o-o-o-o-w." Instead we mean a single-minded focus on pursuing the highest and the best, despite temptation, frustration, and bunions. A fine Old Testament instance here would be Moses, who overcame his stammer and his annoying upper-class accent (he grew up inside Pharaoh's palace) to follow God's commands, which came to him from flaming shrubbery. Facing down the most powerful ruler in the world on behalf of a tribe of slaves, he brought them through the Red Sea, then the desert, despite their propensity for whining and worshiping

cattle, not to mention lousy sense of direction. For forty years Moses served as a kind of pope and king of the Jews, keeping them together like a camp counselor leading a pack of individualist "gifted" kids until they reached their promised land—which he never entered but only glimpsed from across the border before he died, presumably of exhaustion.

Long-Suffering. From its name, this spirit-fruit sounds about as appealing as the infamous southeast Asian durian, which smells like a pile of fish that died in a diaper pail but tastes, aficionados promise, much more like rotting venison. The fact that Thais and Malaysians can consume such a fruit and *like* it helps explain such nations' breakneck economic progress; clearly, these people have the kind of Long-Suffering that sustains workers through long, long hours in factories, long after we Westerners would have formed unions, gone on strike, then gone off to earn B.A.s in occupational art therapy while racking up student loans. In the spiritual sense, Long-Suffering is the almost preternatural peace of mind that certain saintly people maintain in the worst of circumstances. For instance, St. John of the Cross. This sixteenth-century Spanish mystic joined the already austere Carmelites only to insist that they revive the most outrageous penances and deprivations, which the order had pragmatically abandoned. His brother friars didn't appreciate such helpful suggestions; they fought him bitterly, reported him as a heretic to the Spanish Inquisition, deprived him of the sacraments, then locked him for nine months in a six-foot-by-ten-foot prison cell—from which he was taken out only to be flogged while kneeling half-naked on the kitchen floor eating bread and sardines. (Those unreformed Carmelites sound sufficiently *kinky*, come to think of it, that we can begin

A real sign from Singapore, forbidding both Long-Suffering and Discalced Carmelite activity on its commuter trains.

to see why St. John thought they needed reforming.) All through it, he never wept or cried out in pain, maintained by an inner life of prayer that frequently sent him into profound religious ecstasies—reflected in the strangely chipper poems he wrote during that period. In the end even his enemies were won over by John's preternatural peacefulness—that and the fact that his body didn't decay when he died. He was quickly acclaimed as a saint, and his works as spiritual classics, even if his life reads to us bad Catholics more like a cautionary tale. (*Note to self:* When trying to restore a religious order to its primitive severity, remember Step 1: Don't.)

Mildness. The best illustration of distinctly miraculous Mildness appears at the very outset of man's journey in faith: with our father Abraham and his dealings with God and with Sodom. Most of us know, in a vague sort of way, why Sodom and Gomorrah were destroyed. But nobody looks far into it—perhaps because we don't much like to think of God raining napalm on cities for sexual sins. (It's easier to imagine, say, Richard Nixon doing this.) If He got back in that habit, what would happen to all the cities with interesting architecture or restaurants? Anyway, how do we explain the persistence of places like San Francisco—where the lack of a law against public nudity has recently led some hygiene-minded locals to foster an ordinance requiring that naked people at least *put down a towel or something* before they sit down in restaurants or park benches? That tempest in a fleshpot raises too many questions[13] for a catechist to answer, but at least we can speak of Sodom—whose evils went far beyond anything that's legal even in Amsterdam. As readers of Genesis 18 will recall, three angels paid a visit to Abraham to inform him that his elderly wife would finally have a son that spring. Scripture recounts that she cackled, "Fat chance" (translations differ), but at least she and Abraham put out a decent spread. Hospitality was a big deal in the ancient world, as the story of the Cyclops in the *Odyssey* reminds us. We can hear our foremother in faith as she piled high the blintzes and kugel for her visitors, "Eat, eat! You three are wasting away to nothing already." The surfeited spirits moved on to the neighboring Sodom to visit Abraham's cousin Lot—who'd moved to the big city to try to "make it." As soon as these Adonises arrived, Lot's house was besieged by sexual aggressors—apparently so jaded by having tried *everything else that's possible* in the bedroom that they wished to . . . gang rape angels. Ever the gracious host, Lot protected his guests by offering the *putti*-posse his virgin daughters instead. But there were no takers. It had to be angels or nothing. The angels made a miraculous escape and warned Lot to get his family out of town before they called in the B-52s. As we all know, Lot's wife looked back at the burning city (she must have thought she'd left something on the stove) and was turned to a pillar of salt—quite a valuable commodity in the ancient world, *so it shouldn't be a total loss.*

But before all this happened, God informed Abraham of the fate that Sodom faced, and Abraham's reaction was one of pertinacious compassion. In noble Semitic fashion, he started to haggle with God:

---

[13] For instance: "*Eeeewww?*"

"Will you sweep away the righteous with the wicked? What if there are fifty righteous people in the city? Will you really sweep it away and not spare the place for the sake of the fifty righteous people in it? Far be it from you to do such a thing—to kill the righteous with the wicked, treating the righteous and the wicked alike. Far be it from you! Will not the Judge of all the earth do right?"

The LORD said, "If I find fifty righteous people in the city of Sodom, I will spare the whole place for their sake."

"Now that I have been so bold as to speak to the Lord, though I am nothing but dust and ashes, what if the number of the righteous is five less than fifty? Will you destroy the whole city for lack of five people?"

"If I find forty-five there," he said, "I will not destroy it."

Once again he spoke to him, "What if only forty are found there?"

He said, "For the sake of forty, I will not do it."

Then he said, "May the Lord not be angry, but let me speak. What if only thirty can be found there?"

He answered, "I will not do it if I find thirty there."

Abraham said, "Now that I have been so bold as to speak to the Lord, what if only twenty can be found there?"

He said, "For the sake of twenty, I will not destroy it."

Then he said, "May the Lord not be angry, but let me speak just once more. What if only ten can be found there?"

He answered, "For the sake of ten, I will not destroy it." (Genesis 18:24–32)

You might be astounded at Abraham's persistence and at God's patience in this exchange, but the latter could afford to be magnanimous; He knew there were only nine.

Still, it's uplifting to think that the father of the People of God was bold enough to act like a litigator with the Lord of the Universe on behalf of a city full of decadent, inhospitable goyim. This was a foretaste of the Jewish people's providential role as a "light to the Gentiles."

Faith. Strictly speaking, Faith is one of the "infused" virtues, which we cannot manage without a special grace (that is, "gift"—it comes from the same root as the "*gracias*" we mispronounce when thanking the Mexican waitress for bringing us a free shot of mezcal along with our margarita; like God, she rolls her eyes but accepts the well-intentioned gesture). So the Holy Spirit is always in the mix. But there's a special kind of Faith that we class among the Spirit's fruits, and it's much more pungent than lime juice: the strictly miraculous Faith that sustains believers when they are faced with fierce opposition from their fellow Christians and persecuted by the powerful for telling the truth. This Faith sustained the sixteen-year-old illiterate shepherdess Joan of Arc when she led armies of once-despondent Frenchmen to drive out the English occupiers who had devastated her country. It helped her stick to her story when she was dragged out of a jail cell and forced to debate the theology faculty of the University of Paris.

And on a much, much, much less heroic note, it helped me back in high school—when I tried to prosecute my religion teachers for heresy. Back in the 1980s, at the local Catholic school my parents had helped to build, a coterie of jaded ex-seminarians and dissident nuns had taken over the religion department, whose bully pulpit they used to teach Catholic kids to reject the Church's teachings on sex, the virginity of Mary, the fleshly Resurrection of Christ, and the infallibility of the pope. Between showing us Sandinista recruitment films and dismissing Pope John Paul II as a backward Polish plumber, they used reeducational methods like standing me in front of the class "to tell everyone how you can support the Church's backward position on birth control on a starving planet." Only the Holy Spirit can keep a sixteen-year-old from bursting into tears at times like this. After my written complaints went from the principal to the bishop, then from him to the papal nuncio, I was summoned to the principal's office alone. I faced him, the religion faculty, and the high school chaplain—who'd actually donned a Roman collar for the occasion. The principal crumpled his face compassionately, and asked, "John if you're so unhappy with what we're teaching here, have you considered another school?" The Spirit answered for me: "If you people are so unhappy with the contents of the Catholic Faith, have you considered getting other jobs? And if that's a threat, you should talk to my attorney—here's his card." Tequila that strong is only poured in by the Spirit.

Modesty. This word can mean several things, including the "aw-shucks" Jimmy Stewart humility that, when authentic, can make a good man (like Stewart) great to be around, and when aped can make a megalomaniac U.S. president. The fruit of the Spirit here refers to something much more concrete and potentially tangible: nubile human flesh, casually flaunted or squeezed into garments that caress every tempting curve and sinew . . . *ahem*! I think we just learned a bit about the importance of Modesty in helping writers keep on topic. In a culture like ours, which is just as beauty loving and cruel as that of the pagan Greeks (without their martial courage or good taste), there are situations where it might just take the miraculous aid of the Spirit to swim against the tide. I'm not speaking of people like me who have no business wearing Speedos on the beach; covering flesh like ours is an act of simple charity. Real instances where divine intervention might be necessary include actors or actresses pressured to do needless, explicit sex scenes of the kind that make

some "R-rated" movies off-limits on a date—it's just too cringeworthy as you squirm in your seat and wonder what your partner is thinking. Other candidates for Pentecostal help would be teenagers (and nowadays even tweens) who are pressured to wear clothes that make it hard for their healthy counterparts of the opposite sex to think straight, or think at all. I remember high school . . . and the Italian-American girls in their five-inch heels. What I don't remember is most of the teachers' names (except the religion faculty, see above).

Continency. Another word for this is "celibacy." We're not talking here about Chastity (that comes next), which can in one context mean earthy, toe-curling acts transmitting the grace proper to marriage, and in another context placid solitude in a hermit's cell. Nope, we're talking straight-out self-denial, which can sometimes be demanded even of the married—for instance, when one party is abandoned by his or her spouse, or when a couple is practicing Natural Family Planning and that oh-so-romantic mucus chart on the fridge shows the grinning "baby" sticker. In these cases, where celibacy is not even proper to one's vocation, the Holy Spirit can visit the heart and mind and loins and weave among them a peace that surpasses all understanding—or at any rate, a truce. Instead of "white-knuckling" it through this stark deprivation, the person who enjoys this fruit of the Holy Spirit sits back and peels it like an orange, enjoying the other good gifts of God that sensual frustration often causes us to miss. Like languorously petting an angora cat or building Minas Tirith out of Legos in your basement . . .

Chastity. The most famous case of Chastity captured by strictly miraculous means has to be that of St. Thomas Aquinas. As you amateur hagiographers all know, young Tommaso, son of Count Landulf, was the great-nephew of emperor Frederick Barbarossa. His family had seven sons and dynastic plans for each of them that entailed marrying heiresses blessed with huge tracts of land. So it came as an ugly surprise when the young man informed his parents that he planned to join the threadbare, upstart Order of Preachers—mendicants who literally walked the streets to beg for their suppers. Tommaso was lectured, manipulated, threatened, then finally kidnapped by his brothers, who locked him in a cell for a year and a half, when they finally got and idea they were sure would drive a stake through his vocation: They sent in the prettiest courtesan they could find with instructions to do whatever it took to seduce the future saint. Tommaso was not . . . unmoved. In fact, his passion was such that he leapt from his bed and seized a burning poker to menace the woman. Convinced that was all he would brandish, she fled the room. At that moment, according to his biographers, Tommaso felt an overwhelming sense of peace and order, as if an invisible flak jacket of

Chastity had been strapped onto his body. He was never troubled by Lust again. Nor did he lose his zest for life or other appetites—remaining ever ravenous for classical learning, sanctity, and risotto carbonara.

CRWORWORWORWORWORWORWORWORWORWORWORWORWORWORWORWORW

FAQs from Your Stoner Neighbor #5
So you're saying that the Holy Spirit only acts in small ways, serving as a spiritual booster shot to needy souls? Or how about this: The Father built the hardware, the Son designed the software, and the Spirit is the tech support you call in Bangalore.

Even allowing for the apophatic (that is, baffling) nature of theological language, those are really atrocious ways of putting the matter. They are at once demeaning, misleading, and even dispiriting. Are you channeling Screwtape today?

Well, aren't you just bubbling over with the Mildness of Father Abraham . . . Go ahead, then, and explain how the Holy Spirit isn't merely the Ladies Auxiliary of the Trinity.

You have stumbled (and I do mean stumbled) upon a widespread theological error, which feminists have used to smuggle androgyny into the Godhead: They point out that in Hebrew and Aramaic, the gender of the word *Spirit* is feminine, and so try to argue that the Spirit can be seen as a kind of goddess-figure. The problem is that the apostles seem to have given zero credence to such a theory. The Gospels use the masculine word *Paraclete* and masculine pronouns in referring to the Spirit—whose gender was never questioned again in Christian circles until the appearance of *Ms.* magazine. After that, the notion of casting the Holy Spirit as feminine became quite popular among groups of ex-Catholics who now practiced Wicca and (no kidding) the Branch Davidians. Not that this should discredit this theological innovation, of course. Not at all.

A more significant problem with conceiving of any person of the Trinity as feminine is this: The primary use of sexual metaphors in Christianity is to convey the balance of activity and passivity, initiative and response, between the Lord and a human soul. We call the Church the "bride" of Christ and Jesus the "bridegroom" of the soul precisely because of what these terms convey to psychologically normal people with conventional sexual expectations. To be a bit more blunt, it is God Who picks us up and carries us over the threshold, Who overwhelms us like the bride in the Song of Songs, Who plants the seeds that we must nurture. Those people who want to make God feminine are really trying (whether they admit this themselves or not) to make themselves the dominant partner in the relationship, to flip things over and make the soul the master. In this context only, the Church insists on the missionary position.

Of course, in other linguistic contexts that don't connect to the marital act, there are places in the Bible where God's love is compared to maternal solicitude and tenderness—which, believe me, is quite a relief after reading stories like Sodom's. But the primary use of sex metaphors in scripture is yoked to the sharp distinction between transcendence and immanence that we discussed in chapter 2, and for that reason the entire orthodox Christian tradition has spoken of God (metaphorically) as male. If it's any consolation to outraged readers, that means that the whole of the human race (the pope included) is theologically female. We're all in this together, girls, and sisterhood is powerless.

No, that doesn't help at all. In fact, it just makes matters worse.

It sure does, if you are intent (as Descartes was) on making human beings "the masters and possessors" of creation—an ambition that the misogynist Simone de Beauvoir extended to include women, too. Read Karl Stern's *The Flight from Woman* to learn how it was her contempt for women's work (especially nurturance) and her loathing of docility, humility, and a long list of other Christian virtues that led her to pioneer the ideology of modern, pro-choice feminism, which is essentially atheist existentialism in drag. For a wholesome response by a more balanced woman whose husband actually loves her, read Carolyn Graglia's *Domestic Tranquility: A Brief Against Feminism*, which (besides being a raucous read and a brilliant intellectual history) boils down to a rapturous essay on the joys of surrender. That's a theme that recurs with great regularity in the writing of Christian mystics, male and female. You know a motif that doesn't pop up in the works of a single saint? The importance of asserting our equality with God, demanding equal rights or autonomy. You'll find much more along those lines in *Paradise Lost*, or *The Inferno*.

ꝏꝏꝏꝏꝏꝏꝏꝏꝏꝏꝏꝏꝏꝏꝏꝏ

8. OK, OK. Back to the Holy Spirit. How would *you* characterize His role?

He is the motive force, the breath that moves our limbs, the gasoline that runs the ambulance . . . He is, to return to the Hebrew image of the *Shekinah*, the immanent presence of the transcendent God. We are shown the Father through the person of Christ, but we don't encounter Him directly on this earth. We encounter Christ primarily through the Eucharist, though He's also present in a more diffused way in the Church itself. We can even see Him in the face of other human beings if we remember that they are images of God, and we try really, *really* hard. But most of us don't. However, the Holy Spirit, as I indicated above, is present whenever we follow the promptings of grace, do some act of kindness with God in mind, or settle down to pray. Which is to say, for most of us, not very often. But He's always waiting for us, right at our elbow, ready to come when called. Think of the Spirit, if you will, as the butler Jeeves, while each of us is Bertie Wooster. We are technically in charge, but Jeeves is the brains of the operation and all the best decisions come from him.

9 . And all your best theological arguments come from P. G. Wodehouse?

Just as Aquinas's came from Aristotle.

10. By the way, where does the Holy Spirit come from? One version of your creed says that He proceeds from the Father—the other from the Father and the Son. Which is it? Or is it neither? Perhaps he just kind of gurgles up from the ground of Being like the "bubbling crude" in *The Beverly Hillbillies* . . .

This issue is a sore point for many Christians for many reasons, principally because the question of from whom the Holy Spirit proceeds (from the Father, or the Father and the Son) was what split the Eastern and Western churches in 1054.[14]

---

[14] CCC, 246-248

Those of us whose families hail from places such as the Balkans know how much innocent blood has been spilled by fanatical nationalists in service of distinctly unholy spirits. Of course, there was much more at stake in the East-West schism than an excruciatingly fine point of Trinitarian theology. In the stormy marriage between East and West, the *filioque* controversy was the final burnt dinner or flirtation with a waitress that precipitated a long-awaited divorce. To put things bluntly and briefly, the Christian East was the source of most of the sophisticated theological distinctions concerning Christ that we slogged through in chapter 3. As the "brain" of the Church, the East was also the source of most of the heresies, whose sheer complexity left successive popes scratching their heads and dispatching anathemas. However many saintly Eastern Fathers defended the orthodox position, all that a dedicated heretic really needed was the support of the Byzantine emperor—who held the local church in the palm of his hand. He needed to have it there, since theological differences were enough to start street riots in Constantinople, Antioch, or Alexandria. In fact, there were two main dissenting factions of Christians whose theories concerning Christ were denounced—the Nestorians and the Monophysites. They treasured opposing errors, and it won't surprise students of Church history that each group seemed to hate the centrist (orthodox) bishops even more than they hated the other. Various emperors tried to conciliate each faction at various times, afraid of estranging entire provinces full of their subjects. Which was, of course, what happened. The Christians deemed heretical by councils would later prove disloyal when Byzantium was fighting the mighty armies of Islam, and the efforts the emperors made to fudge essential doctrinal truths would alienate the pope, who had cultivated powerful, newly converted kingdoms like that of the Franks—who were far enough off not to meddle in theological questions.

Well, not meddle much. It was the Frankish Holy Roman emperors who insisted on introducing to the Creed the idea that the Holy Spirit proceeds "from the Father *and the son* (*filioque*)." That adapted creed was first used in Spain to force the residual Arians in Spain to clearly and unequivocally acclaim Jesus as equally God with the Father. Important theologians such as Augustine (in the West) and Maximos the Confessor (in the East) had taught that the Holy Spirit proceeds from both the Father and the Son, and this theory at first raised little controversy in the East—which was quite preoccupied with yet another patched-together heresy (Monothelitism) that the Byzantine emperor had sponsored to try to win the hearts of his dissenting subjects. It was one thing to teach Augustine's theory concerning the Spirit—but adding words to the Creed itself, on papal authority that overrode the decrees of an ecumenical council . . . now them wuz fightin' words. Eager to pick precisely that fight with the Byzantines, the Franks began the practice of singing the revised Creed at Mass—something that didn't yet happen in Rome, where a long string of popes tried to keep the peace through the expedient of leaving the Creed out altogether. But by 1014, relations between East and West were thoroughly frayed over half a dozen jurisdictional disputes. Each of the churches spoke, wrote, and prayed in a different language, competed for authority from Kievan Rus to Ruthenia, and had little incentive to conciliate each other. The Byzantine emperor continually pressed the patriarch to defy papal authority, while the Western Holy Roman emperor goaded the pope into insisting on papal supremacy. In 1014, the papal Mass at last featured the Creed, which now included the *filioque*. Thus Rome affirmed its long-held understanding of the Trinity and, much more important, its right to overrule mere councils of bishops (something the East had accepted, tacitly, for centuries). This led to open schism in 1054, a split that continues to this day.

11. Um, OK. But which side was right?

The best theory is that the Eastern and Western understandings insist on a distinction without an ultimate difference. There's plenty of biblical evidence that the Holy Spirit was sent at Christ's command to guide and "console" the Church after His Ascension—thus it proceeds from Him as well as from the Father. There is also plenty of reason to insist that the Father is the essential origin, the wellspring of the Trinity, from whom both the other Persons eternally flow forth. There's a widespread Western theory that the Spirit is generated by the perfect mutual love of the Father and the Son, but it isn't dogmatically mandated. The Eastern Catholic churches, which came back at various points to unity with Rome, were never required to say the *filioque* during the Creed, and Pope John Paul II finally forbade them to. But we still say it in the West. The Orthodox churches began by saying that adding words to the Creed merely exceeded the pope's authority; by now their position seems to be that the *filioque* is heretical, since it somehow (though I can't see it) derogates from the Holy Spirit's dignity. In reality, what they object to is the primacy of the pope, whenever and however it's exercised, but the *filioque* "heresy" is their story and they're sticking to it. Given that birthrates are plummeting in every Orthodox country, as Allen points out in *The Future Church*,[15] the sheer size of the Eastern Orthodox population compared with that of the Catholics (who in Africa and Latin America at least still bother to breed) will soon be almost trivial. But that won't diminish the significance of the Orthodox Church, which to those who know their Church history offers the only plausible alternative ecclesiology to Roman Catholicism. But we'll get into that in the next chapter, which covers the Church.

---

[15] Allen, *Future Church*, 170.

12. Are there any more heresies, real or imaginary, concerning the Holy Spirit?

Sure. But only two are really important. And as usual, they each take one horn of a dilemma and snap it off, running away and claiming they've caught a unicorn. The Church takes the middle position, which means she ends up having to ride the bull.

13. Speaking of bull . . . oh, never mind. Tell me about the heresies.

The history of heresies really does beguile the mind, like a textbook in abnormal psychology, which always gets people trying to diagnose their roommates or their parents. ("Dad, guess what I learned this semester: You're a clinical narcissist." Or: "Britney, check it out—you got a perfect score . . . on the Sociopathy Checklist.")

The most dangerous of the remaining pneumatological heresies—

14. Wait a minute. What the heck is pneumatology?

Ever heard of etymology? Now put it into practice.

15. So these are heresies that make you cough?

In a manner of speaking. They center on how the Spirit ("*pneuma*" or "breath") circulates in the Church, and each of these theories has Him blowing through the wrong side of the bagpipes, so "Amazing Grace" sounds more like a song by Nirvana.

First there's the heresy named for Joachim of Fiore, a pious but batty monk who developed a whole new interpretation of the Church. The very fact that some 1,100 years after Pentecost somebody thought he finally had a handle on what the Church really was is enough to make one suspicious. Joachim had been reading between the lines of the Book of Revelation and thought he'd figured out the real significance of the Trinity in history: The Old Covenant with the Jews was the age of the Father. (So far, so good.) The New Covenant with Christ was the age of the Son. (We're still with you, Jojo.) But that left the Holy Spirit entirely unaccounted for. As a full-fledged member of the Trinity, surely the Holy Spirit deserved His own epoch in history. What is more, there was widespread corruption in the Church because (surprise!) it was still composed of humans. The graces that came from the sacraments clearly weren't doing their job of making people saints, so surely God must have something more decisive in mind: a new age of the Spirit, which would come at some point in the future and put an end to all the sinful practices and institutions that still existed throughout the world—such as warfare, serfdom, inequality, Jewish moneylenders . . . Joachim's followers tended to fill in the blanks with whatever they objected to, and his theological ponderings were quickly adopted by the medieval equivalents of the Bolsheviks—from the bands of meandering Flagellants, who'd flog themselves into frenzies then rouse the townsfolk to plunder the Jewish ghetto, to radical Franciscans who'd been excommunicated for denouncing private property. (This last group took St. Francis's nickname, *alter Christus*, all too literally and proclaimed the thirteenth century and thereafter the age of St. Francis—which neatly dovetailed with Joachim's age of the Spirit.) Norman Cohn in *The Pursuit of the Millennium* sees Joachim's prophecy of an impending "third age" where all evils will be exterminated on earth as the forerunner of later, crackpot revolutionary theories that would erupt in the Reformation, the French Revolution, and the brain of economist Karl Marx. Even Hitler's Third Reich, which turned the land-pirate fantasies of pretzel-chomping bigots into a pseudo-redemptive religion, can trace its origin back to the seemingly harmless wonkery of poor Abbot Joachim.

Closer to home, there were many Catholics who looked at the phenomenon of Vatican II as a pretext for hitting the RESET button on the entire Catholic faith, an attempt to reboot the Church from DOS in Safe Mode. This, too, amounted to a Joachim-style misreading of Catholic history, casting the safely distant "early Church" as the first age, the dark and oppressive Church created by Constantine as the second, and the new, "postconciliar" Church as the final, perfected version: Christianity 3.0. Some even took to calling Vatican II a "second Pentecost," as if the title of the council had made it a movie sequel: *Vatican, Part II*: "Jesus Is Back, and He's Wearing a Rainbow Dashiki."

The actual documents of Vatican II made only modest adjustments to the mode of the presentation of the Catholic faith, apart from the question of religious liberty—where a real development of doctrine was promulgated. (See chapter 5 for more on that.) But these facts didn't stop thousands of priests from celebrating Mass on coffee tables, or laymen from deciding that somewhere, between the lines, Vatican II had approved of their adopting . . . the exact same social and sexual mores as the non-Catholics all around them. For once—indeed, for the first time since Pentecost—the Church had looked at the state of the world and instead of accusing mankind of sinning and falling short of the glory of God, she ostensibly decided that everything on earth in 1965 was pretty much hunky-dory. That message came not in the quickly disregarded letter of Vatican II but rather in its "spirit," which was channeled through the Sibylline oracles of Jesuits at

Georgetown and tenured, la-
icized Dominicans still teaching theology at Louvain. The
letter, you see, is a downer,
while the spirit's the life of
the party.

**16. I can see that such
thoughts are hazardous.
But how are they a heresy?**

Because the logical inference of Joachim's theory is that the Holy Spirit has essentially been silent since Pentecost, biding His time while the grimly imperfect age
of the Son went through its worldly paces—with a Church still corrupt and man
still ineffectually or incompletely redeemed. But in fact, as our catalogs of Gifts
and Fruits made clear, the Holy Spirit is what works in the world each day, urging
us toward the sacraments, away from occasions of sin, and toward whatever con-
tentment we find in a world that is still—and will be until the end of time—scarred
by the side effects of Original Sin. This is the best we're going to get, and we work
with the flawed materials at hand to "restore all things in Christ," without much
expectation of earthly success. Expect something else from God and you're all too
likely to snap at the chance to follow power-hungry or delusional human beings
who promise to provide heaven-on-earth on the cheap—if only you're willing to
wink at a few "necessary crimes" along the way, such as theft, murder, conquest,
or genocide. If ideas that have led to toxic consequences like those don't count as
heresies, what does?

17. OK, so Joachimites are the heretics who think that the Holy Spirit's in hiding, waiting for His chance to burst into the spotlight, center stage. What's the opposite error?

It amounts to the theory that the Holy Spirit, far from silent, has been nattering on for millennia—dictating every word ever spoken by any pope in any context, binding Catholics forever to accept even their short-term prudential decisions, even when said pope was put on the throne by a powerful prostitute (also his mistress), or when he was excommunicating entire cities for resisting his land grabs on behalf of his nephews.

This attitude is mostly displayed by enthusiastic devotees of recent popes—who, unlike their Renaissance forebears, showed actual personal sanctity, but like them were merely guardians of the existing Deposit of Faith, not oracles privileged by God to unveil vast new swathes of public Revelation. (That ended, as you'll remember, with the death of the last apostle, after he finished his last book—which was conveniently titled "Revelation.")[16] It turns up in pious superstitions like the popular idea that the Holy Spirit chooses the pope—which elicits the question of whether there wasn't, in the entire world, a single man better qualified to serve as Vicar of Christ than the adulterer Alexander VI (1492–1503) or Stephen VI (896–897), who dug up the corpse of his predecessor Pope Formosus and tried it for heresy.

Instances of this credulous heresy abound among well-meaning, would-be orthodox Catholics. For instance, Pope Paul VI opined in *Populorum Progressio* that high taxes on the First World to fund state foreign aid to the Third World seemed like a good idea, even a moral imperative. The next forty years of experience have shown that such aid tends to freeze poor countries in poverty while fattening the Swiss bank accounts of postcolonial dictators in leopard skin hats. But some Catholics persist in attributing to one pope's prudential judgment the force of infallibility. The worst example came in a press conference where John Paul II (or one of his less-skilled speechwriters) said that rich countries must welcome immigrants in the same way that parents must welcome the unborn child in the womb—apparently equating prudential worries over mass migration with the murder of millions of children through abortion. When I differed with a prominent Catholic psychologist over this catastrophic non sequitur, the conversation went as follows:

"You know that the pope was only speaking in his capacity as a private theologian there, don't you? The Church has never taught that countries must have open borders, and it still doesn't. Read the *Catechism*. Immigrants have the right to leave their country of origin, just as I have a right to move out of my house. That doesn't mean somebody has to let me move into his house, rent-free."

"When someone as holy as Pope John Paul says something, I listen."

---

[16] CCC, 86.

"Whereas a child has an absolute right to be born, and not get pulled apart by forceps. Right?"

"The Holy Father saw a parallel, and that's good enough for me."

"OK, but you know that's not infallible, right? It's not an ex cathedra statement, or even part of the ordinary universal magisterium."

"I think that the Holy Spirit guides Pope John Paul II in a special way."

"In a way that He didn't guide any previous popes before him—who said quite contrary things?"

"Yes. That is what I believe."

"Congratulations. You've just invented a brand new heresy."

Later on, the doctor's male patients would learn that their real route to recovery lay through joining a paramilitary strike force he planned to lead, which would combine Marian devotion, Israeli martial arts, and advanced weapons training—all of which would help them resist international jihad and close down the global sex-slave trade.

When you hear something like that, it might just be time to log on to Psychology Today.com and find another therapist.[17]

---

[17] On the other hand, if you are involved in the global sex-slave trade, and you see a bunch of high-strung guys in blue berets and turtlenecks coming at you brandishing rosaries, watch out! Those guys know karate.

The Church

1. The problem I have with what you've been explaining isn't so much with the details. They all seem to follow, once you grant a set of very strange premises.

I'd say that we humans reside in some very strange premises, which we didn't build ourselves but blundered into, like those hapless Eisenhower voters who used to visit the Addams family. By the way, I've always considered that a deeply Catholic show: Here's a bunch of aristocratic, history-obsessed homeschoolers who live in a gothic house full of torture devices and actual relics, trapped in an uncomprehending Protestant suburb. Watching the reruns as a kid, I developed a real "thing" for Morticia. She ruined me for any woman whose veins don't show through her skin.

Image courtesy of Wikipedia Commons.

2. Thanks so much for sharing.

Here we are, shaped a lot like chimps and inclined to act like baboons, but unlike them we're capable of building La Sagrada Familia and making films like *Annie Hall*—to cite just two of the high points of our species. But beyond the arts, some of us do astonishingly non-Darwinian things, like giving all our worldly goods to the poor (St. Francis of Assisi); crossing the world to care for unbelieving foreigners (St. Damien the Leper); or giving up reproduction to educate other people's children (those thousands of sisters who used to man our Catholic schools, before they encountered Carl Rogers and absconded). We also engage in outrageously useless acts of evil, like setting up death camps (Hitler) or famines (Stalin and Mao) to attack the most productive members of our societies; or aborting our own kids by the millions, then spending billions to generate new kids in laboratories, only to leave most of them sitting in the deep-freeze like

shrimp dumplings we forgot about. Any account of man's fate that didn't sound a little bit *strange*—for instance, those chipper "just-so" stories of inevitable human progress and rationality they came up with in the Enlightenment—would obviously be nonsense. Like whistling in the infinite dark. Pascal said, "Man is a reed, but a thinking reed." More important, maybe, is the fact that he's a self-immolating, mass-murdering, icon-painting, and warmongering reed. We need some account of that. As that commie hack playwright Arthur Miller said, "Attention must be paid!" Or not. We could just drink another Twisted Ice Tea and settle back to watch *Tosh 2.0* on Hulu till the barbarians come. Your call.

3. You certainly like to rub the ugly truth in people's faces.

I'm practicing the converse of what Christians call apologetics. That's the art of making faith appear as reasonable as possible. What's needed now is to show that unbelief is unreasonable. Or at least it will lead you to madness, if you think about things hard enough. Consider what I do the art of apoplectics. And it's as serious as a heart attack.

4. It must have really helped you with getting second dates in college.

Yeah, those were thin on the ground. (Real college nostalgia quote: "You're John *Zmirak*? But you seemed . . . nice!") It's my own fault, of course: I acted prickly (that's an adverb). The mood always broke at the moment where, apropos of nothing, a fetching young coed would volunteer that she was "pro-choice." I'd shrug, give her a really candid look, and explain: "You know, when I say I'm 'pro-life,' that's not entirely accurate. I mean, life is cheap—and they're only babies. What I really want is to *restrict women's reproductive health care options*. Fetuses are just a pretext."

5. How did that work for you?

Pretty well, actually. It filtered out the women who were into Reiki and polyamory. But that was just a side benefit. Nor was the point just to watch that oddly constipated look pass over their lovely faces. My real intent was to peel off the scab on the unexamined caricature they carried in their minds, to make them listen to their own rhetoric on someone's else lips. They usually laughed. And that's the point: The chipper, individualist theory most modern people have is just plain funny—at least when you try to square it with everything else they claim to think. The average person you run into at a classical music concert or organic grocery store believes at the same time:

Image courtesy of Wikipedia Commons.

(a) That each human being is endowed with inalienable rights, which begin with life, liberty, and the pursuit of happiness, but continue through infinite, tortuous emanations to include freedom from want, freedom from fear, and freedom of choice, then extend to things like a living wage, health care, housing, educational opportunities, racial and gender equality, and handicap-accessible restrooms.

AND

Not (a) That human beings are the accidental result of billions of years of random cosmic and planetary accidents, followed by millions of years of undirected genetic mutations; that our brains are organic computers whose unreliable constructs result from deterministic electronic events on the submolecular  level; that our altruistic instincts are driven by DNA's drive to replicate itself; that the most successful human being in history must have been Genghis Khan, who left behind several million direct descendants; that the biggest failure had to be Jesus Christ, who lived without sex or money and died without having children.

Try holding both these thoughts in your head at the same time and you'll have to keep them in tightly sealed containers so they don't spill together and annihilate themselves, like matter and antimatter in a particle accelerator. To ease the strain and give the world a little glimmer of numinous "meaning," you'll meditate sometimes or read mystical literature exclusively (and this is key) from religions about whose doctrines you are blissfully ignorant (hence Rumi, the Kabbalah, or the Tibetan Book of the Dead). You'll wince when evangelicals say that Jesus got them their mobile homes, and nod benignly when Oprah says that the "universe" wanted her to write her latest Tweet. You'll give money to Planned Parenthood and to ferret shelters. You'll think like Darwin but emote like Rousseau. Of course, when the chips are down, the meaninglessness of life will win out in the end. When *Annie Hall* is over, and Mia Farrow is shouting at you, "You're not supposed to BLEEP the kids," you'll shrug and say, "Why not? We're consenting adults."

6. So the Church offers an alternative to both (a) and Not (a)?

More like she offers an integrated worldview that takes account of the true parts of both and reckons with the tragic paradoxes we face—instead of pretending they aren't there.

7. So even if a personal God exists, why would I need an organized religion, much less a Church with a long and historically spotty track record, to manage my communications with him?

It sounds like what you'd prefer is a perfectly individual religion, customized to your own particular needs. And believe me, I feel your pain. I'd prefer a personalized planet where nobody but good-looking people were even tempted to go out in public and anyone nattering on the subway when I'm trying to read sounded instead like soothingly chirping crickets. Oh yes, and I wish they all smelled like pesto sauce.

However, it seems that God has other ideas, that He does not, in fact, wish to negotiate with each of us like Job but rather considers salvation social. We won't get anywhere near Him by hunkering down and focusing inward or wallowing in existential angst. Instead, perhaps as a way of forcing us out of the cozy cell of solipsism each of us secretly craves, God insisted that relating to Him entailed accommodating ourselves to each other, submitting to authority, accepting inequality (and sometimes even injustice), and focusing *on how we can serve*, rather than tapping the cosmic (half-empty) water glass to complain about the service. Because the *maître de l'univers* will not rush over and apologize.

So God revealed Himself to a father, Abraham, and promised His protection to a people. It was as a whole that this people received the divine promises, and as a body that it was judged and sometimes punished. It wasn't just the pious Jews who got delivered safely from Egypt, or the irreligious ones who were sent into exile. It was the nation as a whole.[1]

8. So you're saying that souls are saved or damned in batches, like pallets of Mexican Viagra impounded at the Arizona border?

No. The promises and threats that the Israelites encountered were merely earthly, and their effects were felt collectively. In the afterlife, each of us (sheesh) gets what he paid for—or else he gets what Jesus paid for in his stead. It's our job as a Church to swell the ranks of the latter. But while Jesus would have died, we're taught, for any one of us, He in fact died "for the many"—that is, for all who would be humble enough to accept His grace when it is offered. And it is offered lavishly. St. Faustina spoke of "oceans of mercy" sufficient to drown the pitiful matchsticks of our sins. But we have to be willing to drop the match before it burns our fingers.[2]

---

[1] CCC, 62
[2] CCC, 211

However, while the outcome of the life of grace is experienced personally—our souls don't dissolve into some gray, pantheistic smoosh—the process of obtaining and cooperating with grace is intensely social. But that's true of everything else we value, too. None of us develops a brand new language to speak as a child, or founds his own civilization and institutions. We don't (except for sociopaths) invent our own code of morality and laws. Neither do we have a long talk with God and work out the mode of salvation best suited to our own cognitive style and personality quirks. We are grafted into a lively, thriving tree that was planted before our births

and will go on growing once we're dead. That plant is the only beanstalk that reaches to heaven. We can climb it or not. In that sense, and in that sense only, God is pro-choice.

9. So I should think of the Church as a tree?

The Tree of Life, yes. But as the actual *Catechism* explains, there are many other images that work equally well to evoke how the Church sees herself—or much more to the point, how God sees her.[3]

10. So now the tree is a "she"? You're bollixing up your biology there, I think.

No, just mixing metaphors. And the Church uses a very long list of images to grasp for an explanation of her own nature. She's the Ark of Salvation, the True Sheepfold, the Temple of the Holy Ghost, the Sacrament of Salvation, the City of God, the Vine that is grafted into Israel . . . I really could go on all day. But you get the idea that this is something very hard to pin down. It might sound like a grab bag of incompatible attributes, when in fact we're looking at something whose nature is so unusual, at once enormous and close at hand but also extending into dimensions we can't even see, that we do the best we can. Remember the elephant and the blind men trying to talk about the Trinity? Well, there's something like that going on here again.

---

[3] CCC, 751–757

11. That seems less elephantine than fishy. You'd think that an organization would know what it was about and have a clear core of premises from which its structure and operations would proceed. Of course, you guys have been muddling along for centuries, so maybe you're more like the Habsburg Empire than you are like Google . . .

Or the Communist Party or existentialism. The Church is not ideological or even philosophical. It's not an organization so much as an organism, one that individuals can choose to graft themselves onto or not.

12. More like *Star Trek*'s the Borg?

I think some militaristic popes in the past might have wished we could impose that level of uniformity on Catholics, and the Church does have real teachings she tries to convey. But no. We aren't interested in fostering a hive mind among all those Italians, Nigerians, Germans, Irishmen, Koreans, El Salvadorans, and Australians we have baptized. What we're building is more like a communal, participatory soul. With the Fall, Adam and Eve lost the original privileges God granted to humanity—and He made it clear that this kind of gain or loss comes not to the one but the many. It was only with Abraham that God began to offer some tangible means to reestablish the good relations between us and Him, and it entailed collective bargaining; Abraham negotiated on behalf of his descendants—the first of whom, Isaac, he came close to sacrificing in the process. The blessings and punishments God sent the Jews rained on the just and unjust alike, and He promised the Messiah not to a tiny elect of faithful Israelites but to everyone.

When Christ came, He didn't act like a pundit or spiritual guru and arrange for a sit-down with the Henry Kissingers and Dr. Phils of his day, or even the Jewish Vatican (the high priests). Instead, He walked the dusty roads of Palestine preaching to high and low alike, healing Gentiles as well as Jews, attracting harlots and traitors along with dunderheaded fishermen, and even some sincere Pharisees. After

Pentecost, the Spirit sent the apostles speaking many tongues to Jews from all over the world, and to cap things off, Christ appeared to the natural activist Saul of Tarsus, beginning him on his career of preaching to every sort of creature in that great *Star Wars* cantina that was the Roman Empire. Within less than a hundred years, Christians were evangelizing from Spain and Roman Britain to Ethiopia and India. The Church has been universal ever since—but what it's important to remember is what she is becoming: a worldwide family that builds up a new humanity to receive the very particular blessings first granted to the genetic descendants of Abraham. In doing this, the Church creates a new human race, one that claims its true descent not from Adam but from Christ. For this reason, the titles that the Church puts the strongest emphasis on are these two: the People of God, and the Mystical Body of Christ. If you like, these are looks at the elephant from the ant's point of view, then the eagle's.[4]

First, the People of God. I know this comes as a left-handed compliment to those who adhere to contemporary Judaism, but the Church sees herself as the New Israel, the heiress to all the messianic promises proclaimed to all mankind via the Israelites. Repeatedly throughout Jewish history, despite the prophets' warnings, large numbers fell away from faithfulness to the Covenant. As the Church sees things, St. John the Baptist was the last such prophet, and when he proclaimed the coming of Christ, the same thing happened again: a large proportion of God's people didn't hear or couldn't accept the message, leaving a faithful "Remnant" who kept the faith.[5] In this case, that means the apostles and every Jew who joined them. One big difference here—and this helps us to be not simply more charitable but more just to the rest of the Jews—is that this prophetic message was different in key respects from those that had come before.

13. Ya think? A redeemer who claims divinity, puts himself above the Sabbath and the Temple, and tells people to eat his flesh and drink his blood? I'm amazed that anyone listened at all.

Yes, it is rather miraculous, isn't it? But those weren't the hardest things, I think, for the Jews to accept. (Each of them was heavily prefigured in the Old Testament.) No,

[4] CCC, 782 & 1474
[5] CCC, 711

I think what made the Church so unpalatable to Jews was the fact that it started recruiting Gentiles. The floodgates opened when St. Paul convinced St. Peter and the other apostles to make circumcision and the rest of the kosher laws optional. Soon the gatherings of Christians were overrun with Syrians, Romans, Greeks, and all sorts of other assorted pagan riffraff whom the faithful Jews had spent many centuries carefully shunning. Indeed, the parts of the Law that weren't moral or liturgical were designed in part precisely to accomplish this, to mark off the Jews from every other people and keep them from mixing religions. Now here these apostles were, opening the gates to the heirs of the Philistines, of the Greeks who'd hunted the Maccabees, of the Romans who burned the Temple. The Jews who followed Christ would soon find themselves lost in the mix—no longer the proud and lonely soloists belting out the message of monotheism but now mere choir members chanting in unison the praise of the Trinity. It must have looked suspiciously like apostasy. So the Jews turned even more firmly inward, rejecting the Greek translation (Septuagint) of the Torah and building a new religion not of sacrifice (the Temple lay in ruins) but of learning, remembrance, and waiting—for the "real" messiah to come and reestablish the Kingdom of Israel.

The Church, for her part, believed that she had become the New Israel, one that embraced implicitly all humanity. By doing that, she inadvertently alienated most of the Jews. Since it seems this was all unavoidable, it begins to look like part of God's Providence—as St. Paul suspected.[6]

14. This is way, way weirder than I'd imagined.

You'll find no argument here. Now in arguing that it's organic, I don't deny that the Church shares some bits of DNA with every other sort of human institution. That shouldn't surprise us into suspicion; if the Church is made of men, then she will do some of the same things that men do in other contexts. So the Church acts at various points in time like a sales force, a social club, a philosophical debating society, a 12-step "recovery" group, a hospice, a grammar school, a graduate school, a government, even an army. To the unsympathetic outsider, this can make her look like hydra-headed beast, or seem to render her eschatological claims merely . . . scatological.

But if they are, then we'll all end up in a world of s***t, since there's no other plausible candidate for making earthly life add up to much. The "atheist humanist" plan to free our race from its long childhood by banishing the oppressive Father in the sky ended up in Gulags and terror famines. The cult of national and racial rebirth that so captivated the pointy-heads of the early twentieth century—from H. G. Wells and Margaret Sanger to George Bernard Shaw—bled to death in the fields around Stalingrad, and now the very races these high-minded honkies hoped would rule the

---

[6] CCC, 839

planet are too blasé to have babies and too ashamed of themselves to apprehend the terrorists in their midst. So 1984 came and went, and we're left in the Brave New World where Ivy-educated ethicists tear their hair out over the rectitude of testing AIDS vaccines on chimpanzees, while human embryos—the afterthoughts of middle-aged couples determined to undo decades of birth control—are shipped to Harvard to be cannibalized for parts. The embryos, not the couples. Science has not yet found a use for middle-class, middle-aged white people—though if our pension plans keep going bankrupt, I'm confident that future generations will someday stuff us into their walls as insulation.

Image courtesy of Wikipedia Commons.

But back to the Mystical Body of Christ. It's hard for us to see the Church as something celestial when she is so clearly and plainly earthy. Then again, it's mighty hard to think that most of the human beings you run into every day have an eternal destiny, either. That hot young thing you're ogling on the beach, the "wide-load" who's blocking your way up the escalator, the sullen and slow-moving postal clerk, other people's sticky and stinky children, the creepy old guys with tattoos at Dunkin' Donuts in New Hampshire who would like to kill you with farm implements. Are these motley, imperfect primates possessed of indestructible spirits that extend out into forever? A Flannery O'Connor character once complained of the Christians he met, "You don't look redeemed to me." Likewise, if human beings have an infinite, ineradicable dignity conferred by almighty God, they sure don't look that

way to me. Neither do I. In fact, the only people over twenty-five who seem remotely godlike are Olympic athletes and actors, whose austere, artificed beauty would not be out of place in a Nazi recruiting poster. Now you know why those posters were so effective....

The Church, then, has the arduous task of revealing the hidden glory in every person and building up a glorified Body of Christ on earth out of lumpy raw materials. She isn't the Platonic ideal of a recipe you read in a glossy, food-porn cookbook before microwaving your burrito, or even the glamorous hostess who seats you in the restaurant. The Church is the sweaty, exhausted chef who's covered in blood and flour. She needs knives and spoons, sauté pans and pasta machines, missionaries and monarchs. And she needs to get herself dirty. Watching her work in the kitchen won't do wonders for your appetite, especially when she starts to grind the sausage. But without her, the menu wouldn't mean much.

The recipes are all written down: those are the scriptures. And the basic practices of cookery she learned from Christ were passed down by imitation: the sacraments. But the techniques for making the recipes work, for whipping up holiness out of the pantry were passed down from chef to chef, in what we call sacred Tradition.[7] These were clarified (like butter) in a series of heated councils and cool papal decisions, so what we have now is less like a mustard seed and more like the company that manufactures Grey Poupon.

And yet the entire thing is not in fact a corporation, or a philosophy, or an army, empire, or tribe. The Church is something quite unique in history. And what makes it stand out is the way it transmits its authority and its energy, its power to sanctify

Image courtesy Wikipedia Commons.

---

[7] CCC, 78

followers: It does that through this strange system called "apostolic succession," which has no parallels, I believe, in any other kingdom, conspiracy, or creed.[8] The Church is all three, of course, and a thousand more things besides—which is another way of saying it exists in more dimensions than we experience day to day, so when we try to describe it we will always be getting things wrong. But that's OK. All we can do is try.

15. So you claim that the pope is the successor to St. Peter. Big deal. The emperor of Japan claims he is descended from the rice god.

Well, he did, until 1945, when General Douglas Macarthur insisted on a sudden *ciaobella*-ment of doctrine[9]—not something Shintoism had experienced before, nor will it need to again; the revelation that the emperor was merely a very short, near-sighted marine biologist pulled the teeth from the bushido code. This admission, and the Allied bombings that left much of the country a cinder, rendered pacifism suddenly popular and redirected Japanese energies to the peaceful pursuit of techno-logical innovation—pioneering better means of mass-producing automobiles, com-puters, and sex robots.

The papacy never underwent this kind of transition, as even secular historians will admit. However many popes were kidnapped, imprisoned, or even martyred, none of them reversed a basic teaching of the Church, not even to save their skins. In fact, no pope has ever formally taught a heresy or innovation in almost two thou-sand years. If only the U.S. Supreme Court had stayed so faithful to our country's founding principles, we'd be living in a very different country today—namely, one where a frustrated President Roosevelt had expanded and packed the Court with 150 justices chosen from left-wing labor unions, and each American now had a constitu-tional right to seven weeks paid vacation from their jobs (which no longer existed), but that's another story.

That track record, of consistency almost to the point of monotony, is the stron-gest argument for taking the papacy's claims seriously. Given how corrupt have been some of our pontiffs, how preoccupied with power, how cowardly or stupe-fied with wine, art collecting, and nepotism, it may be a literal miracle that not one of these men messed with the Church's deposit of faith—clipping out some books of the Bible he didn't like (see Martin Luther), shedding their least-favorite sacra-ments (see John Calvin), or making room in middle age for men to collect extra wives (see Joseph Smith). It's almost as if the devil has been playing a game with God, trying to paper over the truth or scissor it up—but the Rock always comes out on top.

---

[8] CCC, 1576
[9] Technical theological jargon for that moment when you wave a doctrine goodbye.

FAQs from Your Stoner Neighbor #6:
I read two books by one of the leading Catholic intellectuals in America, Garry Wills—*Papal Sin and Why I Am a Catholic*—where he proves that the papacy hijacked the Church and turned it into a corrupt, worldly institution for dominating people through spiritual blackmail. What do you have to say about that?

Those two books are at once so shoddy and so skillful that I'm almost afraid to take them on. I have never before encountered someone so well-informed about what the Church really teaches, and so committed to lying about it. Garry Wills employs his Catholic training in exactly the way some fanatically anti-Zionist Jews use their ancestry: as a license to body-slam the truth, and throw it under the wheels of the juggernaut of elite opinion. But then, as St. James once said, "the devils also believe, and tremble" (James 2:19). So in that sense, I am willing to stipulate that Garry Wills is, indeed, a Catholic. And while considered as literature or history the books are nothing special, they do a fine job of compiling in one place all Planned Parenthood's talking points, so I might as well address them.

In *Papal Sin,* Wills presents as "news" the old, dark moments of the papacy as proof that its claims to consistency are not a mistake but a conscious fraud. Of course, Wills wields the old, trusty weapons of contemporary liberalism: *ad hominem* attacks, feigned shock that the Dark Ages were *barbarous*, plus rank disdain for the foreign, the poor, and the dead. This comes out clearest in his treatment of the church's teaching on birth control, a subject with which Wills is nearly obsessed. He bluntly equates periodic abstinence (i.e., natural family planning) with the use of foams, latex contraptions, and abortifacient chemicals—since they all aim at childless intercourse, as if we didn't all know perfectly well that the difference between moral ends and moral means was covered in the first freshman philosophy class Wills took with Jesuits back when Buddy Holly was still alive.

Looking at Pope John Paul II, Wills heaps ridicule on that pope for glorifying the goodness of marital sex and urging Catholic men to see to their wives' orgasms—while insisting that sexual acts can only be "holy" when they are subject to "self-control." Wills mocks him for prudishness, as if any act could be *human*, much less "virtuous," when done as a spastic response to compulsion. It seems one side effect of the Pill is to make men forget their Aristotle.

The writer whom Wills has the gall to claim as a mentor, G.K. Chesterton, saw the church as especially glorious when she resisted public opinion and refuted popular heresies. But Wills denounces the popes for refusing to follow the press and the Zogby Poll. Where Newman honored doctrines that develop over time, Wills veers wildly between archaism and chronological snobbery.

In his next masterpiece, *Why I Am a Catholic,* Wills answers a chorus of requests from readers troubled by *Papal Sin,* earnestly asking how he can remain in that church, having demolished its authority. He admits that a few notes came from those who disliked the book—whose authors all (all!) confessed that they hadn't read it. These pious biddies he dismisses with a pat on the head and proceeds to dig among the Roman ruins to build a church worthy of him. Yet even here, two-thirds of the book consist of still more attacks on the papacy. Wills simply cannot resist. The last third of the book is all that Wills affirms as a positive creed—a milk and water gruel that Hugh Hefner could cheerfully serve at the Playboy Mansion for breakfast.

If the past is "another country," Wills tramps through it as an Ugly American, sneering at practices that confuse him (such as physical mortification, commended by thousands of saints—which he dispatches in a line or two); feigning surprise that contemporary prejudices did not prevail a thousand years ago; obscuring and skewing evidence—all to build up a high school debater's brief against Catholicism. But for most readers, that will be quite enough. None of Wills's charges *quite* proves his point—that church teaching on faith and morals has zigzagged recklessly. But he will simply adduce another charge and another, drawing hasty (always hostile) conclusions in a glib paragraph. Where scholars disputed for centuries, Wills ends the question in a sophomore's summary:

- Pope Honorius, who wrote a private letter around 637 too tolerant of heretics. Condemned by the church for laxity, Honorius is made out here as a full-blown heretic himself, and his note an infallible pronouncement.
- The Council of Florence, which declared infallibly that there is "no salvation outside the church." That doctrine, which later popes carefully nuanced—noting that *membership* in the church is a mystery known only to God—Wills calls a simple lie, one revoked at Vatican II.
- The popes who urged Catholics to rebel against Elizabeth I. Wills damns these men for fomenting treason. A later pope told Catholics *not* to rebel against the Russian tsar—so Wills condemns *him* for fostering tyranny. Wills drubs popes for supporting King Louis XIV's autocracy, and then for *opposing* Napoleon's. The stark, awful power of infallibility in faith and morals Wills smuggles into *politics* and inverts: The papacy is miraculously wrong about everything.

- Pius IX and Leo XIII, who denounced the separation of church and state—in their day, always the first step toward persecution—are drawn as monsters, and Vatican II recast as a caucus of the ACLU.
- Pius X who taught that dogmas cannot evolve. Against him Wills cites Newman. But the "doctrines" whose development Newman discerned are bluntly different from "dogmas," which (unlike doctrines) must always be understood *in the exact sense originally intended.* Pius X noted the difference and praised Newman accordingly. How can such a distinction—as stark as that dividing an American law from an Article of the Constitution—escape sophisticated readers, or the writer? Easily: Notice how similar are the sounds employed—dog, *doc*, doc, *dog*. Remember how lazy and busy people are, how eager to soothe their sneaking bad consciences. Recall how many souls abandoned the Eucharist thanks to the slogan *"hocus pocus,"* that cheap pun on *"hoc est corpus."*

Wills never does provide a clinching case of dogmatic self-contradiction—or indeed, any argument that could withstand a patient Google search. But he doesn't need to. These books are finely tailored for reading on Jetblue: free of ambiguities, brightly mirroring the prejudices of their public, always focused on a single guiding principle: the infallibility of the Baby Boom.

Wills accepts no Catholic teaching that might offend his comfortably secularized readers. Rejecting popes, councils, and ancient interpretations of the Bible, Wills adverts again and again to the "sense of the faithful" as his infallible authority. But of course, he defers to nothing of the kind. The vulgar masses he pretends to defend adore such wonders as the roses of Guadalupe, the dancing sun at Fatima, and the virginity of Mary. Wills dismisses such mysteries with a sniff, noting that "the New Testament is a book of theology, not of obstetrics or gynecology." It is not the hordes of pious Mexicans and or persecuted Sudanese who must be consulted but Westerners who own Kindles, who only buy books they have seen recommended on Salon.

Wills makes a big point of noting that he still says the rosary—the prayer chaplet favored by peasant saints. But read attentively, and see how very *proud* Wills is of his humility, and how he preens about it. In his exegesis of the prayers, the reader can't help noticing just how *very learned* and wise Wills is, how much more nuanced and polished than those dreary, drooling popes. And in a final touch, Wills simply cannot withhold the information that he frequently says the rosary in biblical Greek. Humility such as this is quite at home in hell.

CR∞CR∞CR∞CR∞CR∞CR∞CR∞CR∞CR∞CR∞CR∞CR∞CR∞CR∞CR∞CR

16. Didn't the popes rise to power over the other bishops just because they were at Rome—the capital of the empire? By that standard, the archbishop of Washington, D.C., should be running the Church, though he'll have to relocate to Beijing when the Chinese finally cash those checks.

You've got the facts exactly backward. When the city of Rome was at its height and the center of power, the see of Rome was a low-key, after-hours, catacombs kind of affair. If Rome was anything to the Christians, it was the nerve center of mass persecution, in which thousands died in ugly, public ways depicted on walls of churches like Santo Stefano Rotondo and in movies starring Victor Mature.

The numbers of Christians at the center of pagan persecution remained comparatively small. The Roman church's main claim to fame was that it had been founded by St. Peter and evangelized by St. Paul. That gave it the same "apostolic" status as Jerusalem (St. James) and much more populous Christian centers Alexandria (St. Mark) and Antioch (also St. Peter). Still, the leading centers of Christianity in the West were for centuries cities like Carthage and Milan, whose economies were heavily outperforming the bureaucratic, crime-ridden backwater that was Rome. The bishop of Rome had a primacy of honor among his peers but little practical influence. If closeness to secular power had been the defining factor in which a bishop would rule the Church, then the patriarch of Constantinople would certainly have taken over—he was the one who sat in a glittering palace and consulted with the newly Christian emperors. By this point, the city of Rome was a faded-glory backwater, the kind of place that would soon be prone to roving bands of barbarians. So the pope was in a worldly sense much more like the archbishop of Detroit.

17. So what does explain the rise of the papacy?

The fact that it was needed, but first I want to clear something up. The Church doesn't start with the pope, the way you might think. It began with the apostles Jesus called, who were made both priests and bishops at the Last Supper, which also began the Eucharist. Christ did say something rather cryptic to St. Peter about being "a rock," but it took several centuries for the Church to see precisely what He meant: that among the bishops, there had to be someone in charge, a figure who could put an end to arguments, who could (if you will) be the "here" where the "buck" could stop.[10] Since councils of bishops split, and competing councils popped up to denounce each other, there had to be some earthly locus of authority, an executive branch of the Church. (Try to imagine America functioning without a president—however wretched—being run just by the Congress. There wouldn't be two rocks left standing on top of each other.) The Church couldn't live without it, and Christ meant His Church to live on, so He gave her what she needs. It became gradually apparent over several centuries that this is what He meant by making Peter the "rock" as the various bishops began to look to the bishop of Rome—the heir to St. Peter.

The power of the papacy grew as the Church did, in order to serve her—not the other way around. Most popes in the fifth and sixth centuries were so busy evangelizing barbarians and taming the Roman mob, scrambling to keep that fractious city from ending up like Pompeii, that they hardly had the energy to intervene in the endless theological conflicts that kept erupting among the highly educated Byzantines.

But time and again, the bishop of Rome had to step in to settle disputes or champion ancient truths against contemporary heresies—such as iconoclasm, the rejection of sacred images.[11] One Byzantine emperor, deeply impressed by Islamic success at crushing his armies, got the idea that God was sending the Muslims victories because the Christians had flouted the Ten Commandments by using imagery in religion. He convinced (or arm-twisted) the patriarch of Constantinople, and soon the exquisite productions of centuries of piety were being smashed and burned as monks gouged out Our Lady's eyes, and crowds cheered the stripping of churches. The bishops of the east turned to Rome, and the pope condemned the assault on sacred art—which gave them the moral authority to say no to the emperor. Providentially, the collapse of the Western empire had left the popes almost independent agents, beyond the reach of kings or emperors who wished to tinker with mysteries, co-opt the Church's doctrine for his interests, or otherwise try to secularize her mission. That was the advantage of the pope ruling much of central Italy. (The downside emerged in the Renaissance, when astonishingly corrupt pontiffs used their religious authority to act as worldly princes, conquering cities and excommunicating their enemies over petty squabbles or secular questions.)

For the past two hundred years, we've had a string of popes who were mostly holy, sober, and wise—especially by the standards of previous centuries, like the tenth (when Roman whores pulled the strings in papal elections from behind the red velvet curtain) and the late fifteenth (when popes in love with great art, good wine, and mediocre prostitutes waged aggressive wars and sold indulgences). If the bad popes tempted people to turn into Protestants, this long string of good ones

---

[10] CCC 880-888
[11] CCC 1159-1162

has transformed some well-meaning Catholics into Mottramites (see Introduction), attributing infallibility to nearly everything any pope says—even when it's a purely private opinion, such as Pope John Paul II's reflection that modern prisons are much more effective than those in the Middle Ages, so the death penalty is almost never necessary. He could be right . . . but one thing he wasn't being (or claiming to be) on that occasion was infallible.[12] Popes have only very rarely invoked that level of authority, and only when they made dogmatic an ancient teaching, like the Immaculate Conception or the Assumption. When a pope recommends a prudential course of action that turns out to be disastrous—like all but one or two of the Crusades that pontiffs called—Catholics are not required to believe (as Mottramists would) that the pope's plans turned out well "spiritually, only we're too sinful to see it." The pope is a guardian of tradition, who hands it along like the baton in a relay race—not a Delphic oracle, pouring forth from time to time some new decree of the gods.

Image courtesy, Wikipedia Commons.

But none of this makes any difference, or proves the Church is anything more than quirky, until we understand precisely what the apostles were passing on. It wasn't a set of secret rituals, like the mystery cults or Masonry, or an esoteric message whispered by Gnostics or Scientologists. In fact, what the apostles gave the next generation of bishops were the gifts that God had conferred on Moses: the *power* to offer sacrifice and the *authority* to rule the Church.[13] Just as Moses gave the Jews their laws and commissioned their temple priesthood, so each bishop would rule his local church and confer on all his priests their sacramental powers. These "charisms" were passed down from apostle to bishop, and from that bishop to the

---

[12] CCC, 891
[13] CCC 1086, 1575

next, in an unbroken chain from Jerusalem down to Steubenville, Ohio, by the laying on of hands. To become a bishop, a man must be ordained by a bishop himself—and then it is he who ordains the priests. The power and authority that Christ handed on to the apostles can't be generated spontaneously from the soul of a holy man, any more than the best biologists can build a mouse from the relevant chemicals. Like life, it must be passed down from life. The people might vote on who would be made their bishop (this happened in the early Church), but the charism he would take on didn't come from them; it came from God, and had to be passed on sacramentally. The pope is there to oversee this complex genealogy of authority, but he doesn't rule it as a dictator. He is bound by the teachings of his predecessors, and his role is to hand on faithfully—and sometimes more fully unfold or better explain—the revelation that was complete with the death of St. John the Apostle.[14] What the bishop is for his diocese, the pope is for the Church as a whole.

All the key doctrines that mark off orthodox Christianity from the various heresies outlined at painful length in chapter 3 were clarified and laid out by councils of bishops, who when they meet in a doctrinal council with papal approval are protected by infallibility from teaching error.

18. So are individual bishops infallible?

Theoretically, yes. Theologians say that bishops "partake" in the infallibility of the Church as a whole, but only when they repeat *exactly what the pope and previous Church councils have already said*, which is something laymen can tell by checking the statements of their particular bishop against the Church's official documents—which are thankfully available online.

Until then, they don't know if a bishop is tapping into the Church's infallibility. And once they've found out, they're probably going to pay more attention to the Church documents (which have religious authority) than to the bishop's newspaper columns (which don't). That's how American Catholics deal, for instance, with periodic statements by bishops on immigration. Like the time when newly appointed Los Angeles archbishop Jose Gomez compared Americans worried about uncontrolled immigration with . . . Julian the Apostate. (For you history buffs, Julian was the neo-pagan emperor who tried to stamp out the Catholic Church.) In his 2008 speech at the Missouri Catholic Conference Annual Assembly, Gomez made the apostasy charge and by way of explanation said: "In Catholic teaching, the right to migrate is among the most basic human rights. It's very close to the right to life. Why? Because God has created the good things of this world to be shared by all men and women—not just a privileged few."

There are several problems here. For one, the "right to migrate" means the right to *leave* a country, not the right to enter any other country of one's choice. (I'd like

---

[14] CCC, 66

to move to Switzerland; if the Swiss say no, are they sinning?) Of course, no Catholic supports a Berlin Wall holding unhappy citizens in their home countries, any more than we favor placing innocent people under house arrest. Does that mean we must allow anyone, for any reason, to move into our homes? We oppose abortion; does that mean we're morally obliged to adopt indefinite numbers of children?

Gomez went on to assert that those who oppose immigration were guilty of xenophobia. As he helpfully explained: "The Christian word for 'hospitality' is like the antidote to that. *Philoxenia* literally means 'love of strangers.' This is who we are called to be— 'lovers of strangers.' Lovers of the immigrant, the alien, the undocumented. This love is not some sentimental affection. It's a radical love in which we open our hearts and our homeland to the stranger in need."

In fact, Christian love consists first in praying and acting for the eternal salvation of someone's soul (the spiritual works of mercy) and second in caring for those in desperate straits (the corporal works of mercy). It does not extend to *every action that might possibly be of material benefit to people who* (for whatever reason) *have less money than you.* Even if you imprudently choose to do that yourself—to hand out all your cash to anyone who asks—you do not have the right to force your neighbors to do the same, to clog the public hospitals with thousands of strangers who never paid taxes, the public roads with people who haven't insured their cars, the voting rolls with poor people who will vote to redistribute your neighbors' wealth. To confirm that I wasn't taking crazy pills, I went from the text of Gomez's speech to the *Catechism of the Catholic Church*, which posits in classic Catholic fashion a pair of obligations that are inextricably linked:

> The more prosperous nations are obliged, to the extent they are able, to welcome the foreigner in search of the security and the means of livelihood which he cannot find in his country of origin. (2241)

And:

> Immigrants are obliged to respect with gratitude the material and spiritual heritage of the country that receives them, to obey its laws and to assist in carrying civic burdens. (still 2241)

This reminds me of other Catholic teachings: A worker has a right to a living wage but only if he actually shows up and does the job. Likewise, if the immigrants don't do B, we aren't obliged to offer them A. Are illegal immigrants who take part in foreign elections, who demand bilingual education, who vote as ethnic blocs, and who commit identity theft to work here illegally fulfilling their side of the bargain? If not, then we are dispensed from ours.

Many American bishops have essentially given up on passing along the Faith to the next generation of native-born Catholics and are relying instead on a steady influx of people who have not yet been fully exposed to the acid effects of modernity—including the dominance of "dissenters" in many Catholic schools, the blandness and vagueness of religious instruction, the unrelenting banality of most parish liturgies (with music and rituals that would not pass muster at gatherings of the Boy Scouts), and the dismal quality of education for would-be converts. I like to ask "conservative" Catholics who favor virtually open borders because it will "help make America Catholic": Do you think that uneducated Mexican peasants are more likely to save their souls in Guadalajara—or the slums of Los Angeles? Which is a more wholesome atmosphere for their children? Likewise, I say to those who

blandly suggest that we will "restore American culture" through the influx of "pro-family" immigrants: That's like flooding a whorehouse with virgins to try to raise the moral tone. It works—for about fifteen minutes.

On the other hand, when one's bishop does faithfully repeat the official teachings of the Church, individual Catholics are bound to listen to him. Increasingly, recently appointed U.S. bishops are starting to do just that, so I'm guardedly optimistic. But just out of habit, I'll probably always listen with ears akimbo, and one eye on the official documents over at *www.vatican.va*.

19. Did you enjoy that self-serving digression?

Yes, quite a bit. Thanks for listening.

20. So I'm guessing that bishops' policies toward priestly sex abuse also fall outside the "infallibility safety zone"?

Tragically, yes. It's important that faithful Catholics not blow smoke up their own skirts or pretend that the scandal that erupted in 2002 and has dragged on for another ten years was somehow invented or exaggerated by anti-Catholic journalists. In this case, and perhaps this case alone, those anti-Catholic journalists were doing their jobs, and thank God for them. While only a tiny percentage of priests—no higher than occurs in other groups that deal with young people—proved to be offenders, the *Dallas Morning News* documented in 2002 that *two-thirds* of U.S. bishops were involved in cover-ups of sex abuse. Most of those bishops are still in place, and only one (and far from the worst), Cardinal Bernard Law, was forced out of office for this

Drawing by Carla Millar

kind of blatant disregard for the safety and souls of children. The rest will retire in peace and go off to play golf until they meet their eternal reward. (So will the many cops who refused to investigate parents' complaints.) Which just goes to show that the pope's day-to-day decisions aren't infallible, either.

Another unspoken, tragic aspect of the sex abuse crisis is the negligence of prosecutors. That is the only explanation why at least a few of those faithless shepherds aren't wearing their proper garb: bright prison orange.

There were several factors at work in the sex abuse crisis—including misguided compassion for abusive priests, a "magical" attitude toward the effects of repentance and confession, and an erroneous faith in the power of pop psychology to treat incurable diseases like pedophilia and deadly sins like Lust. But the main driver of the scandal was simple *worldliness*: As Philip Lawler has noted in *The Faithful Departed*, a vast and powerful Church infrastructure was built up by heroic missionaries and fiercely faithful, impoverished Catholic migrants—who came here legally (it should be noted) when the U.S. needed an almost infinite supply of strong Sicilian ditch diggers and chaste Irish nannies. The kind of men who founded the American church were a lot like the men who founded the U.S. government—heroes willing to risk life and limb, to face ridicule and thankless toil in a cause most people thought hopeless. (Imagine George Washington in a miter.) The Church continued to grow as faithful men sternly schooled in Jesuit spirituality and Thomist theology faced down hostility and anti-Catholic mobs to build a massive network of Catholic parochial schools and resist evil laws imposing Prohibition and eugenics. (You might think of these men as the Andrew Jacksons and Abraham Lincolns of the episcopate.) As time went on, and Americans began to accept that Catholics really weren't filling their church basements with dynamite and scheming to make the pope our king, life for bishops became a lot more comfortable. It started to attract a different kind of man, with another set of priorities—glad-handing, ward-heeling power brokers, more in the mold of Lyndon Johnson. When a crisis of faith erupted over birth control, it turned out that the upper ranks of the clergy were largely composed of men like Richard Nixon or William Jefferson Clinton. Those were the kind of men who were faced with the tough choice of turning an abusive priest over to the police—and facing the public scandal and possible lawsuit—or covering up for him and either bribing or intimidating the victims into silence. The scandal was the love-child born of the world and the flesh, but the Devil did play his part. He served as matchmaker.

21. So the offending bishops are guaranteed jobs for life?

Most will stay in office until they turn seventy-five, unless they "check out" prematurely. There's little lay Catholics afflicted with such a bishop can do—apart from pray, give money judiciously to reliable pastors or solid religious orders, and send said bishop cartons of cigarettes and tins of tasty, smoked meats.

22. Sounds like you don't have much use for bishops.

On the contrary, the Church could use a few thousand excellent bishops, and I pray God will send more soon. It may be that my standards for bishop behavior are too high, but I can't help remembering that bishops in the Dark Ages were not just the spiritual leaders and evangelists of their areas. They often were the only figures providing order, education, and help to the poor—as the Saracens, Vandals, Vikings, or Magyars swept through to burn the crops and rape the maidens. But you needn't go that far back to see how astonishingly good bishops can be at their best. In just the past one hundred years, the Church has been blessed with the likes of:

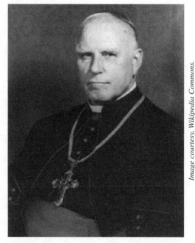

Image courtesy, Wikipedia Commons.

• The Blessed **Clemens August Cardinal von Galen**, who as bishop of Münster began campaigning against Nazi ideology in 1934. His bold attacks on its anti-Semitism and neo-pagan absurdities (he coauthored Pius XI's blistering denunciation of Nazism, *Mit Brenneder Sorge*) and his widely circulated pamphlets condemning euthanasia of the handicapped made von Galen a top Gestapo target. The heroic, quixotic White Rose student resistance movement took von Galen for its inspiration, printing a sermon of his as its first secret pamphlet. Nazi ideologues tried to arrange for his murder or execution, but their superiors feared that Catholics might revolt and so decided to wait until Germany won the war to reckon with Galen—and the Church. Josef Goebbels famously hoped that a victorious Third Reich would try and hang Pope Pius XII, and an SS plan to kidnap that pope in 1944 was only foiled when a crypto-Catholic officer warned the Vatican. Von Galen was beatified by Pope Benedict XVI in 2005.

Image courtesy, Wikipedia Commons.

• **Jozsef Cardinal Mindszenty** of Hungary, who was first arrested in 1919 by that country's short-lived pro-Bolshevik government for resisting the confiscation of Catholic schools. Later, as archbishop of Esztergom and primate of Hungary, he fought Nazi collaborators who were arranging the deportation of Hungary's Jews—and was jailed for four months, under threat of deportation himself. When Soviet troops arrived—and in their wake, another collaborationist government— Mindszenty became the focus for patriotic resistance to the nation's new occupiers. Again, the issue was education: In 1948, the new communist regime set about seizing some 4,813 Catholic schools. In response, the recently elevated cardinal drove around the country with a sound truck, urging resistance. He was quickly arrested, imprisoned, and subject to torture. Paraded through the streets dressed as a clown and presented with a long list of invented "counterrevolutionary crimes," after months of brutal interrogations Mindszenty finally signed a false confession and was made the defendant in a communist show trial for treason. He was sentenced to life in prison, and moved from jail to jail until the Hungarian uprising in 1956 set him free for a time. When Soviet tanks crushed that abortive attempt at glasnost, Mindszenty took refuge in the U.S. Embassy in Budapest, where he remained a focal point of patriotic dissent until Pope Paul VI (in a bungled outreach to the Soviets) arranged for his removal to the Vatican. Undaunted, Mindszenty moved to Austria—as close to Hungary as he could get—and traveled extensively to preach against attempts to accommodate totalitarians of any stripe.

Image courtesy, Wikipedia Commons.

• **Ignatius Cardinal Kung Pin-Mei** of Shanghai, who was consecrated in 1949, at the height of the Chinese civil war—which Mao Zedong was already winning. When Mao (who considered Stalin too moderate and timorous and urged the Soviet leader to launch a nuclear war over Korea) expelled all missionaries and tried to corral the three million Chinese Catholics into a puppet "Patriotic Church," Kung urged them to resist. Along with thousands of others, he was arrested in

1955—and later sentenced to life in prison. His crime? Clinging to the authority of the pope, which the schismatic Patriotic Church rejected. As the Cardinal Kung Foundation recounts: "During his years of captivity, Bishop Kung was asked to denounce the Holy Father and to cooperate with the Patriotic Association. He was told it was not necessary to say the words; a nod of his head would release him from prison. His answer was: 'I am a Roman Catholic Bishop. If I denounce the Holy Father, not only would I not be a Bishop, I would not even be a Catholic. You can cut off my head, but you can never take away my duties.'" In 1979, Pope John Paul II made Kung a cardinal in secret, a secret Kung kept at the pope's request (even from his family) long after his release from prison in 1987. It was not until 1991 that the pope thought it prudent to publish the news of Kung's elevation. The ailing eighty-nine-year-old Kung came from his American home in exile to Rome, climbed out of his wheelchair, and stumbled up the stairs to kneel at the foot of the pope. When the pope raised him up, it was to receive his cardinal's hat.

• Archbishop **François-Xavier Nguyễn Vân Thuận**, who was appointed coadjutor archbishop of Saigon in 1975, six days before the North Vietnamese armies conquered the city. Thuận, who had never engaged in politics, was seized by the communist authorities and (like so many thousands of those America left behind in its retreat from the ill-starred war) imprisoned in a brutal reeducation camp. There he languished for thirteen years, nine of them in solitary confinement—held because he refused to renounce his authority as bishop. In fact, he tried to continue acting as shepherd to the beleaguered Catholics of a united Vietnam by writing tiny pastoral messages that he managed to smuggle out of prison. In one, he wrote, "I am happy here, in this cell, where white mushrooms are growing on my sleep-

François-Xavier Nguyên Van Thuân

ing mat, because You are here with me, because You want me to live here with You. I have spoken much in my lifetime: now I speak no more. It's Your turn to speak to me, Jesus; I am listening to You." As AsiaNews reports, "These messages were then hand-copied and circulated throughout the Catholic community. They were collected in the book *The Road of Hope*. Another book, *Prayers of Hope*, contains the prayers he wrote in prison. He even made a small Bible on pieces of paper. Some jailers who sympathised with him smuggled him a piece of wood and twine, for a small crucifix." Thuận was finally transferred to house arrest, then allowed to go to Rome. But his plea to return to his see (now Ho Chi Minh City) was refused by the communist government, so he served out most of his remaining years as a Vatican official addressing Third World poverty. He is on the road to beatification, the first step toward being named a saint.

The takeaway message of this catalog is all too clear: If you want to produce saintly bishops, arrange for an anti-Catholic regime to come to power, especially one that produces widespread poverty and hunger and places inordinate power over the lives of ordinary people in the hands of rabidly secular bureaucrats. This conclusion is deeply consoling; it makes sense at least of the political and economic pronouncements that have been coming out of the U.S. Conference of Catholic Bishops since the early 1970s—which it turns out were aimed at creating the conditions for holy bishops and heroic laymen. Who knew?

23. Maybe the Protestants are right and you don't need this elaborate, sleazy hierarchy of men in silk robes, from the priest up through the bishop to some Pole or German in Rome, to stand between us and God.

If you want to eliminate sleaze, there's a simple way to do it: Keep human beings out of the process altogether, including yourself—unless of course you alone are immune to low motives and self-serving rationalizations. But then you wouldn't need a Savior, would you? Immortals don't frequent hospitals, and that's what the Church is on earth: a trauma ward full of bloody cots and doctors who smoke, nurses who struggle with obesity, and orderlies who like to swipe pain meds from the dispensary. Unless you want to go Japanese and staff the whole place with robots—who, if sci-fi movies are to be believed, are likely to go berserk and start transplanting brains—you're going to need a human institution. And that means sleaze.

Priests and bishops are sinners, just as doctors and nurses are someday going to die, but they can still work together to help us keep the Grim Reaper at bay. Like your parents, they're far from perfect ("You want me to give you a *reason* to cry?"), but without them your life just wouldn't be the same. It would be . . . someone else's.

Without the Church hierarchy, the faith wouldn't be the same from one Christian to the next. It would be "yours" in the same sense as your fingerprints, perfectly personalized because you yourself would have made it up. Sometimes that seems like what Westerners really want, given the thousands of Christian denominations that appeared in the Reformation's wake like bulk letters jamming a mailbox, each with the one true interpretation of Christianity, each one marked "urgent" and "personal." Within sixty years of Luther's Ninety-five Theses, Catholic scholar Christopher Rasperberger had compiled so many different Protestant theories of the Eucharist that he could publish a book called *200 Interpretations of "This is My Body"*(Ingolstadt, 1577). Luther's initial theory that the Holy Spirit would guide any honest Christian to understand the Bible on his own was quickly crushed by the onrushing crowd of new one, true, holy, and apostolic churches. Lutherans quickly organized under bishops, who would inform honest Christians what the Holy Spirit was really saying. After five hundred years of this, in our own time, gatherings of scholars like those found at the Jesus Seminar use their expertise to prove that He never speaks at all.

If we human beings were more like angels, deathless and bodiless spirits that sprang fully informed from the hand of God, communicating with Him via literally instant messages and learning what He expected of us firsthand, then of course no mediation between Him and us would be needed. It might not even be possible; the fallen angels don't benefit from the Passion of Christ, and the unfallen ones don't need it.

But you and I picked up most of what we know about the universe secondhand, beginning with the warmth and nurturing we got as infants that "told" us that the world is a welcoming place where we can live and thrive. (Kids placed in Romanian orphanages who were never picked up and held got the opposite message, and promptly died.) Then we learned language, without which human thought is a vague, disconnected series of sensory perceptions. After that, we learned to identify and name other people, and the fact that they are every bit as real as we are. Our parents and teachers explained the basic rules of how we ought to treat those other people, some of which are encoded by the government—which if we violate them too flagrantly will helpfully send those nice men in blue with guns and nightsticks to offer fraternal correction. In every single area of life, our experience is mediated and interpreted through the words and deeds of other people. We learn to "believe" that the world is round (it doesn't look round) and that it spins through space (why don't we throw up?) on the *authority of others*. We trust that when the doctor sticks a needle into us, he is giving us not botulism but some helpful compound created by men whose training (at the hands of other authorities) taught them to know the difference. We

even trust the testimony of our grandparents that World War II didn't really happen in black and white.

Wouldn't it be bizarre if the one thing we learned without any outside help was how to pray and relate to the God who made us what we are—utterly social creatures, who communicate with words? I suppose God could have revealed Himself to us this way, individually, in a blinding flash of insight that drove each one of us to write his own Book of Revelation. (He can do anything that doesn't contradict the laws of logic or His own nature.) But it would have seemed out of character, and it might very well have fed into our pride—which if you recall is the root of our problems in the first place.

24. So you're saying the Church is above the Bible?

A thousand times yes, but then again, no. The Church is the only reason that when you pick up a Bible there are 73 books in it, instead of 147 or 4. It was bishops who prayed to saints, baptized infants, venerated icons, and treated the Eucharist as the real presence of Christ who gathered in 382 A.D. to decree which books were divinely inspired, as opposed to merely inspiring or (worst of all) "inspirational."[15] The so-called "Gnostic" gospels, which keep turning up in abandoned outhouses throughout the Levant, were dissident documents drawn up much later than the canonical scriptures and express a very different view of the universe.[16] Think of them as revisionist histories, written by elderly Germans in Argentina and distributed at gun shows in rural Idaho.

So in one sense, the Church is like the Constitutional Convention, and the Bible the document they produced. Except, of course, that bishops weren't writing the thing—its author was the Holy Spirit, speaking through varied human voices over the centuries. The books existed before the bishops, and they were subject to its dictates before they'd taken a vote. Their individual salvation depended on conforming themselves to its message. These lawmakers, at least, were not above the Law. The Church judged what the Bible was, and tells us what it means—but in its turn it is judged against the standards the Bible contains, which it lacks the power to tinker with. That is why no committee of bishops can "expand" the sacrament of marriage to include homosexual couples and why no pope can add a fourth Person to the Trinity.

---

[15] CCC, 120

[16] This view amounted, in brief, to the following: The material world is evil, bearing children is criminal, death is a blessing, and we are much, much smarter than the rest of you. Indeed, the name they took for themselves, "Gnostics" (knowers), tells us most of what we need to know. That and the fact that they kept their doctrines secret, whispering them only to a chosen few. "The first rule of the Gnostic gospel is you don't *talk* about the Gnostic gospel. The second rule . . ."

25. OK, so you needed some authority in the early Church to get the whole process rolling and determine what Christianity was and what it wasn't. We needed a Constitutional Convention to get America started, too. But we don't have one sitting in perpetuity.

In effect, we do. The Supreme Court acts in something like that capacity, determining what the text of that document really means, how it applies—and occasionally, when they just get sick of the thing, deciding to invent new rights out of thin air, like "privacy" (abortion). The Court doesn't have divine guidance to step in at critical moments the way the Church does. We are solemnly promised by Christ that if a pope tries to teach something heretical, he will have a brain aneurysm on the toilet the night before. That's in the Bible.

26. Where in the Bible?

I don't remember. Ask a Protestant.

27. But it seems like the Church slid away from its primitive purity the further it got from the time of the apostles. Could it be that the early Church, whose members braved persecution to spread the gospel to the four corners of the earth, at some point ceased to exist and was replaced by a different organization with the same name, one that collected mountains of gold to build palaces for cardinals where their mistresses could keep their pornographic art collections?

I'd question some of your facts there, first of all. The particular misconceptions you've picked up about the Church suggest to me that you graduated from a Jesuit university, and that instead of fulfilling your three-credit-hour "religious studies" requirement the smart way—by studying Taoism—you actually took a course in Church history. Am I getting warm?

28. No comment.

Never mind. Your suggestion is an interesting one. Sometimes, in dealing with Church bureaucrats, obstructionist dissenters with mullets, or grumpy old dry-drunk Irish misanthropes in Roman collars, I've found myself wishing that it were true—that I could, when I got fed up, hoist the Jolly Roger and sail off on my own to find in one of those unadorned Baptist buildings full of nicely dressed, polite and patriotic Americans (and buxom blondes named "Dixie") the austere, pure, primitive Church. Then Dixie would drive me home in her Jesus-fished BMW to drink ice tea with her parents. At times, it's really tempting to imagine that this present-day institution lost its lifeline to the early Church of saints whom the Holy Spirit guided in choosing the books of the Bible and in determining in councils what Christians must think of the nature and mission of Christ. But when exactly was that rupture supposed to have happened?

Some reformers choose as a logical breaking point the conversion of Constantine. In 312 that pagan emperor reportedly had a vision, in the middle of a civil war, of a Chi Rho (Christ's initials) in the sky with the motto "In this sign, conquer." He shrugged and decided it was worth a try. He had his army's banners and helmets marked with the Christian symbol and promptly won a devastating victory. Soon after his victory march into Rome, Constantine legalized the Church and gave it favored status over other religions. When the doctrinal squabbles over Christ's divinity threatened to start civil wars in cities across the empire (see chapter 3), Con-

stantine ordered the bishops to convene in what became the Council of Nicaea, which condemned Arius and adopted the Creed we still say at Mass. Soon bishops went from being treated as criminals to serving as advisers to the emperor. Constantine funded the building of vast, magnificent basilicas and leaned heavily on the Church to help him keep order in the empire. His successor, Theodosius, went even further (too far) and outlawed every other religion, giving the Church a power she never ought to have had—the arm of the state in repressing heresy. It was at this moment that the Church became the Whore of Babylon, according to hardcore Calvinists like the Rev. Ian Paisley, leader of the Ulster Protestants, who made his name picketing papal appearances with effigies of the pope conveniently labeled "Antichrist."

Here is how Reverend Paisley sums thing up on his website:

> Then Satan changed his tactics, and set on that baptized heathen Constantine to profess to become a Christian; and he, for reasons of statecraft and subtle policy, made Christianity the national religion, and this struck the most fearful blow at the vitals of Christianity. The union of Church and State is a fatal blow to true religion. The king's hand, wherever it falls upon the Church of Christ, brings the king's evil with it; there never was a Church whose spirituality survived it yet, and there never will be. Christ's

Kingdom is not of this world, and if we try to marry the Church of Christ to a worldly kingdom we engender innumerable mischiefs.

So it happened that when the Church became outwardly glorious she became spiritually debased. Her communion table glittered with gold and silver plate, but her communion with Christ was not so golden as aforetime. Her ministers were enriched, but their doctrine was impoverished; for every ounce of outward gold which she gained, she lost a treasure of grace. Her bishops became lords, and her flocks were famished; her humble meeting-places were exchanged for grand basilicas, but their true glory was departed. She became like the heathen around her, and began to set up the images of her saints and martyrs, till at last, after years of gradual declension, the Church of Rome ceased to be the Church of Christ, and that which was once nominally the Church became the Antichrist.[17]

If Paisley is right, how do we explain what happened over the next seven centuries—the evangelization of the still mostly pagan West? On this account, it was the Whore of Babylon, ruled over by the Antichrist, that brought the gospel to France, Spain, England, Ireland (north and south!), Germany, Hungary, Poland, Scandinavia, Russia . . . you get the idea. Indeed, every one of the countries where the founders of the Reformation were born was converted after the Church embraced "the dark side." Furthermore, most Protestant churches still accept the decisions of  Church councils held after this dark event—beginning with Nicaea. Were the bishops who reaffirmed the full divinity of Christ doing so in service to Satan?

More critically, we have abundant records of the doctrines, liturgies, and sacramental practices of the Church before Constantine and after. They were . . . exactly the same. The jump from adoring God to worshipping Satan seems to have had *exactly no effect* on the way Christians practiced their faith. As someone who has had the misfortune of running into Satanists and occultists over the years, I can tell you this doesn't ring true. People who open themselves to the power of evil do not, as a rule, continue to:

- open hospitals for the poor,
- preach the New Testament to hostile pagans,

[17] http://www.ianpaisley.org/article.asp?ArtKey=metro

- confess the faith in the face of death at the hands of Muslim conquerors, or
- painstakingly recopy the great works of antiquity while leading lives of poverty, chastity, and obedience.

Instead, they tend to invent their own ugly rituals, which center on weird sex, violence, and blasphemy. It seems Satan lacks the patience required to allow his followers to emulate, for centuries, the holiness of Christians while covertly (even unknowingly) preaching heresies that will send souls in giant boatloads down to hell. Those who serve him directly can sometimes (briefly) appear as angels of light, but the effects on the soul and intellect of embracing the devil are so overwhelming that his minions can rarely keep their disguises straight or their pants on—much less evangelize a continent. For that much, we can be grateful.

What is more, it was the dark, perverted, post-Constantinian Church that converted St. Augustine—the very man whose theology of grace John Calvin took to its logical extreme, producing the beliefs that Ian Paisley liked to shout through a megaphone in Belfast. Logically, Paisley should toss out St. Augustine, too.

It's the central assertion of Protestantism (why else protest?) that the visible Church turned evil at some particular date and passed her divine mantle to tiny groups of proto-Baptists or embryonic Pentecostalists. To students of the Bible this ought to seem kind of strange. Whenever the Israelites committed some act of apostasy, God always sent a prophet to call them back, and punishments to remind them Who was in charge. There was always a clearly identifiable "remnant" keeping the faith, holding fast to the faith of Abraham and the law of Moses. Where were those people all through the Dark Ages (500–1000)? If they were good Protestants, why didn't they spread that faith (instead of the Roman corruption) through Western and Eastern Europe? Why do the oldest churches outside the Roman communion, in Ethiopia and India, have shockingly similar sacraments and nearly identical creeds (apart from a Christological heresy here or there), none of which reflect Luther's or Calvin's (or Zwingli's or George Fox's) supposedly apostolic doctrines?

There is no such breaking point. However far back you go in Christian history, deciding to set the cut-off date *here*, you will always find something the Church did after that which you can't attribute to Lucifer. So the quest for a clean, crisp moment of transition turns into a hopeless muddle. Those who reject a hierarchical Church but want to hold on to the doctrines

it promulgated have sawed off the limb they were sitting on. But no one wants to admit something like that, so Protestants speak of "orthodox" Christianity, citing the acts of councils presided over by popes, whose proceedings were opened and closed by the celebration of the Mass. In other words, they're sitting on the ground, still clutching the tree limb and looking up at the sky. Sorry, Dixie.

29. So there's no value to Protestantism—these people just emerged out of nowhere and rebelled for the sake of causing trouble, because they couldn't understand simple arguments like those?

No, not at all. The most profound truths are simple (God is absolutely simple, St. Thomas explains), which means that the deepest errors will be, too. To say that isn't to accuse the person who makes an error of being simple-minded. There were reasons why a Reformation erupted, and we've already talked about the most obvious ones, in the form of papal mistresses, their bastard children made cardinals, and their habit of denying the sacraments to cities that stubbornly refused to let papal armies conquer them. But there was a deeper issue at stake. The great theologian Louis Bouyer was raised as a French Huguenot (a Protestant group that barely survived the cruel persecutions of French Catholic kings) and later joined the Church. He wrote *The Spirit and Forms of Protestantism* as a kind of insider's guide for Catholics to what motivates Protestant faith—and maybe to teach those of us who were so blessed as to have the Truth rammed down our throats since early childhood not to preen about it or sneer at those who weren't. Because for our part Catholics are not entitled to pretend that the many millions of sincere Christians who grew up as Protestants over the centuries were themselves in service to Antichrist or utterly cut off from God.

For one thing, anybody validly baptized with water in the name of the Trinity becomes—perhaps unwittingly—part of the Catholic Church. Whatever beliefs he adopts that depart from orthodoxy remain between him and God, and it's not up to us to decide that people are culpable of sin for adopting mistaken opinions. But on a much more concrete level, we can't dismiss all the good works done in the name of the gospel by people with a mistaken ecclesiology or sacramental theology, any more than Calvinists can say that St. Augustine served the Whore of Babylon.

What Bouyer says is that there was something much more fundamentally wrong with Christendom in 1517 than Church corruption and discount indulgences. He notes that the theological synthesis of faith and reason achieved by St. Thomas Aquinas had largely broken down in universities and been replaced by a tendency called Nominalism. Without going into philosophical depths ill-suited to a book full of silly pictures, the Nominalists said, in essence, that there is no real connection between words and things, faith and reason, theology and science. The realm of prayer and piety has no overlap with the world of clear and rational thought; God and all His works are an unfathomable mystery, which our reason can shed little light on. So

with one half of our brains we should read the Bible and pray, while using the other to work out scientific and rational solutions in the realm of practical living. The Church should give way to the power of the state in most realms of life, and clerics should stay in their rectories, instead of blocking the road to progress. If this late-medieval worldview sounds eerily modern to you, you aren't wrong: Such a divided mind became increasingly widespread in subsequent centuries, ironically in part because the Reformation widened (rather than bridging) the gap between faith and reason, until by the nineteenth century good churchgoing factory owners (Catholic and Protestant) could sit with a clear conscience through a long service on Sunday, then on Monday go back to paying starvation wages for child labor.

The other toxic addiction of late-medieval Christians was to something that Luther rightly called "works righteousness." Now the Letter of St. James does say that faith without works is dead—and that's the reason Luther dismissed it as an "epistle of straw." The Church always taught that good works, made possible by grace, were useful in making partial restitution for sins that had already been forgiven. To put it simply, if you stole something and went to confession, part of repairing your relationship with God entails giving it back. But you can't unring such bells as sodomy, adultery, or murder. If salvation really consists of God healing our self-inflicted wounds and uniting our human nature with Christ's in the form of His Mystical Body on earth, then it won't do simply to pop into confession and pretend that because all is forgiven, it should be forgotten. We have done real and lasting damage to our souls, and perhaps to the community, by our sins, and we are expected to work to make it good.

That's the theory, and it's a sound one. But just as teenagers can misuse the Theory of Relativity as a pretext for insisting that "all truth is relative," so Christians were tempted to pervert the Church's emphasis on good works to suit their own neuroses or convenience. "Indulgences" started out as a way for the Church to guide penitents into doing works of charity for their neighbors. By the Renaissance, they had become in the public mind a kind of get-out-of-purgatory free card, which wandering friars sold like lottery tickets at festivals. This showed just how far popular piety had swung in the direction of Pelagianism—the heresy that teaches that we must save ourselves by our own efforts while Jesus stands on the sideline like a football coach who (two thousand years ago) Himself won the Heisman trophy.[18]

As Bouyer explains slowly and patiently for us papists, this is not Christianity. Luther was right about that, and when he rebelled against this kind of self-help, bootstrap theological capitalism, his heart was in the right place. But because he himself had been formed in the Nominalist tradition, Luther was much too quick to abandon the Church's attempt to synthesize the facts of revelation with the dictates of formal reason—a faculty he once impatiently called a "whore." He was also too proud to submit to the Church's authority (as St. Francis had) and patiently endure misunderstanding and abuse (see St. Joan of Arc, St. Catherine of Siena, St. John of the Cross). Instead,

when the pope excommunicated him, Luther took the papal letter and burned it in the public square, to the cheers of the crowd. When his own readings of St. Paul were shown to contradict not just papal bulls but also the decrees of ecumenical councils, he dismissed the latter too—assuming, in effect, the mantle of infallibility.

Luther was so keen to reject Pelagianism that he rushed to the opposite extreme, denying that man had any free will at all, asserting that the human soul is a like donkey—which is ridden either by God or by the devil.

For Catholics, the salvation of a soul is not a one-time, slam-bang event, like dropping a grape into liquid nitrogen, then smashing it with a hammer. That's what Luther's rival John Calvin thought, insisting that our nature is irredeemably corrupt and our wills must be simply replaced with the irresistible will of God. That's a literalistic misreading of St. Augustine, but the Church never taught it, for very good reason: if the only reason a soul were sent to eternal bliss in heaven or everlasting punishment in hell was that God chose to lavish one with grace and leave the other soul on its own, there's no way you could call God "just" and mean it. You'd have

---

[18] CCC, 406

to mean something else, as in "He's in charge, He's the one who's holding the pistol, so He's whatever He says He is. OK, He's 'just.' I just wish He'd point that thing somewhere else." St. Thomas Aquinas insisted that terms when applied to God must at least be analogous in their meanings to what they mean for men—or else instead of "just" or "loving," we might as well say that God is "Cheerios" or "paint thinner." Such an arbitrary God who only saves men from the sin they were born with by overriding their wills and occupying them like the Germans did France would have had no reason to make independent creatures in the first place. And in fact, He wouldn't have. The human race would be a vast array of robots—some driven by grace, others by original sin—that He capriciously cherry-picked to people heaven with saints while keeping the rest around to torture eternally. If that's the God we're expecting to meet in heaven, I respectfully return my ticket.

Instead of smashing a grape, the way grace works on a soul is more like the process of training a stubborn, intractable tree—snipping here and there, attaching stakes and wires, guiding by slow, inexorable force the direction a living thing will take. The Holy Spirit offers constant assistance, the sacraments infuse a soul with the graces needed at particular stages of life, and the Church with her teachings and prayers over time unites our imperfect natures with the Perfect, transforming our corruptible natures into the Incorruptible. We walk up Calvary slowly, like Simon of Cyrene, falling beneath the cross. Christ lifts us up and leads us gently in His footsteps. He doesn't carry us on His back or step on our faces. He came to give us life, and that more abundantly.

The Sacraments

1. What is all this business of "sacraments"? Why set up all these complicated rituals to stand between man and God? It looks to me like a system set up by priests to guarantee you would always need them.

First of all, you don't need priests for all the sacraments, strictly speaking. They proved that in Japan, where the samurai killed all the clergy and most of the laity, so the surviving "secret Christians" had to make do with just baptism and marriage, teaching their children Latin prayers whose meaning they'd long forgotten. The Church continued in that residual form for more than three hundred years, until the first missionaries returned in the nineteenth century—right after American gunships pounded Japanese ships and forced the "opening" of that country to the world. (That's a melancholy theme, the recurring role of U.S. firepower in Japanese reform, but it's for another day.) But yes, the clergy play a central role in Catholic worship, which sets it apart from other human religions exactly . . . how?

2. Ah ha! You just admitted that yours is just another human religion like all the others. Nothing divine about it.

No, I didn't. Logic is a sadly neglected subject in American public schools—and even the Ivy League—but I won't insist on the point. Why do you think the Christian sacramental system can only be uniquely true if it were distinctly quirky? Given that man has a certain nature, with inborn and engrained habits and a fixed routine of life (you get born, you eat, you grow up, you get married, then you die—and through all of it, you sin), doesn't it seem more likely that the true religion would address each of these points along life's way and show us how to use them as means to get closer to God? Imperfect religions, even those that dabbled in evil, would pretty much have to work with the same raw materials, and so they'd be bound to center their rites on the same basic events. So yes, other faiths bless food and have rites for birth and marriage, coming of age and dying. Would Christianity somehow seem

truer if it picked the minor, marginal moments of life and affixed its critical rituals to those? Such sacraments would attach, I guess, to things like flossing, farting, taking the SATs, and switching from T-Mobile to Verizon. Come to think of it, I can see now why a postmodern smart-ass might prefer that kind of creed. It fits in with how trivial they've concluded life must be, and covers the resultant, heaving despair with a thin icing of irony, a smiley face on the door of the cosmic euthanasia room.

3. So the Church realized that man needed signposts along the road of life and sat down to figure out how to mark them in an emotionally satisfying way, attaching to each of these key moments some ritual by which the community signified and recognized the progress of the individual. I can see how that makes sense.

You've just described the merit-badge system in scouting, not the sacraments of the Church. There was no point at which some Archbishop Baden-Powell picked up a notebook and sketched these things out artificially, as some useful if arbitrary system for marking time and rewarding people for developing character virtues and tying intricate knots. The sacraments arose directly from things that Jesus said, or did, or told His disciples to do.[1] The apostles and those who followed them did their best to follow instructions, adding here and there a prayer of thanks, sometimes adopting a more solemn or dignified way of doing things to mark such actions off as sacred. Over the centuries, saints added a few more prayers or elaborated the actions to make absolutely sure no one could mistake these Christian rituals for ordinary, practical actions. Once a saint had added a prayer or a ceremony, nobody really had the heart to cut it, so these tended to add up over the centuries—till a rite that began at the Last Supper, with Christ, and probably took ten minutes, grew into something as grand and grueling as the Russian Easter liturgy, which keeps you chanting, droning, and standing for more than four hours. I know this firsthand because I've been to it several times—one year getting so weary that I leaned back on an icon lamp and set my hair on fire. Given the organic mode in which liturgies develop, I'm sure that if this kept on happening to people, within a few hundred years it

---

[1] CCC, 1131

would be stylized and included in the rubrics—attributed to the shadowy, possibly mythical, "St. Michael of Neverland."

4. So when it comes to ceremonials, the Church acts like a hoarder?

Think of her more like a librarian who treasures every volume. There are periodic cleanups when things that have gotten out of hand are pared back for the sake of clarity. At the Council of Trent, some long and elaborate "Gallican" prayers were respectfully sent to the dugout. The urge to go "back to basics" can go too far, of course. In the wake of Vatican II, reformers went hog-wild and pig-crazy, ripping out hugely important things like most of the Offertory prayers, adding in banalities like the Reportorial Psalm[2] and desacralizing the rituals willy-nilly. For the past forty years, there's been a war inside in the Church between those who want to repair the damage and those who'd like to knock out the last few pieces of stained glass left in the windows. Recent popes have made it clear that the vandals won't win in

the long run, but by the long run the Church means "centuries," so for our lifetimes at least, you'll still see people in T-shirts holding hands like four-year-olds at the Our Father, waiting for their chance to sing "Blowin' in the Wind" as they stroll up to palm the Eucharist from some divorcée wearing a track suit, then hightailing it for the parking lot. It makes you grateful that we're only stuck down here for threescore and ten. But I'm sure that within five hundred years, Catholic ritual will have recovered from the 1960s and '70s. In fact, I'll bet you five . . . no, *ten* thousand dollars. (We should probably make that payable in *yuán* or in robot currency.)

What makes the Christian sacraments unique is that they are neither of the two things they closely resemble:

(a) merely symbolic representations of "deeper" truths, designed to generate lofty thoughts and remind us through what we can see of things we cannot—like a flatscreen installed in a tombstone at a Beverly Hills cemetery, which plays in an endless loop the dead guy's favorite Eagles song while cycling through his old photos, watercolors, and haikus;

(b) acts of magic, by which men wield shibboleths, sacrifices, and fetishes, binding forces of nature or the occult to work their wills, smite their enemies, or score with "death metal" chicks.

---

[2] Now, repeat after me: "Happy is the one who takes your babies and smashes them against the rocks!" (Ps. 137:9)

The Reformers feared that the Church had stumbled into treating her sacraments like (b), so some of them eviscerated their rituals and theology, ripped out altars and altar rails, then lumped in priests with laymen, until finally what most Protestants practiced amounted to (a). By overreacting against the "magical" heresy that arguably beguiled some Catholic peasants, devout men like Luther and Calvin unwittingly embarked on a massive secularization of the West that prepared the way for men like Descartes and Spinoza. Instead of a pope, however flawed, whose powers were traced to the apostles, the churches were now dominated by princes and kings—in other words, by the state.[3] Christians traded sacraments that reliably channeled the grace of God through the rituals of the Church and anointed priests for symbols that lay ministers enacted, which at best served to dramatize the individual's lonely struggle with the complex demands of the gospel. Theology began to give way to psychology, and it was only a matter of time before the confessional gave way to the therapist's couch.

5. So they're not just symbolic dramas, but they aren't incantations—I get it, no *Hamlet*, no voodoo. So the sacraments are . . . what precisely? If you duck behind the word *mystery*, I'm going to have to smack you upside the head.

Sacraments are the ordinary means by which God promised we could get His help.[4] If we go to a priest who was ordained by a real bishop, and he uses the right words with the right intention, we receive the grace we're asking for—so long as our own intention is at least moderately sincere. As you can tell from this list of conditions, things could go wrong at almost any stage of this process. It's much less like magic in that sense than like mathematics: If you get the wrong value for "x," it won't compute with "y." There are all sorts of exceptions, exemptions, and specifics, but they're much better dealt with in context—so we'll go through this one sacrament at a time.

---

[3] For a detailed account of how this happened, see Scott Hahn and Benjamin Wiker: *Politicizing the Bible* (Chestnut Ridge, NY: Herder and Herder, 2012).
[4] CCC, 1116

6. So God has kind of boxed himself in with these sacraments?

No. God is bound by the laws of logic because they're intrinsic to Him, and He is bound to keep His promises because He's just that kind of Person. But the sacraments are created thing He willed into existence, and He can go above and beyond them whenever He likes. God can and does send His messages where He likes, as He likes, to men of goodwill who seek Him. But the sacraments are always there.

7. Like the Post Office, which can't go on strike.

But Fedex can. Except that the sacraments are also more reliable, quicker, more certain than any other conceivable means. It's more like having your mail delivered by the Secret Service every day. Sure, you could ask a neighbor's teenager to drop off your note across town. Provided he isn't distracted by some loud noise or shiny object, it might get there. You never know.

It's this greater certitude, a big shiny divine promise that Jesus left us under the Christmas tree, that Catholics consider a privilege and want to share with the rest of the world. That's why we're so busy evangelizing society at every street corner.

8. Where? What are you talking about? Compared to Protestants and Mormons, I've always thought of Catholics as being in kind of a sleepy religion. They don't try to get new members, but if you show up, they'll stick you in some boring classes pitched at a fourth-grade reading level, and if you still haven't gone home by then, they'll let you join.

Sigh. Things weren't always like this—see the conversion of Europe and the Jesuit missions to China—but I have to admit you're right. One unhappy side effect of all that certitude and complexity that make the Faith attractive to peasants and intellectuals is that for the folks in between (we sturdy bourgeois), there's a tendency to torpor. At least we're not like the Greek Orthodox, who if you ring their doorbell and ask about Jesus Christ will come back by asking, "Are you Greek?" For a long time, when we virtually banned mixed marriages, we attracted whole rafts of male converts who couldn't resist those sensuous Italian and willowy Irish girls. So they agreed to convert, or at least to raise all the kids as Catholics, and the outcome was frequently happy. The power of flesh as a salvation bait for the spirit goes all the way back, actually. St. Augustine was one of many kids born to pagan fathers and

Christian moms. In the late Roman Empire, morals had plunged so far that the only way a senator could be sure his kids were . . . you know, *his*, was to marry one of the Christians. That's how we converted the upper class of Romans before the mob. (The Latin word *paganus* translates, roughly, as "redneck.")

9. OK, so you people start by spritzing water on a baby's head. Then you give him a cookie. Then you make him tell his sins to an unmarried guy while kneeling inside a box. Then you have the bishop smack him across the face. Then you marry him off— or ordain him. Then when he's dying, you have a healing ritual that never seems to work. Am I missing anything?

Font (def. 1)

Well, that was a nice, respectful summary of the sacred rites of another man's faith. Using your real name, why don't you offer a similar rundown on the Internet of the central beliefs of Islam? Come on, why not? I notice that you just turned a whiter shade of pale. You're kind of quiet. So I'll launch into our first sacrament, baptism.

The ritual for this sacrament actually predated Christ—that's how John the Baptist got his name.[5] Jesus came up to the Jordan River and took part in it, predicting that a new and more potent form of baptism would be coming downstream in the very near future. Soon enough, Christ would be telling His disciples, "Unless a man be born again of water and the Holy Ghost, he cannot enter into the Kingdom of God" (John 3). That tells us that something a lot more profound is going on than a simple scrubbing off of particular sins. In fact, the Church sees baptism as a kind of death and rebirth. The sinful, fallen son of Adam and Eve drowns in the font, and what emerges is a redeemed man whose nature is now joined to Christ's. That symbolism is a lot more powerfully vivid in the original form of baptism, which is still used in some Eastern churches and entails submerging someone's entire body three times—once for each person of the Trinity. Nowadays (since the Middle Ages), we in the West anoint a newcomer's head with oil and pour water over it three times. That's perfectly valid, and much more convenient, but to onlookers it does tend to emphasize the cleansing from Original Sin over the equally important fact that the person is being born again. Emerging squinting and squalling from a water bath is a lot more reminiscent of the "miracle" of childbirth—at least as much as I've seen of it accidentally on cable

[5] CCC, 536

before I could grab control of the remote.[6] Some Christian churches still baptize newcomers in rivers, but experience has shown that the sacrament, performed this way, tends to produce Pentecostalists (see chapter 4).

Baptism is at once less gory and more decisive than natural birth. Made possible by the bloody sacrifice of the Cross, it's a painless transformation from one spiritual species to another: from just another example of *homo lapsus* to a freshly minted instance of *homo electus,* one whom God has chosen to remake on the model of Christ, to divinize gradually, and with his own consent—filling up his emptiness with His superabundance. That's why the newly baptized are clad in white and treated like saints; for the moment they are. Even bloody-handed adults like Emperor Constantine are purged of every sin and every stain of guilt, such that if they died right then, they would wing it straight into heaven. Baptism really is the only "Get Out of Purgatory Free" card in our deck.[7]

10. So why don't you drown everyone in the font and send them right up to God? That way you wouldn't be taking any chances. No one would go to hell.

Except for you, since you'd murdered the next generation of the human race. Regardless of your motives, that might count against you. I wrote a whole book on this subject, the graphic novel *The Grand Inquisitor*. It was based on a Russian novel, composed in Miltonic blank verse, and illustrated like a death-metal album cover, reducing its potential target audience to approx-

---

[6] Why in heck is it now de rigueur for fathers to "take part" in the birthing process? In every other culture I'm familiar with, childbirth was a ritual conducted by women, which the dads stayed far away from. This arose not so much from squeamishness—though that would be my motive—as from a sense that this was a peculiarly feminine mystery, which men ought not to monkey with. Then in the 1970s, some hippies got the idea that it was "beautiful" for fathers to kneel down with a catcher's mitt and watch their wives get turned inside out and unstuffed like a turkey. Like every other idea that stemmed from the '70s, it was a bad one. If I ever con some woman into marrying me, she will give birth while I smoke a cigar out in the hospital parking lot. In return, she doesn't need to come and cheer on my colonoscopies. Fair's fair.
[7] CCC, 1262

imately "John Zmirak," so I have plenty of free "author's copies" in my apartment if you'd like one . . .

11. So the only reason not to turn baptismal fonts into Cuisinarts is a selfish concern for your own salvation, at the expense of everyone else's?

You know, I've had precisely the same thought when dealing with people who try a little too hard to be otherworldly, to the point where they're happy to make a complete botch of this one—then justify the awful effects of their bad ideas with a shrug: "Well, suffering is good for the soul!" I met a lot of these Potato Famine Catholics[8] in New England who were traumatized after forty years of dominance by the likes of Cardinal Cushing, Teddy Kennedy, and Barney Frank. They're so disgusted by the unprincipled, hedonistic social climbing of their lace-curtain cousins that they climb back into the shanty and nail the door shut behind them. They think that in order to care about eternal life, you need to neglect the legitimate goods of this one. They scoff at people's God-given instinct to seek out happiness, health, and pleasure— forgetting that these things are good in themselves, while suffering is evil. The only thing worse is actual sin.

I'll never forget the grimmest wedding I ever attended, which joined together two Faminite friends of mine—fine, hard-working people, but blighted by bad theology. The Mass wasn't irreverent or disrespectful—quite the contrary. They had arranged for a lovely Tridentine liturgy in a New England Gothic church that had somehow escaped the wreckovators and liturgists, the pedophiles and the plaintiffs. The choir sang exquisitely. The bride was glowing, the groom was gloating, and all seemed as it should be. Then the specially chosen priest (they'd flown him in) mounted the pulpit to give the homily. He took as his theme the unique value of suffering and offered the theory (cribbed from the gloomy, campy Rev. Frederick Faber) that willfully accepted suffering is the *only* currency acceptable in heaven. He spoke of the many and heavy crosses that married people must carry and illustrated his message by pointing to the bride and then to the groom—explaining that each of them would serve for the other *as the heaviest cross in life*, the deepest and most enduring cause of suffering. "It is thus, as we embrace the Cross, that we work our way in fear and trembling along the narrow path to Heaven." *Victim soul, embrace your cross. You may kiss the bride.*

---

[8] By this I mean Irish-Americans (like my mother) whose ancestors leaned on their Faith to survive devastating poverty and suffering, who inherited a vision of Christianity somewhat warped by the experience—such that the descendants saw good health, comfort, and prosperity as near occasions of sin. Of course, as they watched some Catholics assimilate to the American "mainstream," and trade their religious heritage for a mess of suburban pottage, that only seemed to confirm the theory: If you aren't eating grass for sustenance, you're probably somehow angering God .... Wondering if someone is really a Faminite? Here's an easy way to tell: They believe in the "fewness of the saved," but they also condemn Natural Family Planning; apparently it's our duty to help stuff hell to the rafters.

A few weeks later, the affectionate couple sent out the announcement that they were already expecting. Apparently, they'd assisted in the procreation of a brand new human soul on the first night of their honeymoon. A good friend of mine, who teaches at MIT and so has all the emotional intelligence of a Vulcan, wrote them a goofy note: "You really hit the bed running, huh? *Vroom, vroom!*"

To this the merry couple replied:

> We are happy that you share our joy in the news that Dymphna may be expecting. It is sad that today it is very common, if not easy with the corruption of our culture, to minimize the blessed gravity of these events by characterizing them through the distorted prism of our modern world which only sees worth or value in vanities.
>
> So often today this causes us to see the coming to life of a new child, indeed created in the Image and Likeness of God, albeit through His imperfect instruments in the Sacrament of Holy Matrimony, as an occasion for immodesty, if not puerility.
>
> We are grateful for your prayers and your friendship, and only ask that you express your genuine joy for our recent happiness in a more subdued fashion.

My friend was mortified, and it seemed to me some response was in order. So I penned the couple this note:

> I have been informed of the news of your recent conception. While I hope it does not provide for you an occasion of the sin of Vainglory for me to say so, I feel obligated to laud you both for stoically shouldering the solemn duty of those Christians called to the (lesser) vocation of marriage to graciously accept all children whom God, in His Providence, deems fit to entrust to you. Were we worldings, it might seem fitting for me to join with you in a merely fleshly celebration of the continuation of the species. However, given the grim reality of the Fewness of the Saved (a fact attested by St. Leonard of Maurice), one must acknowledge that the conception of a human soul is a hazardous undertaking, and one not likely to end well. Nevertheless, it seems that it has, in your case, been tolerated through God's permissive will. Given that fact, I know that you will embrace this cross as courageously as you have the arduous cross of matrimony, and I hope that your mortifications as parents will be many and edifying, and I will pray for the unlikely event of your son or daughter's eternal salvation.

> Yours at the Foot of the Cross,
>
> John Zmirak

I guess the note had the intended effect, because they didn't end up naming their kid "Stigmatus." Mission accomplished!

12. OK, and your point is . . .?

That God could easily call each of us to Himself by striking us dead the moment after baptism. He takes an enormous risk by creating us with free will that allows us to sin and cause Him suffering—at least in His human nature, in the flesh of Jesus Christ. (Every sin committed before His birth or after His death was visited on Our Lord upon the Cross, and as St. John Vianney said, every time we repent we are pulling a nail from His crown of thorns.) But God clearly thinks our earthly life is important enough to allow us to take this risk. So we need to honor that life and live it well. It's more than just a placement exam we're taking to see which class we get to enter next—like those grueling admissions tests that Japanese kids have to take to get placed in the "right" kindergarten, since the alternative means working as a janitor in a sushi joint, mopping up fish heads for the rest of their lives. Life is not just a shadowplay whose only significance comes with its ending. As C. S. Lewis observed in *The Great Divorce*, for the saved heaven begins on earth, while those who refuse salvation drag hell up to earth and trail it along behind them through the decades. We're meant by our prayers and good works to pour the cement for the City of God while we slog through whatever muck (or fields of flowers) we encounter in this mortal coil. Baptism provides the water for mixing that cement. Suffering offers the sand.

13. You claim that every baby is born as a bad seed, corrupted with "Original Sin." Every time the real world doesn't match your theological fancies, you don't blame your theories—you blame the world and claim that it is "fallen." (That tactic reminds me of people who say that communism is "beautiful in theory, but too impractical"—as if any false, useless theory could be beautiful.) How does any of that make sense?

The great advantage of Christianity over competing faiths is its technology for *rendering suffering meaningful*. Beginning with the book of Genesis, divine revelation seems to me less an answer to speculations such as "Where did the world come from?" (the Greek myths' "just so" stories were equally satisfying) than to the vexing question "Why do bad things happen to good people—especially to me?"[9]

Genesis answers this neatly by explaining that none of us is quite as good as we think, that we're flawed copies of a rogue prototype who lost us the right to paradise. Some people find it troubling that the tale of Adam in Eden in some ways mirrors pagan accounts of a Golden Age, equally free of suffering—as if that proved the Jew-

ish revelation carried no more authority than those. Instead of worrying over this, I'd like to ask a deeper question: *If we weren't created for something better than the perilous life we face, where on earth would man have gotten such a crackpot idea?* None of the animals dwell in safety, live forever, or enjoy perfect abundance. No aspect of existence in a planet with scarce resources, of nature red in tooth and claw, would suggest that things had ever been any different. But there is a widespread human tradition assuring us that our lives were once idyllic. Perhaps that means something. I'm willing to wager that it does.

While we have no direct evidence that paradise ever existed, we do have daily reminders of the reality of the Fall. A few minutes spent surfing the Internet will prove to the bleakest, most dogged optimist that, however man was originally programmed, a pretty serious virus has worked its way into the code. I challenge the most intrepid evolutionary biologist to find the "survival value" of the instinct that drives fertile men to obsess over pictures of college girls kissing. And what aspect of natural selection is served by dressing one's mate up as a show pony? I really could go on all day, and prove my point with images, but this is a family book . . .[10]

While subsequent narratives (Noah's and Abraham's) show a cause-and-effect connection between serving God and receiving an earthly reward, the Book of Job backtracks a little—warning us not to see in every trial the shadow of punishment. That profoundly unsatisfying book of the Bible reminds happy people whose lives are going well not to jump to conclusions that those who suffer must somehow deserve it. This point Christ would make explicitly, noting that God "maketh his sun to rise on the evil and on the good, and sendeth rain on the just and on the unjust" (Matthew 5:45). But, of course, the story goes on, and prophetic predictions of a saving "suffering servant" come true in the person of Christ—who echoes the pains of Abel and all the innocents ever to perish throughout the ages.

---

[9] CCC, 407
[10] CCC, 2354

The story of Jesus's passion is not a tragedy from which we can all take valuable lessons, or a cautionary tale for aspiring founders of religions. (And from this we learn: snazzier miracles, less puzzling parables, and for God's sake don't mess with divorce.) Too many film adaptations present Christ's life as the career of a noble moral reformer, with piercing blue eyes and a stoner's blank affect, needlessly cut short by intolerance. But if this were true, then Peter would have been right to draw his sword, and Christ would not have rebuked him. He would have beat a hasty retreat from Jerusalem, as Muhammad fled Mecca, and Latter-day Saints founder Joseph Smith fled the mob in Carthage, Illinois, that shot him to death. Instead of "Father, into thy hands I commend my spirit," we might remember as the last words of Christ the stirring "Feets don't fail me now!"

We aren't to draw from Jesus's story the lesson to seek out martyrdom—though some unbalanced saints made that mistake. We do not fetishize suffering or consider it good in itself. If we did, the Church would be betraying her worldwide mission by running hospitals, schools, and pregnancy centers all aimed at alleviating human misery; she could save herself all the trouble by leaving folks to their fates and advising them, "Offer it up!" Indeed, if suffering were in itself redemptive, we could sanctify souls by *purposely inflicting it*. I made this point imprudently to my students, and for the next few days the guys were walking around punching each other in the arm and saying with a smile, "Offer it up!"

No, the proper Christian attitude toward suffering is that it is evil, the fruit of the Fall, almost the worst thing in the world—except for sin. The only reason on earth to embrace suffering is to avoid committing a sin, or to atone for one. Christ Himself didn't rush to the cross like a suicide bomber, but pleaded with His father to let the cup pass from His lips. Only because there was no other way to atone for men's sins did He bravely, and with a fortitude we cannot fathom, carry the cross.[11]

---

[11] CCC, 1808

We can gain such fortitude for our own daily trudge by interrupting our self-pity sessions to think about the Passion. By uniting our own sufferings to Christ's, and offering them in reparation for sin, we gain an astonishing cosmic power—to turn the useless, toxic substance that is suffering into the balm that heals the soul. So it turns out that the essence of Christianity is its mechanism for recycling. Who knew?

14. So to counter the effects of the "Fall," baptism is absolutely necessary—for salvation?

Yes, because Christ said so. And so we try to provide a full, sacramental water baptism to every person on earth, whenever possible.[12] Obviously, this can prove a challenge when the parents are unwilling, have never heard of Christianity, or have no reason on earth to think it's true.

15. So those people are damned to hell?

Those who reach the age of reason, who don't embrace Catholicism, whether or not they've heard of it. Or so the Potato Faminites like to think, but for centuries the Church has taught that there is more than one form of baptism:

- the ordinary form, with water, that requires a paid photographer and results in silver rattles from Neiman Marcus;
- baptism of blood, which happens when believers who haven't yet been baptized are martyred first;
- baptism of desire. We call such desire "explicit" when we refer to someone who's planning to be baptized—who maybe has even registered at Neiman's—but drops dead first. We call it "implicit" when we speak of peo-

[12] CCC, 1257-1260

ple who either haven't heard of Christ (think of pagans in Central Asia) or haven't had Him preached to them persuasively (think of lawyers living in Boston) who nevertheless follow their consciences, seek God honestly, and obey the natural law (see chapter 1). Such people, who are ignorant of the truth of the Church through no fault of their own, may enjoy the grace of baptism and be Catholics without even knowing it. Though it would be really nice if they started sending checks to their local parishes anyway.

16. So that's the loophole you people use to avoid damning, for instance, every human being in Korea who lived before 1700?

Yes. Because without it, it would be impossible for any honest person to believe the central message of Christianity: that Christ loves every soul enough to die for that one person alone, to save him. To that we'd have to add the much more counterintuitive loophole "except for all the Indians, Asians, Africans, Eskimos, and Pacific Islanders who lived before the missionaries came. He sends them to hell by the boxcarload. His justice is not our justice. Shut up," we'd explain.

I once knew a devout Faminite who'd joined a religious order devoted to preaching the narrowest possible reading of the doctrine "There is no salvation outside the Church." I asked him, "Before Christ came, what happened to virtuous pagans when they died?"

"They went to limbo, and then when Jesus rose from the dead He took them to heaven."

"So what about a virtuous pagan who died the next day, Easter Monday?"

"He wasn't baptized. He went to hell."

"So on your view, the resurrection of Christ was not the Good News but the worst imaginable news for the vast majority of the human race for at least a thousand years. OK then, thanks for explaining things."

If that were what the Church taught, I would persecute it myself. Through sarcasm, though, not violence—I believe in religious liberty, thanks to Vatican II.

17. Wow. Did you just say something positive about the Second Vatican Council?

Treasure the moment, pal. It won't happen again.

18. So what's the deal with "limbo"? I thought Pope Benedict XVI closed it down.

The way you phrase that suggests a Mottramite understanding of papal authority. Limbo isn't the branch of the Catholic franchise located in North Dakota, which the pope can downsize because the herds of buffalo won't shop there. Limbo is a theory that theologians came up with to answer the question of what happened to miscarried fetuses and unbaptized babies.[13] They couldn't have had baptism of desire, since they never reached the age of reason, so it was hard to see any way for them to get into heaven. But any God who punished them for that would be a monster, unworthy of love or worship. How to square the circle? Imagine a third place, neither heaven nor hell, where souls forever enjoy perfect natural happiness, deprived only of the vision of God—which they don't know about anyway, so they don't mind.

19. So what happened to limbo?

Personally, I think too many Catholics asked, "Where do I sign up?" Perhaps I'm not the most otherworldly soul, but if you offered me perfect natural happiness forever,[14] with no risk of damnation, in return for surrendering what sometimes seems a slim hope of heaven, I would take it in a heartbeat. So would every person who can stand spending time with me. (The others have flounced off long ago, and thrown this book across the room, so I needn't fear offending them.) Now it doesn't seem very edifying for the Church to teach a theory that makes us baptized Christians envy the souls of stillborn babies, does it? In any case, Pope Benedict XVI approved a document by a theological commission that stated that limbo was not the most persuasive theory for what happened to souls like these, and instead expressed hope (not certainty) that they might go straight to heaven. Let's hope they do—that will leave more room in limbo.

---

[13] CCC, 1261

[14] Defined, in my case, as a comfy personal library stocked with Basil Hayden bourbon and several beagles, atop the Chrysler Building.

20. Moving right along to your next improbable sacrament, let's talk about Holy Communion. To quote one of the first Holy Communion hymns I've heard about, it seems to boil down to:

"Eat His Body, drink His Blood
And we'll sing a song of love."
How many second-graders have woken up with nightmares thanks to songs like that one?

Oh, don't shed too many tears for those little carnivores. If there's a group more ruthlessly devoted to creating social hierarchies, shaming outsiders, and crushing dissent than second-graders, I've yet to see it. By that age at least, you can see the proof of the Fall in 3-D high-def color. Besides, children that age gobble up fairy tales rife with witches baked in stewpots and evil stepmothers dancing to their deaths in hot iron shoes. Doesn't seem to do them any harm—anyway, not compared to creepy pieces of social engineering like *Heather Has Two Mommies* or sick, masochistic fables like *The Giving Tree*. I think it was a good and healthy development for St. Pius X to extend Holy Communion to children as

soon as they hit the age of reason. In the Christian East, infants are baptized, confirmed, and given Communion all at once. We in the West prefer to do things by stages; maybe it's our Roman sense of good order that prefers solid, discrete steps to tangled chutes and ladders. You have to get your card punched in a certain predetermined sequence. Even our deepest mysteries can be laid out on a flow chart.

You needn't be an eight-year-old to be scandalized by the Eucharist.[15] A good swathe of Jesus's followers greeted the announcement of this sacrament by turning tail and scurrying back to Zabar's, and who can blame them? At first blush, and second, it sounds like He's calling for human sacrifice and ritual cannibalism of the lowest, pagan order—a giving in to the dark, obscure human craving for that sort of thing the Jews had been heroically resisting for millennia. Apart from that close call with Abraham and Isaac, and the ugly incident of Jephtah, the Hebrews refused to purchase divine favor with human blood. But let's look a little more closely: In Genesis, Abraham is not rebuked by God for offering Isaac; he is rewarded. True,

---

[15] CCC, 1333–1340

the sacrifice is made needless when God provides a ram instead. But in showing his utter obedience to God—offering back to God a life He had created and still owned—Abraham passes the test. Likewise, every first-born son (like Jesus) had to be brought to the Temple and offered to God, then "ransomed" back with another, lesser sacrifice like a lamb or a turtle dove (Exodus 22:29–30). For Christians, this is a clear foreshadowing of the perfect sacrifice that founds the New Covenant, which completes and supersedes the one forged by Abraham on Mt. Moriah: God Himself providing the sacrificial victim, in this case His only Son. What's clear from all this—and from the extensive, expensive, sanguinary system of animal holocausts demanded by God at the Temple—is that God does not consider sacrifice for sin barbaric or immoral. In a fallen world with limited resources, we show how much we value something by what we are willing to pay for it. (Cain and Abel put different prices on pleasing God, with well-known results: The lower bidder killed the higher in a vain attempt at price-fixing.) But God in His kindness refused all real human sacrifice—aware at once that we are all too willing to make this kind of offering, and also that any death short of Christ's would have been insufficient anyway. Since all our attempts to repay the debts we run up by sinning are doomed to fall short, God allowed us to make symbolic gestures in the form of sheep and cows until the time came when His Son would offer Himself, the one sacrifice that rendered all others superfluous and silly. It seems to be no accident that He let the Romans tear down the Temple within the lifetime of the apostles—nor that Christians have always feared the reconstruction of the Temple as a sign of the End Times.[16]

21. So the Eucharist is just another instance of human sacrifice, like that practiced by the Carthaginians or the Aztecs?

There's no denying that it taps into the same human impulse. But it turns that dark compulsion on its head. Instead of gods who "need" human blood to stay alive and in a good mood, and so demand that their worshippers provide an endless stream of victims, the true God shows us that He needs absolutely nothing from us. He provides in the form of His Son the single victim, who willingly walks the way of the Cross, dying once for all of us. We don't feed or water God; He nourishes us. His

---

[16] Except, of course, for those Christians eager to bring the End Times on, since they're sure that Jesus will "rapture" them before the going gets tough. Their confidence is as enviable as their foreign policy is regrettable.

action, which reverberates in eternity, never needs to be repeated. The sacrifice of the Mass doesn't enact Calvary all over again; instead it opens a window in time to the moment when Jesus died, and places us all at the foot of the Cross, then seats us at the Last Supper to boot.[17]

22. And he feeds you his body and blood—just like he did the apostles, even though he was sitting with them apparently intact?

That very fact should make it clear that we're talking about Christ's body in a different sense than the bodies of war prisoners whom Montezuma savored in the form of "leg of man, with chipotle sauce." The mystery here eludes our best theologians, and even our mystics (who specialize in that sort of thing), so let me say up front that my attempts to shed light on it will fall far short and suggest outrageous falsehoods if you take my analogies too far. The impenetrability of the Eucharist is infamous for generating heresies. Fundamentalists who take literally every detail of the Bible, down to the number of nails used in building Noah's Ark, will, on this subject alone,[18] casually wave off the plain words of Jesus Christ. Luther rejected the "idolatry" practiced by St. Augustine and the bishops who codified the Bible and argued that, since Jesus is everywhere, He is in the Eucharist too. Calvin reduced the sacrament to a dramatized reenactment, along the lines of suburban gynecologists firing blanks at each other at Gettysburg. Baptists go even further: They're so sure that Jesus didn't mean "blood" that they conclude He didn't mean "wine," so they perform their infrequent "Lord's Suppers"with grape juice.

All these problems stem from the baffling mystery we're marking here, of course. But they're made far worse by a philosophical shift that happened (drumroll, please) . . . on the verge of the Reformation. You might remember I mentioned a movement called Nominalism, which said that there are no "essences" to things, just lumps of stuff to which we arbitrarily pin names, like "wine" or "blood" or "cups" or "plastic." There is no essential resemblance between one cup of wine and another, except some purely accidental connection between the chemicals. The Thomist philosophy that came before made a clear distinction between the physical attributes of a thing (its chemical composition) and its substance—what it was in the eyes of God. In the Mass, Thomas taught, the substance of the bread and wine disappeared and were replaced by the Body and Blood of

---

[17] CCC, 1366
[18] OK, on divorce, too. But I'm not here to take cheap shots at the competition.

Christ.[19] What was left behind were merely the "accidents," what we'd now call the molecules and atoms. So once people stopped believing that essences existed, it was impossible to explain what exactly happened when the priest consecrated the bread and wine—so as good early modern men, the Protestants concluded, "absolutely nothing."

23. Thereby showing that they weren't a bunch of primitive, magical thinkers better suited to voodoo ceremonies than universities. What are these so-called essences except empty abstractions that Aristotle borrowed from Plato, who made them up because he didn't own a microscope?

If you're saying that only chemicals exist, and all our thoughts and actions are merely the issue of electrical interactions, you're going to have a very hard time making sense of most of the rest of Christianity—which helps explain why in most Protestant churches (except among those who bravely refused to think things through), theologians, after rejecting the Eucharist, began a long, uneven retreat from every supernatural assertion, beginning with the miracles of the saints but quickly moving to those attested in the Bible, starting with sexual prohibitions in the Old

Testament, then moving to those in the New, and ending finally by questioning the Resurrection and then the divinity of Christ. The higher you go in the social feeding chain, from Baptist Bible camps to Presbyterian colleges to Episcopal divinity schools, the less real faith remains—and the wine in Jesus's cup is mysteriously transformed into a Skinnygirl margarita made up of one part Che Guevara and two parts Margaret Sanger, neither shaken nor stirred.

Let me point to this spiritual truth through an utterly carnal analogy: Imagine a corpse, just freshly dead. Let's raise the stakes and make it Jesus's. How much has chemically changed about this object in the first five seconds since it went from "human being" to "human remains"? A few electrical impulses have ceased to course through its cranial tissue. The blood no longer moves from place to place. That's it. Otherwise it's exactly the same, at least until the microorganisms and creepy-crawlies get to work. But I think that most of us would say that this transition (from living to

---

[19] CCC, 1413

dead) is quite a bit more *substantial* than these accidental changes would suggest. What was it that existed here, that is no more? A whole human being. It had an essence, composed of body and soul, which now is broken. The body no longer contains that essence, but only reminds us of it, and makes us sad. In a similar way (*note to the Holy Office:* I know this is just an analogy), the bread and the wine are bereft of their essences and replaced with the "substance" of Christ. Which makes us happy.

One helpful way to think about the Eucharist is this: It was a way for Jesus to render His divine invasion of day-to-day life and human history permanent and irreversible. Instead of living in a body for a while, then dying and leaving us just with a memory and a book with gold-edged pages in every backwater church across the earth, He planted seeds that when we water them will grow afresh the Tree of Life.

Image courtesy of Wikipedia Commons.

24. Like a Chia Pet.

Yes, in every way exactly like a Chia Pet.

25. What effects are this noncannibalistic, mystical meal of nonbread and nonwine substances supposed to have on people? Does it slake your spiritual hunger for a while so you aren't tempted to "snack" on sugary prayers or fattening fasts, or is it more like a bowl of pasta that gives you a carbohydrate "high," then when it wears off makes you "crash" so you need an ontological nap?

You've just run through a list of emotional epiphenomena, of the sort we'd expect to have after watching a well-made TV show or listening to an opera. Now there's nothing wrong with emotions or the art that evokes them, and they have their role in religion: They are the icing. People who focus on them to the exclusion of what they represent are binging on bowls of artificially colored sugar, forgetting sometimes that it was meant for a wedding cake. The Eucharist joins the soul to Christ in a way that's closely analogous to what the marital act accomplishes for spouses; regardless of the subjective highs and lows that accompany it, the act objectively forges a bond between them—sometimes in the baldly tangible form of their blended DNA, crawling across the carpet, with his little mouth tacky from candy and his hair full of the Nicorette he dug out of your ashtray. He doesn't care what's in "your heart" at moments like that. Whatever you might be feeling, he will get his sticky fingers all over your cashmere sweater. Make that the baby Jesus and the simile is complete.[20]

The Eucharist offers everyone who receives it worthily—in other words, when they're not pretty sure they've committed a mortal sin they haven't yet confessed (see below)—an opportunity to grow in real, objective intimacy with Christ. As with every such human relationship, it goes much deeper than how we feel, and changes what we *are*.

I really can't speak with requisite eloquence on this subject, so I'll cite the man whose writings I've always considered the "Fifth Gospel." Indeed, in my early teen years, it was his works, along with the 1907 *Catholic Encyclopedia* and the oeuvre of Monty Python, that formed my mind for life. I speak of J. R. R. Tolkien, of course—whose *Silmarillion* I assimilated as dutifully as a catechism, such that I can still rattle off the details by rote:

Q: Who made Middle Earth?

A: Eru Ilúvatar made Middle Earth.

Q: Why did he make Middle Earth?

A: To bring to concrete realization the Music of the Ainur.

And so on.

Anyway, as Tolkien wrote his son on the subject of Holy Communion:

> Out of the darkness of my life, so much frustrated, I put before you the one great thing to love on earth: the Blessed Sacrament. . . . There you will find romance, glory, honour, fidelity, and the true way of all your loves on earth, and more than that: Death. By the divine paradox, that which ends life, and demands the surrender of all, and yet by the taste—or foretaste—of which alone can what you seek in your earthly relationships (love, faithfulness, joy) be maintained, or take on that complexion of reality, of eternal endurance, which every man's heart desires.
>
> The only cure for sagging or fainting faith is Communion. Though always Itself, perfect and complete and inviolate, the Blessed Sacrament does not operate completely and once for all in any of us. Like the act of Faith it must be continuous and grow by exercise. Frequency is of the highest effect. Seven times a week is more nourishing than seven times at intervals.

---

[20] CCC, 2837

Also I can recommend this as an exercise (alas! only too easy to find opportunity for): make your communion in circumstances that affront your taste. Choose a snuffling or gabbling priest or a proud and vulgar friar; and a church full of the usual bourgeois crowd, ill-behaved children—from those who yell to those products of Catholic schools who the moment the tabernacle is opened sit back and yawn—open necked and dirty youths, women in trousers and often with hair both unkempt and uncovered. Go to communion with them (and pray for them). It will be just the same (or better than that) as a mass said beautifully by a visibly holy man, and shared by a few devout and decorous people. It could not be worse than the mess of the feeding of the Five Thousand—after which our Lord propounded the feeding that was to come.

Thanks to the liturgical renewal that followed (and flouted) Vatican II, following Tolkien's advice is easier than ever.

26. Now that you mention it, some of the Catholic liturgies that I've seen—on TV, in weddings I've attended, a couple I've dropped in on out of curiosity—have been completely unlike each other. I remember one had a full-on rock band up there with the priest, who'd bob his head to the music like Stevie Wonder. Except he wasn't blind.

In the real sense he was, but never mind . . .

And the altar girl kept knocking into the snare drum. The crowd were all wearing shorts and faded Pink Floyd T-shirts or sweatpants. Another one I got dragged to by a friend was really elaborate and formal, with the priest facing the wall with his back to the audience, and all the prayers chanted in Foreign.

The music was soothing, I guess, but none of the people said the prayers. All these guys in *Mad Men* suits and women in jumpers and veils just fingered rosary beads or concentrated on smacking their kids. And boy did they have a lot of those, filling up entire pews, spaced about . . . nine months and five minutes apart. They looked almost Amish. Except they were all really pale, kind of veal-colored.

Ah, Trads. I know them well.

So what's going on with your official rituals, then? You're supposed to be this really centralized religion with a top-down authority structure, but your services remind me of a dog run—filled with dachshunds, beagles, and Irish wolfhounds; you find it hard to believe they're all the same species, and you wonder what would happen if they tried to mate.

I'd love to say "our diversity is our strength," but it isn't. Sure, there are twenty-three different rites of the Catholic Church, hailing from places like Syria, Ethiopia, and Ukraine.[21] Each of those liturgies is exquisite in its own way—though you'd surely find them overly formal and, frankly, boring. Like the traditional form of the most common, Latin, rite of the Church, they focus on God and leave the worshiper alone to follow along or not. They're hi-

---

[21] CCC, 1203

eratic, elaborate, and properly sung instead of recited. But none of those partake in the kind of "diversity" you're talking about, which has less in common with a dog run than it does with the Table of Contents of the DSM-IV of psychiatric disorders. Each of those Masses you attended was one form or another of a single, "common" liturgy used in the West—which was stuffed with plastic dynamite in the '60s and detonated just to see what would happen.

27. And that was what Vatican II was all about?

Oddly, no. Among many other things, Vatican II called for a cautious revision of the liturgy that would introduce the local languages here and there—in the Bible readings, for instance—while keeping Latin for the critical parts of the Mass and expanding the use of Gregorian chant. It said absolutely nothing about tearing out marble altars and replacing them with butcher blocks, turning the priest around to face the "audience," or eliminating polyphony in favor of tunes from a lame-ass summer camp sing-along. All that was accomplished in plain defiance of the dictates of Vatican II, by a secret, conspiratorial group that had infiltrated Church circles at very high levels by 1970. Canon law enforcement professionals call them "liturgists." They're a lot like terrorists, with one key difference: You can negotiate with terrorists.

28. It sounds to me like you're one of those people who obsesses over inessentials and misses the meaning of your religion. There's a word for that in the Bible, isn't there? I think it's "Pharisee."

If those of us who care about reverent liturgy are Pharisees, then I guess those who don't care about it would have to be Sadducees—those Jews who sold out completely to the secularism around them. But I digress.

To us fallen folks who schlep through the realm of the senses, inessentials *are* essential. We wouldn't have needed sacraments in Eden, and they won't keep happening in heaven. But here, in a drafty world full of loud noises and shiny objects, where the hope of brunch can crowd the Canon from our minds ("Behold the eggs of Benedict . . ."), we need all the help we can get. The forms that our rituals take should signify their content. We understand this intuitively, and hence men send their girlfriends live flowers in colorful vases, not mackerels wrapped in newspaper.

The *central inessential* for liturgical Christians is the form of our public worship. If we really believe that what we're doing is participating in a sacrament that centers on a miracle ("If it's a symbol, then to Hell with it," said Flannery O'Connor), our ritual actions ought to reflect that. This will help us to go on believing the words we repeat in the Creed and will shape the psyches of the young and the untaught so they conform to the mind of the Church. Rightly reverent ceremonies help us develop the natural virtue of religion, teaching us awe instead of aw-shucks.

The historic liturgies of the Church have proved themselves over centuries very effective at conveying the shocking truth about the Eucharist. Recent makeshifts haven't done as good a job—which is why Pope Benedict XVI reversed the tremendous prudential screw-up of Pope Paul VI and lifted the ban on the old Latin Mass. The reason the new form of the liturgy hasn't served as well as the older form can be pinned down quite specifically: a confusion of symbols. Instead of ordering flowers for Valentine's Day, we have been sending sushi.

The basic ritual action of the liturgy can be described at once as a *sacrifice* and a *wedding*. The priest climbs the altar like the hill of Calvary and acts in the person of Christ, offering Himself to the Father on our behalf—while we chime in with prayers of gratitude, praise, and petition. On another level, the priest acts in Christ's capacity as the Bridegroom, descending from heaven to wed Himself bodily to the Church (the congregation) through the Eucharist. The priest represents the masculine principle, Christ. The people are the feminine principle, the Church. Blurring their roles is like dressing a bride and groom in drag: It doesn't guarantee an annulment, but it confuses people.

Protestant understandings of the liturgy are radically different. Luther and Calvin and Cranmer would each willingly have died (Cranmer did) rather than affirm the Real Presence as Catholics understand it. In "pure" Protestantism, the Eucharist is a group celebration of Christian love and unity, symbolized by a common meal of bread and wine. Christ is "spiritually present" in the hearts of believers, but there's no man standing there filling His sandals. Such rites are all bride, and no Groom.

The Mass that was published after Vatican II—in plain defiance of its documents—was crafted by an ecumenical committee (including Protestants) that aimed at Christian unity. In a creative compromise, the committee cut large sections from the Mass—those that made it screamingly obvious that the Mass was a sacrifice and a wedding. The committee also trimmed away many rituals designed to underscore those doctrines, adding other practices to boost the role of the laity and undercut the role of the priest.

These changes didn't vitiate the sacrament, but they did cloud its clarity. They also reduced its dignity, gravity, and beauty. The *Dies Irae* gave way to "Gather Us In."[22] Or as Joseph Cardinal Ratzinger wrote at the time: "In the place of the liturgy as the fruit of development came fabricated liturgy. We abandoned the organic, living, process of growth and development over centuries, and replaced it—as in a manufacturing process—with a fabrication, a banal on-the-spot product."

The most important elements that distinguish the priest's role from the people's, and hence Catholic sacraments from Protestant prayer services, are the following:

- the priest facing the altar;
- the prayers of the old Offertory (which survive in the First Eucharistic Prayer);
- the exclusive claim of the clergy (priests and deacons) to handle the Sacrament;
- the all-male priesthood; and
- kneeling for Communion on the tongue.

Each practice we add to the liturgy that blurs the difference between the people and the priest adds to confusion about what the heck is going on up on the altar. It's no surprise that after forty years of liturgical "renewal," only 30 percent of American Catholics still believe in transubstantiation. More troublingly, those who are receiving Communion rarely bother with the sacrament of penance. The old terror of blasphemy that was underlined by gold patens tucked like blades against our throats gave way to a shrug and a smile as we take in our hands a wafer from a neighbor.

---

[22] This treacly, insidiously catchy hymn has been rightly called "The Battle Hymn of the Slave Morality," since its sentiments reek not of Jesus but Nietzsche.

Dissenters from key Catholic doctrines of faith and morals took ruthless advantage of the hype surrounding the Second Vatican Council and the symbolic confusion sowed by radical liturgical changes—which seemed to signal, like a new flag flying over a country, a new regime in the Church. Maybe a new Church altogether. Imagine that a newly elected president replaced the Stars and Stripes with the Confederate battle flag. Or that he replaced our fifty stars with the flag of Mexico. Let's say he got away with doing this and wasn't carried off by the Secret Service to an "undisclosed location." What would that signify for his administration? If people accepted the change, what else would they be likely to accept?

That liturgy kept on metastasizing, "renewing" itself seemingly every year. It's no accident that the incessant tinkerings with the liturgy came at the same time as the chaos surrounding the Church's teaching on birth control. As Anne Roche Muggeridge pointed out in her indispensable history, *The Desolate City*, the Church's position on contraception was "under consideration" for almost a decade—which led pastors to tell troubled couples that they could follow their consciences. If the Church could change the Mass, ordinary Catholics concluded, the nuances of marital theology were surely up for grabs. No wonder that when Paul VI reluctantly issued *Humanae Vitae*, people felt betrayed. It didn't help when the Vatican refused to back a cardinal who tried to enforce the document, which made it seem like the pope was winking.

The perception that the Church was in a constant state of doctrinal flux was confirmed by the reality that her most central, sacred mystery was being monkeyed with—almost every year. I remember being in grammar school when they told us, "The pope wants us to receive Communion in the hand now." (He didn't; it was an abuse that was forced on the Vatican through relentless disobedience until it became a local norm, but never mind.) Then, a few years later, they lied again: "The pope wants us to stand for Communion." And so on. The Mass, which had stood for centuries as a solid bulwark of formality and seriousness, was suddenly shifting with every year's hemlines—which is precisely what the heretics conspiring to change the Church's teaching had in mind. That is why they pushed for these futile, pastorally destructive changes of "inessentials"—as a way of beating down resistance to changing essentials. And, in a worldly sense, they almost succeeded.

The same bishops who pushed relentlessly for Communion in the hand, extraordinary ministers of Communion, altar girls, and standing for Communion were the men who appointed feminists and pro-gay, pro-contraception, and even "pro-choice" delegates to dissident conferences such as the Call to Action (1976). Such bishops also persecuted adherents of the old liturgy and clergy who preached against contraception. The same men repeatedly defied Pope John Paul II, even threatening a schism when he tried to discipline the craziest bishops. Instead of risking an ugly repetition of what happened with the Eastern Orthodox, the pope decided to wait them out and replace them one by one with better men as they retired or died. Meanwhile, those of us in the pews learned essentially to ignore what our bishops said and take our instructions straight from Rome. That meant that hostile articles in papers like the *New York Times* were often the best way for average Catholics to find out what the Church really taught: Just learn what the *Times* approves of and oppose it.

29. Well, being a Catholic has gotten pretty complicated. You can't just show up and follow instructions anymore, since they'll be different from parish to parish.

You're absolutely right. Over twenty years, I've had to read maybe two dozen books to get my head straight about all these confusions and abuses of the liturgy. All of that, in saner times, would have been *none of a layman's business.* We have enough on our plates pursuing our own vocations and staying in a state of grace, and we really shouldn't have to shop around for the least sacrilegious parish or fight with our bishop's religious-education office against pastors who edit the Creed. But here we are, still gasping for breath as the smoke of Satan slowly lifts, and there's no excuse for pretending the air has been clear all along. The Bride of Christ has been battered, hounded, and hunted by the Enemy—but she's still standing, as we were promised. Now it's our task to bind her wounds, repair the rents in her gown, and lovingly comb her hair.

To do this, we should view every celebration of the Mass *in whatever form* first and foremost as a *miracle*. In my own snarky experience as an amateur liturgy critic, there's no sense—and probably some sin—in distracting ourselves from the holy sacrifice the priest really is performing by focusing on the flaws in the form. If you're like me, it's all too tempting to sit at a lackadaisical modern Mass (often all that's available) and check off every abuse. Does this advance you in holiness? If so, you're a better man than I. (And, as we've seen from our discussion so far, you aren't.)

Instead, I think of the Church's liturgy as a great Gothic cathedral that was bombed during World War II. Some sections are still intact, while others lie mostly ruined. Some of the people praying are shell-shocked, while others have no memory of what the place looked like in 1939. Large numbers have grown accustomed to makeshift services on broken altars and even actively prefer them to the grand ceremonies we had before the war. It doesn't make sense to shout at them. It's tempting to grab such people by the ear and drag them to a side chapel the bombers missed. But not everyone's ready to make the move. A casual joie de vivre has developed among the rubble. People pray quite contentedly on broken bits of stone, looking up at shattered windows—and who am I to condemn them? I can curse the bombers, of course, but these people here are my fellow victims, so there's no excuse for smugness. When I recite the unhappy facts about the Mass, I try to do it gently—in the spirit of someone who loved the old cathedral, not someone who hates its ruins.

And that is what I tell my friends who are Trads: If we can't make our way across the rubble to one of the intact side chapels, we should pray as best we can where we stand. We should do our best to remember what this place of glory looked like once, and how it can look again. While we do our work of piling stones and piecing the windows back together, we'll be tempted to bitter thoughts of vengeance. But the bombers have already winged away, to face a Judgment more exacting than ours, or a Mercy more magnanimous. It's not our job to throw pieces of rubble at our fellow refugees—but instead, with solemn joy, to practice love among the ruins.

30. So you're saying that I should only go to the old, Latin Mass?

No. First of all, there are all those other, equally rich and reverent ancient liturgies of the Church, many of which are local versions of the rites from Constantinople. I'd never pretend that the Western rite is better than any of those—though the prospect of a forty-minute sermon (complete with parish announcements) in Ukrainian is enough to put most monoglots off. Look for Eastern rite liturgies that are partly or wholly done in English, assuming that you understand it—which I'm guessing, since you've read this far. What is more, an increasing number of parishes are offering the modern Roman liturgy in an ever more reverent, serious form. If you see the priest facing the altar instead of the people, it means you're in excellent hands, whatever tongue is being spoken.

Here's another problem (the human condition is crawling with 'em, like fleas on a rescue dog): Too many parishes that have revived the Old Mass have also dug up and reanimated old abuses—like the priest at a Sunday Mass muttering incomprehensibly into the altar, with the people saying the rosary or reading the parish bulletin. Such "low Masses" were only ever meant for sparsely attended weekday rites and were actually forbidden on Sundays by the rubrics—which priests for centuries duly ignored. (Are you seeing a pattern here?) This movement "back to the worst of the past" goes against not just what Vatican II but even what Pope St. Pius X had in mind.[23] The goal of real liturgical restoration is to keep all the beauty and dignity found in healthy monasteries (chanted prayer, reverence, and awe) and to get the laity active in doing our part. Not the priest's part (handing out Communion), but ours: actively praying and singing the Mass. As the manifestation of the Church in her liturgical wedding with Christ, we must "play" her not as a zombie but a Bride.

31. Wait, I thought you were against liturgies that ordinary people could understand?

Where did I say that? Latin was once the vernacular in Rome, and the increased use of English (or French, or Pidgin—whatever) really was encouraged at Vatican II. Nor is there anything wrong with an increase in "active participation" by the laity. That was another good goal laid out at the council. By all means, let's have people responding to prayers and learning chant and delving into the rich, exotic weirdness that's rife in our ancient liturgies. ("Dewfall?" What's a "dewfall?" Is that the opposite of a "RuPaul"?) In fact, they could translate the whole old Mass into English and I'd be delighted—so long as the translation was done by poets and theologians, instead of (as in the 1970 *Novus Ordo Missae*) by Babel Fish. Moreover, there is a proliferation of "extraordinary form" Masses around the

---

[23] CCC, 1141

world that is inspiring (or pressuring) pastors to make their "ordinary" Masses more solemn and . . . sacramental. Consequently, few kids today are likely to undergo what I did: hearing Bob Dylan for the first time in the Communion Hymn and thinking that "B. Dylan" must be some really talented nun in Milwaukee.

If you do decide to check out a traditional Latin liturgy, make sure it's a "sung" or "high" Mass attended by all the beauty proper to the mystery. It's your first "date"; you should both wear your best. Ignore the Latin and follow along in English, but make sure to keep your eyes up front most of the time and watch the priest. You will probably find the language barrier humbling—likewise the fact that the priest is facing the tabernacle, behind an altar rail that clearly marks his province (the sacred) off from ours (the profane). The rituals may seem strange to you, even over the top. But its message will run crystal clear: a *sacrifice* and a *wedding*.

32. Do you think I'll like it?

No. I hated it, not just the first but the sixth through the sixteenth time. But something might keep you coming back, some sense that you're peering through a window out of time, seeing through a glass not quite so darkly into another world far realer than our own. You'll feel a little alienated, maybe even offended. Who is this guy in the shiny robe to turn his back on me and talk to the crucifix instead? You'll resent the calisthenics, the hopping up and down then falling back on your knees, and you'll likely find the prayers archaic and strange, like a quote from the Magna Carta:

> P: If anyone holds of us by fee-farm, either by socage or by burage, or of any other land by knight's service, we will not (by reason of that fee-farm, socage, or burgage), have the wardship of the heir, or of such land of his as if of the fief of that other; nor shall we have wardship of that fee-farm, socage, or burgage, unless such fee-farm owes knight's service. We will not by reason of any small serjeancy which anyone may hold of us by the service of rendering to us knives, arrows, or the like, have wardship of his heir or of the land which he holds of another lord by knight's service.

> S: And with your spirit.

Any traditional rite will be thoroughly off-putting, just like cardio, mathematics, or parenthood. But if you stick with it, you'll learn to "see" something profound and true: a sacrificial ritual enacting a solemn marriage between the fallen muck of earth and fire falling from heaven. The consolations come later.

33. Well, thanks for the tour through the past forty years of bitter intra-Catholic factional warfare. I thought your Church was supposed to be some sort of bulwark against the fissiparous chaos of modern life.

It is. (Among other things.) But the point of a bulwark is to defend something worth attacking and block off all angles of assault. The Maginot Line protected the wretched Third Republic, so when the Nazi invaders' GPS sent them on a sharp right turn, avoiding the detour, the French threw down their guns, gave a collaborative shrug, and lit their Gitanes. The Church has its share of battle scars, but it's still standing—as you can tell by the regular efforts made every day to bulldoze it. Some confrontation between the Church and late Western modernity was inevitable, and if it hadn't happened at Vatican II, it would have occurred some other way. The Eastern churches didn't vandalize their liturgy; have they been spared the ravages of secularization? Not according to my Greek Orthodox friends, who show up for the last ten minutes of liturgy each week to pick up blessed bread and join their friends for baklava and gossip. The liturgy is miraculous, but it doesn't work like magic: Teilhard de Chardin said the traditional Mass for decades even as he cooked up Catholic Scientology; at the same time, his housemate at New York's St. Ignatius Loyola, the holy Rev. John Hardon, obediently switched missals with every tinkering that came to him from the bishops.

Of course, there's something to be said for a liturgy whose very nature resists and defeats abuses. The new Mass evokes the same old fearful reverence when it's said by a holy priest. But with all its Build-a-Bear options, the 1970 liturgy virtually begs to be abused. The Tridentine Mass was like the Navy: A machine built by geniuses so it can be operated by idiots. The old liturgy was crafted by saints, and can be said by drunks and schlubs without much risk of sacrilege. The new rite was patched together by bureaucrats and can be safely celebrated only by saints. And in case you don't read the papers, we seem to be running kind of short.

34. From the size of the lines at Confession, you'd never know that the Church was not a regular termite colony of mystics dancing on the edge of perfect union with God.

Which brings us to the third sacrament, and the one that's currently the least popular—probably because it's the only one that never involves throwing parties or getting gifts. If sinners could register at Tiffany's and get some kind of swag every time they were shriven (a silver-handled whip for doing penance?), I bet more folks would take the trouble to get their sins forgiven. Maybe we ought to disguise penance as therapy, keep each person in there for fifty minutes, deny him absolution, and charge him $150. That would fill the churches up every Saturday afternoon.

People are nowadays much more willing to think of themselves as sick than sinful, and there's certainly some truth underlying this trend. Many cases of what our ancestors might have seen as possession are really schizophrenia, and most suicides are caused by what medievals might have damned as despair but in fact is the tragic outcome of clinical depression. Much addictive behavior that is objectively gravely sinful is so compulsive, it's barely culpable. Thank God (and the rational mind he gave us, which gave birth to science) for our *genuine* advances in self-understanding. But most of the people popping Prozac nowadays don't have inborn imbalances in their brain chemistries; they're just kind of sad. Likewise, the folks who cheat on their wives or steal from the boss then march off into therapy or rehab are missing the whole point of being human: that some of our actions really do have consequences, for which we are held responsible.

Here's a fun modern paradox: The most popular way to try and weasel out of being blamed for your mistakes is nowadays to step up, once you've been caught, and announce: "I take full responsibility for . . ."

(a) driving that school bus while high on meth;

(b) spiking the punch at the prom with all those roofies, and for each of the consequent pregnancies;

(c) sneaking into the U.S. and committing identity theft, thus screwing up some veteran's Social Security benefits;

(d) downloading thirty thousand pictures of "Trampy Cougars" on the diocese's computer;

(e) blowing $3 billion of our stockholders' money on South Indian elephant futures,

which you taxpayers will now have to refund in the form of a bailout, or else we will crash the economy and each of you will lose his job.

You say this in the hope that manning up and taking the blame will get you absolved of the punishment—as if all adult life were modeled on the charming old fib about young George Washington. ("I cannot tell a lie. I did order the ethnic cleansing of Bosnia.") On some level, you're hoping to get a slap on the wrist and a pat on the head. You don't want forgiveness but amnesty. In fact, you feel entitled to it.

35. Come to think of it, that does sound a lot like confession. All you have to do to get out of your sins is to kneel before some priest, admit what you did, say you're sorry, and promise not to do it again. Ten Hail Marys later, you're good as gold.

It's a lot more demanding than that, you know—but I'll grant you that most modern Catholics think otherwise. And yet they still can't bring themselves to do it.

So what is that about?

We are each individual, unique and perfect snowflakes, absolutely special in exactly the same way. We don't commit sins. Or if we do, they're little, teensy-weensy ones that we were forced into by sinful social structures, habituated to by our dysfunctional parents, or driven to by wholesome instinctual urges that the Church has no business repressing. So why should we get on our knees to scrape and crawl and apologize for expressing what is inside us, for insisting on our inborn right to fun and food and fooling around? You might as well blame a dog for pulling a lamb chop off your counter; if you didn't want him to eat it, you shouldn't have left it there. If God didn't want us to sin, He should have made us differently. A tempting theory, especially if (like me) you like dogs better than people.

But there's the rub: We don't blame dogs for licking each other's privates or turning a dog run into a prison yard with their cringeworthy dominance humping, because we know they aren't human. They don't have consciences and hence can't sin—in fact, like other animals (even, some speculate, *cats*) they are free from Original Sin and their every action is perfectly pleasing to God. Nice work if you can get it. Their moral status is higher than ours (absent grace), but their link on the Chain of Being is lower. That's why it's OK to neuter them, clone them, and put their "quality of life" first when they're sick. Having seen each of my parents die slowly and painfully of cancer, I've wondered if they ever envied pets who can be morally "put out of their misery." Suffering isn't redemptive for animals. They don't have a purgatory to burn off the lingering effects of sin along the way. Lucky dogs.

So we embrace both sides of the post-Christian paradox: We are infinitely pre-cious, absolutely autonomous, and dripping with rights and dignities—little gods— and at the same time we're hapless, innocent, furry pets whose misadventures are cute enough for YouTube. I'd take that deal in a heartbeat.

36. So which is it, then?

Both and neither, because each horn of that dilemma is papier-mâché. They're part of a costume we Westerners crafted once we couldn't standing thinking of sin. And each is a subtle perversion of something importantly true. We are indeed a little lower than the angels, made in the image of God and then raised to a still higher state when God became man—in order to help us graft our natures onto God's. For this very reason, our deeds take on a significance one cannot grant (for instance) to the shift of tectonic plates or a baboon's self-abuse. Our actions, tragically, matter. That means that sometimes we sin. Because sin got "into our blood" with the first generation, we find it all too easy. Since sin degrades and debilitates us, we need external help to rebuild us.[24] We aren't just hurting ourselves but often each other, and in both ways offending a Person (God). We're tearing down or even destroying our only really critical relationship in the End. We have no more power to fix that on our own than we do to write the IRS and inform them that the income tax is unconstitutional. (Try it sometime. See what happens.)

37. If God finds our behavior so disappointing, why doesn't he lower his expectations to something more realistic?

It might be nice, mightn't it, if God agreed to define our deviancy down? But that would mean surrendering any hope of better human behavior, admitting that heroes and martyrs were basically wasting their time, and accepting as equally worthy the lives of Hermann Goering and Dietrich Bonhoeffer. What sounds at first like a glorious liberation from guilt would in fact render human life a meaningless drear—a sport where no one kept score and everyone got the same tinfoil trophy for showing up. (Think "Olympic T-ball.") That's the logic that leads to grade inflation, fast

---

[24] CCC, 1422–1433

food, "starter marriages," and obesity on nude beaches. We would pretend to try, and God would pretend to believe us.

Unless we want to sink our standards so low that we can enjoy the Brave New World, we must spurn soma and admit to sin. We can either embrace and internalize the fact that we are always falling short of "the glory of God" (Romans 3:23), or else there's no glory at all. Christ knew this, of course, which is why He set up the sacrament of confession: "Receive ye the Holy Ghost. Whose sins you shall forgive, they are forgiven them; and whose sins you shall retain, they are retained" (John 20:22–23). It was the only real alternative to taking the human race to the vet's office and putting us all to sleep.

38. Why do we need to tell our sins, if that's what they are, to a priest in a wooden box through a screen?

First, let me explain the wooden box—the confessionals which so many parishes in the '70s gaily ripped out and replaced with cozy little chat rooms with folding chairs. They were created as part of the reforms of the Council of Trent, both to give penitents privacy and to put a prudent barrier between them and the priest. Apparently, one of the pastoral problems that arose during the Renaissance popped up when priests heard women's con-  fessions and offered them *reassurance*. The poor dear—she's just told you all about her adultery problem, and now she's crying. She needs a little hug. A pat on the back. Another pat, traveling southward . . . and pretty soon you've got a whole new set of sins, and among them the blaspheming of a sacrament. The Church, ever realistic about human nature and its weakness, decided to put up the screens to protect the laity from the priests. Of course, in the wake of Vatican II, pastors came to realize that no such protection was necessary.

39. Ouch. You've been living close to Boston, haven't you?

Too close. Now, as to why we can't confess our sins straight to God, in the privacy of our consciences: It's just too easy, and hence it is almost impossible. In a real emergency, of course, one can make private repentance for sins, which will serve till you get to confession. But here's the hard part: without the sacrament, you're only forgiven if you can muster what theologians call "perfect contrition." That means you're sorry for your sins not out of fear of hell, or of shame at how squalid they were, or of worry that photographs of you with *all those Ukrainian "au pairs"* will ruin your run for the local school board. No, you must hate the sin solely because it's a sin, and therefore damaged your relationship with God. That's a lofty goal, and one that's rather hard to manage on a plane that is going down, a car that is being jacked, or a rowboat full of rednecks who have just started whistling the banjo tune from *Deliverance*. However, when you make use of the sacrament, the ordinary means the Church set up for regular schmucks like us, it's good enough that you have "imperfect contrition."[25] That's the best that most of us can do most of the time: whip up a mediocrity smoothie of liquefied emotions, powdered good intentions, a vague (but real) hope of doing better, with a strong dash of the humility required to kneel down and fess up to a perfect stranger.

You needn't be religious to see the needfulness of telling one's sins to another: It's essential to keep us honest. The world at large understands the need for what evangelicals call "accountability partners." Writers have their editors, alcoholics have their sponsors, cops have the narcs in "internal affairs," newspaper owners have ombudsmen, and dictators have assassins. It's all too easy, when you're staying inside your head and addressing what you think is God through what you hope is your stern, demanding conscience, to shade the truth, sugarcoat, bloviate, make excuses, and at length decide that your ex-landlord's rose garden *deserved* to be sprayed with Roundup™. Those plants were practically asking for it.

Perhaps the most vivid case in which a priest was needed to call a sinner to account came early in the history of the Church—when a bishop had to denounce and humble an emperor. You'll recall that after centuries of intermittently savage persecution by the Roman Empire, Christians received the divine surprise of Constantine's conversion; suddenly, instead of being snitched on by pagan neighbors for refusing to worship the emperor, then ending up as food for the bears in the third century's version of "ultimate fighting," Christians now could worship in peace. In fact, the Roman government began to favor the Church and subsidize the building of new churches. So far, so good. The pagans still had their temples, the Jews their synagogues, the members of "mystery" sects their kinky little coves where they could play cosmological "truth or dare." But one of Constantine's successors, Theodosius I, could not leave a good thing alone. Upon becoming emperor, he decided that all this religious diversity offended his sense of tidiness

---

[25] CCC, 1451–1454

and good government. He enacted increasingly savage laws against the ancestral pagan religion of the Romans, as well as against Christians who'd blundered (understandably, see chapter 3) into heresy. Starting in 389, Theodosius began pulling down ancient temples, persecuting pagan priests, and even arresting people who held pagan rituals in their homes.

This is the point where the Church's relationship with the state began to get ugly, quick. Instead of rejecting this primitive (but effective) form of totalitarianism, many Church leaders endorsed the forcible suppression of their competitors, acting like Big Three automakers trying to keep Toyotas off U.S. highways. The position of the early Augustine—that all the Church asked of the state was the freedom to preach and live Christian lives in peace—gave way to the stance the saint took in later life, when he asked the state to help repress heretics such as the Donatists.[26] This fourth-century precedent was followed with grim consistency by Catholics, then by Protestants, and then by anti-Christian revolutionaries, for more than a thousand years. It took until 1965, and Vatican II's Declaration on Religious Liberty, for the Church to admit that while "error" might "have no rights," erring people did.[27] Created with an inviolable dignity in the image of God, the person and his conscience are not the playthings of the state—not even of one that wraps itself in the papal flag. True to form, this single, fruitful development of doctrine at Vatican II is the one teaching that some irate traditionalists still reject, effectively drowning the council's baby in its bathwater.[28]

As you might have guessed, Theodosius was not a man of a delicate conscience. This came out even more clearly in his handling of an uprising in Thessalonica, one of many Roman-ruled cities where chariot races were considered essential to daily life. In fact, these races amounted to fourth-century Facebook: the races were how you had fun, met people, learned civics, formed your political opinions, and ran into

---

[26] Surely Augustine did not foresee the prisons and pyres that churchmen would later endorse for use against heretical believers, but it is a grave and sickening scandal that Christians went so quickly from complaining of religious persecution to indulging in it themselves. Many of the cruelest assaults against innocent Catholics in subsequent centuries—for instance, the massacre of hundreds of priests and nuns and hundreds of thousands of Catholic peasants in the Vendée—were excused in the name of avenging the Inquisition or keeping the Church too weak to revive it again. Of course, the atrocities committed with approval of Church authorities never approached those launched by antireligious rulers in Mexico, China, or Russia; based on the scrupulous records its friars kept, it seems that the most infamous Inquisition, the one in Spain, killed at most five thousand people over the course of 350 years. The Bolsheviks were famous for joking that they killed that many each day. But shouldn't the followers of Jesus be held to a higher standard than Lenin's thugs?

[27] CCC, 2108

[28] Traditionalists who accuse Vatican II of heresy or apostasy like to point to medieval and nineteenth-century papal statements endorsing the use of force against heretics; what they seem to forget is that papal infallibility only covers the body of the original, public Revelation, which consists of the scriptures and the oral traditions passed on by the apostles (such as the Assumption of Our Lady). There is absolutely no evidence, in the first three centuries of the Church, that the popes or bishops were secretly passing on the idea that the Church ought to gain control of the Roman Empire and use its soldiers and torturers to punish erring Christians or unbelievers. This means that papal statements endorsing such activities were fallible and subject to later correction by a council of the Universal Church.

old girlfriends for whom you could leave your wife. Well, in 390 the most popular charioteer in Thessalonica was arrested for rape and sodomy. When his thousands of fans and "friends" found out from his Twitter feed, they were outraged, insisting that an athlete's private life was none of the government's business. (They may even have anticipated the ruling in *Roe v. Wade* and argued that what the charioteer did with his body was covered by a constitutional right to privacy; legal historians differ on this point and the exchanges were never recorded in Westlaw.) So the charioteer's supporters erupted in public protest, and the most radical members of Occupy Thessalonica killed both the magistrate and several members of his staff. Enraged that a flash mob could challenge his authority, Theodosius invoked the *Patriota* Act and sent in a Roman legion to impose shock and awe—to the tune of some seven thousand dead civilians. While he thought his troops might have gone a little far, Theodosius felt sure that preserving the rule of law was worth a few thousand empty seats in the bleachers. He went to sleep with a clear conscience. But the next time he returned to his headquarters in Milan, he was accosted at the gate by none other than St. Ambrose, the gifted orator whom Christians had drafted into become bishop of Milan. The bishop actually blocked the gate of the town, challenging the all-powerful emperor:

> You do not reflect, it seems, O Emperor, on the guilt you have incurred by that great massacre; but now that your fury is appeased, do you not perceive the enormity of your crime? You must not be dazzled by the splendor of the purple you wear, and be led to forget the weakness of the body which it clothes. Your subjects, O Emperor, are of the same nature as yourself, and not only so, but are likewise your fellow servants; for there is one Lord and Ruler of all, and He is the maker of all creatures, whether princes or people. How would you look upon the temple of the one Lord of all? How could you lift up in prayer hands steeped in the blood of so unjust a massacre? Depart then, and do not by a second crime add to the guilt of the first.[29]

Ambrose told Theodosius he could not receive Communion, or even set foot in a church, until he had repented. Within a few days, the emperor was kneeling before the bishop, confessing his sins. Ambrose gave him absolution, along with a serious penance: From then on, whenever the death penalty was imposed upon a criminal, there would have to be a thirty-day "cooling off period," at the end of which the sentence would be appealed and reexamined, to make sure that Theodosius hadn't imposed it in a moment of mindless rage. The ruler of the known world accepted these conditions and changed the law accordingly—then the next time he went to Ambrose's cathedral, Theodosius "prayed neither in a standing, nor in a kneeling posture, but throwing him-

---

[29] From Theodoret (c. 393–466 C.E.), *Ecclesiastical History* 5.17–18, found in the Internet Ancient History Sourcebook.

self upon the ground. He tore his hair, struck his forehead, and shed torrents of tears, as he implored forgiveness of God. Ambrose restored him to favor, but forbade him to come inside the altar rail, ordering his deacon to say 'The priests alone, O Emperor, are permitted to enter within the barriers by the altar. Retire then, and remain with the rest of the laity. A purple robe makes Emperors, but not priests.' "

The Church's requirement that we bring our sins to a priest, who will serve as Christ's tribunal of justice and mercy, is designed to bitch-slap the bloody-minded and intolerant Roman emperor inside each one of us—the part of our id that robes itself as our conscience and tries (as Theodosius did) to serve as judge, jury, and executioner. Christ knew that such an internal judicial system was just as biased as an all-white jury in the 1940s, prone to bleaching out our own sins and painting those of others in lurid colors. The priest serves as a sternly impartial judge brought in from out of town.[30] He doesn't make the moral law—he just enforces it. And chances are he isn't outraged by your sins so much as he's bored by them, but also (if he knows his business) honored to stand in the person of Christ and dispense absolution. That doesn't make you any happier having to stand before him. Still, it beats hell[31] out of facing Christ as judge at the end of one's life still dripping with unrepented sins.

40. So when do you know that you need to go to confession?

Whenever you're pretty sure you have committed what's called a mortal sin.[32] From the name, you'll guess that such sins can be spiritually fatal. Once you've gone and done something like that, you're obliged in your own best interest to seek out a priest as soon as possible—and until you do, you should not receive

[30] CCC, 1465
[31] Literally.
[32] CCC, 1856–1863

Communion, ride the Chinatown bus (or any other rattling, unlicensed jitney), or "stand up for yourself" when taunted for reading Mauriac in a honky-tonk by guys with Lynyrd Skynrd tattoos. Ironically, lesser (venial) sins and imperfections can actually be forgiven by going to Holy Communion or performing some act of penance or charity.

Image courtesy of Wikipedia Commons.

41. Like taking the Chinatown bus or punching some bar bully's lights out?

Just for instance, yes. But none of that's going to help you—in fact, all your good actions and prayers go into a kind of spiritual escrow account—once you have committed a sin that meets the Three Preconditions:

- **Grave Matter.** Your sin touched on something important, say, some other person's rights or a part of life that God has marked out as sacred. Right off the bat, you'll see that this will include large sums of money, real "whopper" lies that affect someone's finances or reputation, sacrilege or blasphemy, and pretty much all acts of sex and violence. (My Irish-American mom taught me a simple rule that made this easy to remember: *Sex, like killing, is almost always wrong, except in special circumstances such as self-defense or marriage.*)

- **Sufficient Reflection.** An act you commit impulsively, almost reflexively, will rarely rise to the level of mortal sin. So, for instance, spontaneous fantasies of beating your landlord to death (I have also lived in New York City) will be only venial sins. They turn mortal when you've consciously given in to them, decided to ride them like a pony to see where they lead, and maybe set up a blog where you can record them and get better suggestions from the public. ("Dude, don't use a baseball bat—it'll be over too quick. Tie him up with wet leather straps and gag him with styrofoam peanuts, then . . .") Apply a similar logic to other . . . *passionate* thoughts and actions. The same standard here applies as the legal distinction between first- and second-degree murder: Was it pre-meditated? Did you plan it out, maybe buy some equipment? If so, then the eternal Jack McCoy will press for the spiritual death penalty, so you might as well come clean in return for a much lighter sentence.

• **Full Consent of the Will.** Like the legal system, theology makes allowances for impairments of self-control; this is not a coincidence, but influence. The Common Law, that masterful hybrid of Germanic libertarianism and Roman authority, was born in the Middle Ages and catechized by the Church. Things like doctor-patient confidentiality are shadows of the seal of the confessional, just as exceptions for madness in the law were first made by confessors. Of course, since the Church is not responsible for keeping lawbreakers off the streets or naked lunatics off my lawn, confessors can be more generous and apply a more nuanced standard than the cops or the courts can afford. Besides, the goal of penance is mercy and reform, not punishment and justice. So you need not be obeying "the voices" in your head

for your guilt in God's eyes to be mitigated; extreme psychic distress, a deeply engrained habit or addiction, and a wide array of other things could turn what might otherwise be a mortal sin into something a little more venial. But you really can't make this kind of call on your own, which is why it's handy that there are priests at hand to take over.

42. So you play the prosecutor, and the priest acts as the judge?

Yes, but he acts in the person of Christ. It's like when a kid talks to Santa: He doesn't make his requests of an underemployed, obese actor but of St. Nicholas, bishop of Myra and Coca-Cola. The priest then imposes a sentence, in the form of a "penance" that entails some act of charity or a prayer.[33] These used to be quite extensive in the early Church; adulterers would have to sit on the church steps for months at a time, wearing sackcloth and covered in ash. You can see the pastoral problems this kind of thing would create—for one thing, in countries like Italy or France, the sheer number of adulterers could block access to the church; and it turned the front

---

[33] CCC, 1460

steps into a kind of freak show or (still worse) a meet market. So the Church, in her wisdom, opted for mostly private penances.

43. It seems like a pretty sweet deal. You can go in there and confess to killing the president and walk out with a string of Hail Marys and Glory Bes.

Believe it or not, at some point over the centuries the Church encountered this issue and came up with an answer: Sins that are also crimes, which entail the violation of the rights of innocent others, are absolved only on condition that the sinner turn himself in to the police and do his best to restore whatever damage he has done. If he fails to follow through, his absolution will be invalid.

44. But the priest can't turn him in, no matter what he has admitted to. If Timothy McVeigh had slipped into a booth at St. Barbara's and confessed to the Oklahoma City bombing, the priest couldn't say a word?

Not even if the sinner had made a threat to go on and kill someone else, or even the priest himself. Whatever the priest hears in confession he has to treat as if it had been *told in private to Christ*.[34] He can't even act on it silently—for instance, by trying to stay away from the sinner who threatened to kill him. That's how solemn the seal of the confessional is meant to be. Violating it merits instant excommunication for a priest, who is expected to go to jail or even die instead.

45. So is this why so many American bishops (see chapter 5) engaged in cover-ups for clerical pedophiles?

Absolutely not. That was a criminal conspiracy to hide their own culpable failures to protect innocent children, based on reports that the bishops received *outside of confession*—for instance, in letters from parents, reports from their own psychiatrists, hard drives full of kiddie porn confiscated by police, or suicide notes from victims who had been raped as toddlers, then fallen into lives of prostitution after which they died of AIDS. There is no excuse, no mitigation, abso-

---

[34] CCC, 1467

lutely nothing that can be said in defense of such bishops. But you're right that some of these false shepherds used the confessional as a hideout; one bishop even tried to fend off prosecutors' subpoenas of seminary records by inventing a so-called seminarian-rector privilege, claiming that anything learned by the head of a seminary was sacramentally protected. As I said, there are a lot of retired prelates out there who shouldn't be swinging nine-irons but hammers on roadside chain gangs. The only consolation here is hell—whose floor, according to Church Father St. John Chrysostom, is "paved with the skulls of bishops." Now we know what he meant.

46. On that festive note, are there other sacraments? I seem to remember you people picked a lucky number. What are there, eleven?

Close. We stuck with seven. Or rather, Christ did. Whenever it was that the actual forms or attendant theology sprang up, each of these rites is the way the Church found to obey a mandate from Jesus Himself. The next one, chronologically in most folks' lives, is confirmation.[35] In the West, people usually get confirmed when they reach adolescence. It's a way of reaffirming in your own words what your baptismal sponsors said on your behalf while you were peeing your christening gown: You affirm the Creed, renounce the devil, and state your full agreement to live out a Christian life. The Holy Spirit is called down from heaven to "seal" you, and the bishop lays hands on you, anoints you with oil, and (traditionally) gives you a little smack across the face.

47. Why a smack?

These are adolescents, remember. Think of the teens you've known, and what you were like at that age. You deserved a solid smack, didn't you? I know I did. But that's not in fact the reason. Instead, the slap is a reminder that you're enrolling as a "soldier" of Christ, a role that might well entail persecution. Recall that when these rites took their final form, the Church was being hunted down in catacombs and cellars by the police of the most implacable state then on earth—the Roman Empire. So that's the Church's way of saying, "Listen kid, things can go South. Man up." Since it has emerged (in the West) as the rite of coming of age, it's an echo of the ancient Jewish custom

---

[35] CCC, 1286–1292

of bar and bat mitzvah, in which a young person displays his knowledge and acceptance of his faith, gets to meet Gene Simmons or Paris Hilton in person, then at a climactic moment announces to the world: "Today I am an early-decision applicant to Swarthmore."

48. And the smear of oil on your head is supposed to attract the Holy Spirit? What is that, bird bait?

Anointing with oil is an ancient symbol of blessing, healing, and welcome. Which means that for us moderns, it's a sticky mass you wipe off your forehead, and nothing more. It's hard for us to see how something merely *physical* and *tangible* could possibly carry meaning. After all, it isn't what your *body* is or does that counts. That's just a mass of meat controlled by what really matters—your mind.

Those of us who've been to a modern college all learned that even "gender" is not determined by the structure of those organs that reproduce the species. Gender is a "social construction" so complicated that its study requires thousands of scholars grinding out jargon-laden tomes, while graduate students teach their classes. From these elders we learn that it was only patriarchal religious and economic structures that made women want to nurture their infants rather than become hockey players, and also created the illusion that heterosexuality is somehow biologically normal (an ugly prejudice called "heteronormativity").

Gender is not a fact of life but an ideological figment from which an individual may dissent. Your body may have popped out equipped with a wiener. Does that mean you're male? Let's question that patriarchal assumption. How do you *feel* about your equipment? Do you like the touch of silk against your skin and crave a warm cup of tea, and a nice Jane Austen novel? Then you might be a woman "trapped" inside the body of a man. Doctors will offer you hormones, counseling, and surgery to carve up your body to match your mind.

Until recently, psychologists treated such "gender confusion" as an illness and helped patients mold their cognitions to match the realities dangling from their abdomens. But now we know better and realize that man is neither social nor an animal. He is a spirit that transcends biology and society—a kind of wizard whose mere flesh modern, magical medicine can mold to suit his preferences. As the late Michael Jackson proved, only in America can a poor, talented young black man grow up to become a rich white woman.

The poor souls who undergo full-bore "gender reassignment" can suffer severe health problems from ripping up their plumbing and dosing themselves with massive steroids over decades. But at least they followed their dream.

The Church follows the more ancient theory, asserting that created things have essences that actually carry meanings. So oil is for anointing, although on some occasions it is also for shampoo or salad.

49. OK, so if this little ritual does in fact bring down the Holy Spirit, what is that supposed to do?

The bishop calls down on the person being confirmed the seven "gifts" of the Spirit we talked about before (see chapter 4): Wisdom, Understanding, Counsel, Fortitude, Knowledge, Piety, and Fear. And I think that, Catholic or not, we can all agree that American teens would benefit from a horse doctor's dose of each. That's why I think it's a shame that more and more parishes are delaying confirmation—which in recent centuries was generally done at thirteen or so, perhaps as a supernatural counterforce to the bewildering array of hormones dosing the poor kids at that age, blasting their chastity and ruining their complexions. But I've been told that in the past twenty years, some Catholic schools are pushing the ritual back from seventh grade to twelfth.

50. Why would they do that?

I can think of two decent reasons. First, to dangle one more sacrament in front of the parents, as a means of keeping kids in Catholic school through to the end. As if any such cynical motive were needed where I come from. In New York City, we Catholic school kids knew perfectly well the purpose of parochial education—to keep us alive. The alternative was eight years as practice stabbing dummies in those waiting rooms for state prison with names like Public School 911. The teachers knew this too and dangled the threat of expulsion over our heads. Who said that Catholics don't approve of capital punishment?

Second, the Church accommodates herself, wherever it does not impinge on doctrine, to the culture in which she lives. So in the Middle Ages, when people tended to die off right around forty, pastors were ready to let kids get married at thirteen or fourteen, to give them a chance to reproduce the species. Nowadays, when most of us get our first "real job" and move out of our parents' basement right around age thirty, the Church may have seen that "adulthood" is a concept most of us aren't quite ready to handle. Should we really be held responsible for the money we borrowed, the grades we made, the people we slept with, when we were mere eighteen- or twenty-two-year-olds? It doesn't seem fair, somehow. If the Baby Boomers were allowed to spend forty or fifty years finding themselves, why shouldn't we do the same? It's logic like this that drives single fortysomethings to haunt "young adult" events at local parishes, wear T-shirts with rock bands over our paunches, and use casual profanities to prove that we're still edgy.

If all this is true and confirmation must really wait until a person is on the cusp of psychological maturity, then the age is bound to continue creeping up—as adolescence goes on annexing one decade after another, till it finally reaches senility. Then we'd have to save confirmation till the deathbed—or else make like the Eastern Orthodox and Catholics and get it over with (along with first Holy Communion) by bundling it in with baptism. In fact, some conservative dioceses are actually pushing confirmation back before confession but after baptism—which is a really good idea, since it means that kids will get some extra gifts.

CRWCRWCRWCRWCRWCRWCRWCRWCRWCRWCRWCRWCRW

FAQs from Your Stoner Neighbor #7
The Protestants don't even consider confirmation a sacrament. If you're getting the Holy Spirit, why don't you start speaking in tongues or something? Does confirmation really do anything, or is it just something Anglos do because they're too embarrassed to have a Quinceañera? Does it really do anything?

It did for me—and no doubt for countless other young boys who grew up in the shadow of the thriller flick *The Omen*. When this movie depicting the birth of a cuddly, handsome little Antichrist came out, it reportedly caused countless parents to rush home and check their children's scalps for birthmarks that spelled out "666." My guess is that those kids weren't demonic but simply ADD; then again, I'm no theologian.

On a thirteen-year-old like me, however, the film had a slightly different effect. It sent me scrambling after every book I could find on the Antichrist and the End Times, most of them written by Protestants—but that didn't stop me, because I didn't know what Protestants were[36] and pretty much assumed that all "religious" books were the same. They quoted the Bible, didn't they? One time I brought a parish priest a pamphlet I'd ordered from television that called the papacy the Whore of Babylon and asked him to discuss it.

---

[36] Growing up in Astoria, Queens, I thought pretty much everyone on earth was Irish, Italian, or Greek. When I met my first Protestant in college, I wanted to ask him, "So how do you like our country?"

"Don't read this," he explained, and took it away: But I never brought good Fr. Grisaitis my copy of *The Late Great Planet Earth* or *Satan in the Sanctuary* or any of the other books I picked up here and there, or the lurid exposes of demonology and witchcraft I'd checked out of the public library. Instead, I buried myself in them—desperate to answer one of life's great existential questions: *Was I the Antichrist?*

This question occurred to me early in seventh grade when I was suffused with thoughts of . . . evil. As sexual fantasies swarmed through my head despite every attempt to suppress them, I began to wonder about the nature of these thoughts and dutifully went to my favorite source—a reference book. My parents had lying around an old moral manual from 1945, translated with dogged literality from the Latin, replete with detailed information about the gravely sinful nature of "impure thoughts," "self-abuse," and other forms  of "pollution," and a helpful little section on hell. I looked in vain for mitigations or exceptions, or suggestions on how to stop up this font of evil. But nothing worked. That was when I went to see *The Omen*.

And suddenly, it all made sense.

In that film, young Damien is born as the incarnate child of Satan himself, born evil and unable to choose otherwise. Now, this is a piece of theological nonsense; the Antichrist discussed in the Apocalypse of St. John, when he comes, will be nothing more than a particularly wicked human being. Satan is utterly powerless to emulate the Incarnation, nor can he compel us to sin. (The things done by a person possessed are not attributed to his soul.) But not every Catholic thirteen-year-old knows this.

I sure didn't. As far as I could see, the fact of being overwhelmed with unquenchable desires, impossible to resist, to commit mortal sins was a pretty compelling piece of evidence that I . . . had been born the spawn of Satan, and was doomed to spread evil throughout the world and persecute the Church until I was finally crushed by the Second Coming.

This put quite a damper on seventh grade. I knew enough to realize that mine was the losing side, that some day I'd end up with a Woman Clothed by the Sun crushing my head beneath her heel. And I didn't look forward to it one bit. Nor to the Lake of Fire, the Second Death, or the weeping and gnashing of teeth amid the fire that does not die with the worm that does not sleep. I'd put on a scapular sometimes and wonder why it didn't catch on fire.

I pondered my eternal destiny in hell all through confirmation class, which focused, naturally enough, on penmanship. Each of us had to write a letter to Brooklyn bishop Francis Mugavero explaining why he wished to be confirmed. Since I had terrible handwriting, I was kept after school every day for weeks, retracing the same exact words over and over—all the while pondering St. Thomas's promise that the damned would receive back their flesh at the Resurrection "to perfect their punishment in the senses." I imagined a hot dentist's drill applied to the eyes . . .

And that is when I came up with a way out—or at least a means of finding the answer. Since I had a major sacrament coming up, it could serve as an empirical test of my hypothesis. Surely the spawn of Satan himself could not sit through an entire confirmation service without blaspheming it. The incarnate spirit of evil could not receive the Holy Ghost called down upon him by the descendant of the apostles without reacting like a vampire at the sight of a crucifix. If the promptings of primal evil that filled my mind with thoughts of cleavage, stockinged calves, and secret crevices most waking hours every day were truly invincible, a sign of my destiny and nature, then nothing could stop them—not even the Holy Ghost, since Satan (as I had read) is beyond redemption. He is too fixed in evil to repent. The question, then, *Was I?*

So I made myself an experiment. If I could sit through the entire two-hour confirmation service without once thinking of sex or feeling a . . . stirring . . . of the flesh, it would prove that my nature was not, in fact, demonic. If I couldn't, well that would prove the contrary. As the Jesuits used to say, *quod erat demonstratum.*

As the after-school penmanship lessons drew to a close—the nun despaired and sent my diabolical chicken scratch off to the bishop—and the great experiment approached, I had trouble getting to sleep at night. Something about the embrace of limitless darkness left me feeling too vulnerable. I awaited the day as I imagine the scientists of the Manhattan project did their first tests at Los Alamos—though of course the evil power they unleashed was nothing compared to the monstrosities I would be driven by my nature to commit, should it happen I failed the test. I thought grimly of the mass murders, wars, and persecutions I would have to unleash, and wondered idly if I could spare innocent New York City from the general wrack—particularly the rain of Wormwood with which I would be compelled to poison the seas. Could I at least save my dog?

When the big day arrived and I donned the red polyester robes we'd been loaned, and the stole we would get to keep, I marched into the Church as if to my own murder trial—for millions of murders, really, except that they lay in the future. But God, I had read, is not bound by time .... In a sense, I might already be guilty of them. I sat in the pew among my classmates and tried to ignore the girls—the flouncing hair, the bright makeup of the Italian girls, the rosy skin of the Irish. I sang the hymns in a breaking voice and strained every nerve below the waist for a hint of arousal, of the rising gavel that would mean a guilty verdict.

And nothing happened. Chalk it up to performance anxiety, but I made it through unscathed. For the first time in over a year, I managed to keep my thoughts pure for a solid ninety minutes. The girls might have been bodiless spirits for all I cared. They looked even—angelic. The sweaty, gum-chewing guys were not future victims of genocides for which I would be responsible but just a pack of future cops and firemen. The bishop, I knew for a fact, would not die in prison because of me. My stony heart  was once again a heart of flesh, and the Spirit was in me the same as everybody else, no more and no less. I let my parents take me for ice cream.

So I like to tell people that confirmation meant more to me than it did to anyone else I know. But I don't tell them why.

In retrospect, I realize that I was indulging at once an unhealthy scrupulosity and a positively perilous interest in the Occult—which is to say, I was looking around in the medical wastebins of the Cosmos. This came home to me while thinking about another film dealing with spectacular feats of evil, Anthony Hopkins's fairly forgettable movie *The Rite* (2011).

In my long years as an obscure Catholic journalist (is there any other kind?), I've gotten regular invites from PR companies that specialize in the "Christian market" to preview movies that have some religious "angle." All too often, it's plain from the press release that these are merely "family" movies: moderately interesting, moderately uplifting dramas of ordinary life to which you can bring the kids (though they'll fall asleep) because they are free of nudity and profanity—in other words, they're airplane versions of regular movies. I've nothing against that. Indeed, we need more such films, and I mourn the demise of the companies that used to "scrub" R-rated Hollywood pictures for the benefit of viewers with less-jaded sensibilities. (The auteurs who make movies like *Jackass 3D* sued such well-meaning censors out of existence).

But I'm not going to make a special trip to preview, much less write about, films that are clearly rentals at best. The few times I've made it to such screenings, the audience was packed with Protestant pastors and Young Life leaders and sprinkled with Roman collars and habits. The event always began with a chipper talk by a handsome lady publicist, pointing out the "refreshingly wholesome," "life-affirming" message that pervaded the film, urging the pastors to recommend the movie from the pulpit, with the implicit or explicit argument: "You people are always complaining about all the filth that comes out of Hollywood. Well, here it is, something we've made with you in mind. If you don't support it, and it doesn't turn a profit, we'll just have to go ahead and green-light *Meet the Parents 4*." And they do have a point. But it bothers me that so many of the movies promoted this way are not really "spiritual," much less Christian; they're simply bland and inoffensive.

The Catholic faith is neither. In fact, like really authentic Mexican food (think habaneros and fried crickets), it is at once both pungent and offensive. It offends me all the time, with the outrageous demands it makes of my fallen nature and the sheer weirdness of its claims. It asserts that, behind the veil of day-to-day schlepping, of work and laundry and television and microwaved burritos, we live on the front lines of a savage spiritual war waged by invisible entities (deathless malevolent demons and benevolent dead saints) whose winners will enjoy eternal happiness with a resurrected rabbi and whose losers will writhe forever in unquenchable fire. Sometimes I step back and find myself saying in Jerry Seinfeld's voice: *What's with all the craziness? Why can't I just enjoy my soup?*

The Church's heroes, seen from a worldly point of view, are a pack of self-destructive zealots who embark on crackpot projects like lifelong celibacy, voluntary poverty, and (worst of all) obedience; who leave perfectly serviceable chateaus in France to go preach the Beatitudes to hostile natives in freezing Canada; who volunteer to sneak into Stalin's Russia precisely because he has imprisoned so many priests, then spend decades saying secret Masses in labor camps; who open up prolife pregnancy centers in crappy neighborhoods so they can talk welfare queens into having still more babies we'll have to pay for . . .

And so on. A religion like this doesn't need after-school specials; it needs science fiction and fantasy, horror films and surrealism, to convey the fundamental strangeness that it believes lies just beneath the surface of day-to-day "reality." To keep our sense of perspective, every once in a while at one of our dull, desacralized liturgies, the priest needs to die of a heart attack in the pulpit (as happened at my old New York parish, St. Agnes, some years ago), if only to remind us of the stakes we're playing for. We need—though let me stress, we don't enjoy, and *I do not want*—the occasional grotesque "Flannery O'Connor moment."

So that's why I went to see the preview, a few years back, of *The Exorcism of Emily Rose*. That's why I decided go see *The Rite*, though I had deep fears both of heterodoxy and cheesiness. Such movies, when they are done well, peel back the Norman Rockwell veil we'd all rather stay in place and show us what lies behind it: Hieronymus Bosch. The proper purpose of art (when it goes beyond entertainment) is to show us a glimpse of the deep truths, the kind we can endure only in small and occasional doses. We couldn't really stand it if every Sunday the Host were visibly transformed into a bloody chunk of flesh, as happened at Lanciano; we might not want to bring the kids. And, truth to tell, it would wear us all down. But little glimpses of this kind of thing, peeks into the great abyss of Mystery, dark or bright, are helpful from time to time.

Too often films like *The Rite* don't really serve this purpose but instead feed into a nasty voyeurism of the sort that attracts us to evil. We see that the Enemy really does give tangible, spiritual power to some of his servants. As the author of nature's order,

God is loath to disrupt it, so He grants miracles rarely and dispenses them typically after we're racked ourselves with prayer. Satan, who's merely a vandal, will gladly perform hat tricks and grant instant gratification. Exorcists, in their memoirs, inform us that you really can learn things from Ouija boards, summon spirits who might do your bidding, or cast spells upon your enemies. If you're willing to play with plutonium, you can make little bombs to throw at people to vent your petty spite. But remember that you're an idiot mucking around inside the core of a nuclear reactor, with no idea how the thing works and not the slightest protection against its effects.

The best depiction I've seen of how occultism kills the soul, Robert Hugh Benson's novel *The Necromancers*, details what happens next: a slow, sick burn seeps into your brain. The colors of nature (which you've raped) all fade to a sickly, jaundiced yellow. Having glimpsed the dark underbelly of things, you become utterly cynical. Ordinary knowledge, earned through hard labor, loses all attraction compared to secrets, conspiracies, and gossip. You begin to see other people with that hideous spiritual hunger that demons feel all the time, as if they were healthy animals and you were a parasite, looking for somewhere to batten on them and drain their strength. Soon the glamour of evil fades, and once it's too late (by any human power) for you to escape, you feel deep in your bones the crassness, the foulness, the cheapness of what you have become.[37]

I wish more films that treat the occult would emphasize this point. Evil is a privation, and it lives only by borrowing strength—like a tapeworm, or a tick. We should certainly fear the devil, but he deserves no awe and should exert no fascination. We should not even pity him. What we need to feel is contempt.

But that's enough about unholy spirits. The point of confirmation is to fill you up with the Comforter, who will largely be responsible for carrying you through the rest of life's ordeals.

CRITICAL separator ornament

51. Which brings us to marriage. That's what most people engage in after adolescence—their first marriage, anyway. I know there's a sacrament for that.

Well, that's what Catholics and Orthodox believe. Protestants differ among themselves (surprise, surprise!), though Luther and Calvin were solidly convinced that

---

[37] CCC, 391–395

marriage was not a sacrament but merely a "a good and holy ordinance from God."[38] (King Henry VIII had rather . . . complex and evolving views on the topic, which is rather Anglican, after all.) Now the relevant language in the New Testament is sufficiently ambiguous that both sides can find support in it. The key passage in scripture where St. Paul characterizes marriage is Ephesians 5:32. The King James edition translates it as "This is a great *mystery*: but I speak concerning Christ and the church," while the Catholic Douay-Rheims version reads: "This is a great *sacrament*; but I speak in Christ and in the church." So that's no help to us. I'm sure somewhere there's a sect that translates *musterion* as "banana." Barring a divinely appointed interpretative authority such as a Church, the question must be left up to scripture scholars—and do you really want the faculty of Yale Divinity School deciding how many sacraments there are? Pretty soon the Eucharist would be likely to fall off the list and find itself replaced by either Diversity or Tenure.

This doctrine is important enough that two Church councils (Florence, before the Reformation, and Trent held in its wake) both ruled on it, teaching infallibly that marriage was indeed one of seven sacraments, pointing both to the practices of the early Church and to the gravity with which marriage is treated at key points in the Bible— namely at the creation, when God Himself intervenes to give Adam a spouse, and in the redemption, when Jesus goes so far as to overrule Moses, restore the primitive perfection of marriage as given in Genesis, and rule out divorce.[39] Now this is not a polemic aimed at Protestants, whom statistics say are as willing to marry as Catholics, and slightly less eager to divorce. So rather than wade into hoary arguments that never seem to convince anyone, let's look at the underlying issue: Is marriage of the same order as baptism and the Eucharist? Or is it just a worthy human activity like agriculture or shoemaking? The debatable passage in Ephesians is worth quoting at greater length; just to level the playing field, let's use the New King James version:

> Wives, submit yourselves to your own husbands, as to the Lord. For the husband is the head of the wife, even as Christ is the head of the church: and he is the savior of the body. Therefore as the church is subject to Christ, so let the wives be to their own husbands in every thing.
>
> Husbands, love your wives, even as Christ also loved the church, and gave himself for it; That he might sanctify and cleanse it with the washing of water by the word, That he might present it to himself a glorious church, not having spot, or wrinkle, or any such thing; but that it should be holy and without blemish. So ought men to love their wives

---

[38] But so, Calvin snarked, "are agriculture, architecture, shoemaking, [and] hair-cutting." I don't what's more troubling there—the trivialization of marriage, or the elevation of barbering, one of the many activities, no doubt, that were closely regulated in Calvin's proto-totalitarian Geneva. Luther, for his part, loved marriage enough to extend it to monks and nuns—and even was willing to permit polygamy to sympathetic Protestant lords, like Philip of Hesse.

[39] CCC, 1638

as their own bodies. He that loves his wife loves himself. For no man ever yet hated his own flesh; but nourishes and cherishes it, even as the Lord the church: For we are members of his body, of his flesh, and of his bones. For this cause shall a man leave his father and mother, and shall be joined to his wife, and they two shall be one flesh. This is a great mystery: but I speak concerning Christ and the church. Nevertheless let every one of you in particular so love his wife even as himself; and the wife see that she reverence her husband. (Ephesians 5:23–33)

I'm aware that vast, groaning shelves of books have been written on this subject—perhaps the best recent work being Pope John Paul II's profound meditations on the Theology of the Body—so I won't pretend to do more than add a bookmark to what the great thinkers have had to say. But if you were a Martian or a modern, secular Dane and you came across this passage for the very first time, what would you think of it? Would you say that Christian marriage is something along the lines of cobbling or farming? Would you flip through the rest of the Gospels to find the sec-tions where Christ is called "the sole" of the spirit's shoe? Or would you conclude that St. Paul had chosen marriage because it is one of the most fundamental human relations, something that is by its own nature sacred, which the Incarnation apparently has elevated even further? If God became man so that man might become God,[40] then what would be a more appropriate tool for Him to use in sanctifying us than the most intimate relation possible between one of those spirits He is divinizing, and another one? Even better if that relation were the only means by which still more immortal spirits intended for heaven were to end up crawling the earth, thus forming the basic unit of every human society. If Christ did *not* come to elevate that relationship into a means of growing nearer to Him, that Dane would need to chuckle and ask himself, "Why nøt?"

The Church regards marriage not as an arrangement or even a contract but a covenant—the same term used in the Old Testament to describe the bond of God and the Jews, and in the New for Christ's bond with the Church.[41] St. Paul, in looking for a metaphor to intimate how intimate and irrevocable was our connection with Christ chose not slavery, sonship, or even Roman citizenship, but marriage. Indeed, matrimony is the sole covenant in which any of us will enter in this lifetime. Really, if you have already been baptized and you don't get ordained as a priest, one might say that choosing to marry is the only really serious decision most of us gets to make.

---

[40] CCC, 460
[41] CCC, 1642

52. So the Church teaches that this relationship, more so than any other, such as motherhood, brotherhood, or anything-otherhood, is intended to transform people and make them more godly? I guess you haven't spent much time watching married couples interact with each other (and I'm not even talking about when they're speaking through their attorneys). The only way I can see some point in what you're saying is that prolonged friction between two sharp-edged, ill-fitted objects tends to wear down their sharp edges. Is that what you mean by sanctity—two pieces of sandpaper that have worn each other smooth?

Well, you've got to burn your sins off somewhere. Better in the family room than in purgatory. However, there is a bit more to be said for matrimony than that. For instance, that without it, there would be no need or occasion for any of the other six. And the reason I say that is . . . a *secret*. It's something that nowadays only a tiny coterie of crackpot "social conservatives" know. If you lean forward, I can whisper it in your ear—but be careful to whom you repeat it. First of all, nobody will believe you, and you will seem like one of those losers who picked a date for the End of Time, sold all his stuff, shaved his head, then showed up back at Target the day after The End in his saffron Ascension Robe (it's all he had left) and asked for his job back.[42] So only share this with people you really trust, and those who have already written you off, anyway:

A team of Vatican scientists working in seclusion has discovered that there is a secondary biological function attached to sexual behavior, and hence to the social alliance conventionally known as "marriage." Beyond the agreeable sensations of arousal, the well-documented surge of intense physical enjoyment at climax, and the effects that occur in its wake—which can range from durable emotional bonding to an overpowering "fight or flight" response—there is another, more controversial outcome to sexual interaction, these researchers assert. To find out what it is, please turn this book upside down.

> *Sexual intercourse between humans can result in the conception and birth of human children.*
>
> *Okay, you can turn the book right side up now.*

---

[42] I know whereof I speak. A seminarian I knew from the Latin Mass in New York City became convinced by a self-proclaimed expert on biblical prophecy and private apparitions. The "prophet," whom I'll call here "Ed," spoke in an almost constant stream of profanities like a Martin Scorsese character, but he wore a full-body scapular sewn with hundreds of first-class relics, so he was clearly on to something. Ed swore, among other things, that the Third Secret of Fatima (the real text, not that fake released by the "pope") was a save-the-date note predicting the Second Coming on October 13, 1994. "Our Lady's gonna let her divine Son tear this planet a new one," Ed said with an equable smile. His disciple dropped out of the seminary and moved back in with his mother to wait for the End. I waited too—for October 14, 1994, on which date I phoned this seminarian at the office to say, "That was subtle." Yet we can see the sticky fingers of Providence even here; this fellow never returned to the Fraternity of St. Peter but instead joined the Hare Krishnas, then the skinhead group American Front, but finally announced that he was gay and became a Satanist—at which point I somehow lost his phone number. So the priesthood dodged that bazooka shell, thanks to the apparition I call "Our Lady of Goodfellas."

According to the Catholic Church, this little-considered sexual aftereffect has significant implications. Indeed, the *Catechism* (the real one) teaches that matrimony is "by its nature ordered toward the good of the spouses and the procreation and education of offspring" (CCC 1601). Notice that those two sets of ends are listed together . . . almost as if they had *equal importance*. No wonder the Church is seen as an institutional killjoy. We feel, as modern people, the profound moral conviction that it's *our fundamental human right to do whatever the BLEEP we want*.

Not only does marriage demand that we put the good of another person on the same level of our own—and even be willing to sacrifice own happiness for the sake of a spouse. (That's bad enough, but at least you're taking such trouble for someone you got to pick, who was presumably kind of hot when you made that dark, irrevocable decision.) No, you also have to make those same kinds of sacrifices for a passel of tiny strangers, whom you're linked to through the meaningless twists of chromosomes. In fact, the Church considers it sinful for spouses to alter the nature of the sexual act by artificially rendering it sterile.[43] At this point, most Catholics check out, of course. You can get them to sign on to God

becoming man in order to save their souls (that's kind of flattering), and even to Jesus transporting Himself into a Communion they get to receive (which is also trippy). But start telling us that sex must (a) be reserved to marriage and (b) be open to life, and out comes the shotgun we keep in the garage: "Get the pope the hell off my lawn!"

Now I'm not about to let this book be hijacked by the endless, fruitless arguments over artificial contraception—which frequently turn into squabbles between two sets of people, each of whom misses the Church's teaching in a different direction: the 95 percent of Catholics who simply regard *Humanae Vitae* as something that Vatican II did away with (kind of puzzling since it was published after the council, but logic is *so* preconciliar), and what sometimes seems like the 95 percent of the *other* 5 percent who think the document was a sellout compromise, because it permits married couples to exercise the governing virtue of Prudence in childbearing, by limiting family size for "just reasons" through avoiding sex during fertile times. (The difference between contraception and NFP, as I've written before and will write here again, is no starker than that between bulimia and dieting.) The first group I term, in order to avoid any confusion, "Episcopalians," and there's really not much to say to them beside, "Quit

[43] CCC, 2366-2371

it." They admit to belonging to a Church with a centralized moral authority, and most of them, if pressed, will acknowledge that this office belongs to the pope and not Nancy Pelosi. So I leave it to them to connect this short series of dots.

To the second group, the Potato Faminites, who rely on an old, bad translation of *Humanae Vitae* to insist that one may only limit or space births for "grave and serious reasons," let me point out just this: The Church teaches that the Christian education of children is every bit as essential to the purposes of marriage as their conception. If you can't raise your kids Catholic, you have no business having them. Now, Christian education was a heck of a lot simpler when kids could remain illiterate, learn their catechism by rote, and go out to butcher hogs or glean wheat in a field as soon as they could walk. It was still pretty simple when tens of thousands of religious sisters and brothers ran free Catholic schools to civilize hordes of barbaric Celts and Croats like my ancestors. Nowadays, when Catholic schools are closing by the hundreds every year (and those that remain must keep hiking their tuition), and when soaring taxes and stagnant wages force both spouses into the workforce—even as public schools teach gay "marriage" as normative, and popular culture, pumped into your child's head via his iPhone, or his best friend's iPhone, barrages him with messages that are *less than rigorously Christian*—just how many kids are you sure you can give a proper Catholic education? Well, that's exactly how many kids you should have.

Some Catholics, facing this dilemma, choose to homeschool—and a high percentage of them are actually sane enough to do so. But you really can't homeschool through college, and today a B.A. has become the equivalent of a green card. So for those of us living in developed countries, setting aside some sort of college fund is surely part of what Vatican II referred to as "responsible parenthood." All those factors are surely "just reasons," not selfish, materialist excuses, for having four or five kids instead of twelve. And it's not like NFP, from what I hear, is any kind of fun. Based on the careful study of feminine biology, it's an extremely effective way to determine the precise moment when a woman least wants to have sex—at which point you break out the scented candles/white Zinfandel/pirate costume[44] and get busy. Leave it to rigorist Catholics to accuse marathon runners of being secret hedonists. Quite a few of them don't even

think the fact that your existing eight kids are on food stamps and Medicaid (paid for by your neighbors) is a good reason for reexamining your "openness to life." Some have argued to me, with a straight face, that "the government is run by Jews, Freemasons, and Protestants anyway—why not make them use some tax money to support Catholic families, instead

---

[44] Hey, whatever works for you.

of abortion/birth control/wars in the Middle East? They can underwrite us while we outbreed them, then outnumber them, then rise up to impose a Catholic state."

To such people I like to answer, "Just because you've got St. Michael spray-painted on the side of your double-wide doesn't mean you aren't white trash."

53. Your Church has a very exalted theology for such a primal biological urge. Have you Catholics also invented a sacrament for the crapper?

No, but an Orthodox Jewish friend told me of a prayer they use in gratitude for everything coming out right in the end:

> Blessed are You, Hashem our G-d, King of the universe, Who formed man with wisdom and created within him many openings and many hollows. It is obvious and known before Your Throne of Glory that if even one of them ruptures, or if even one of them becomes blocked, it would be impossible to survive and to stand before You (even for a short period). Blessed are You, Hashem, Who heals all flesh and acts wondrously.

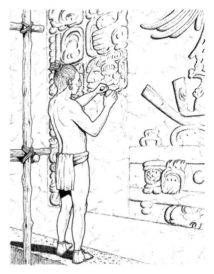

I also love the Old Testament epithet for men: "any that pisseth against the wall" (1 Samuel 25:22). There's something very healthy about that kind of earthiness in religion.

54. Paul's allegory is lovely, but it seems like a lot of weight to put on where one places one's peter. Are you sure the reality is strong enough to bear all that theology?

That's the source of most of the discontent with orthodox Christianity nowadays, isn't it? And of most of the grave matter for mortal sins as well. Most experts agree that sex and marriage predate the New Testament. So does Original Sin, which had plenty of time to implant in various human cultures deep-seated and imperfect understandings of sexuality. Jesus's profound elevation of such a basic fact of life has largely proved puzzling to others:

- the Greeks, who had been taught to think of women as talking animals who could bear them legitimate sons, and so saved their panting *eros* for rippling young boys who'd listen to them nattering on about Virtue;
- the Romans, who by the time of Augustus had moved from a cruel but orderly sexual code—the *paterfamilias* (Dad) could batter his wife and kill disobedient children at will—to a wild and wooly post-*Hustler* culture of easy divorce and orgies enacted on the backs of sexual slaves;
- the Muslims, whose law allows polygamy and the enjoyment of captured concubines;
- the freedom-loving Germanic pagans, who took too many liberties—for instance, they thought that marriage consisted of consummation, and hence that Roman maidens they had taken against their will were now their legitimate wives;

and even

- the Jews, who already saw marriage as sacred, and followed a moral code that showed deep respect for the rights of women and children (a blind spot that has afflicted most other sexual systems). But they did not know what to make of Jesus's celibacy, or the fact that He held that practice up as an ideal for His preaching elite, the apostles. What even the good Pharisees couldn't see was that sometimes, when a worthy thing is being treated with contempt (as sex was among the pagans), it might be necessary for a prophet to renounce it— if only to prove that it something distinctive and noble, which you ought to do without before abusing. I'm thinking here of vegans. No, I'm not going to give up goat's milk, pub cheese, deviled eggs, or even pulled pork. But the fact that some people care enough about the welfare of God's helpless critters to *give up all these good things altogether* has made me—and countless other NPR listeners—aware of abusive farming practices and created a growing industry in humanely sourced animal products.

Christianity was profoundly affected by the bachelorhood of Christ,[45] and St. Paul's wistful musing that he wished all Christians could also lead celibate lives, the better to concentrate on things of heaven. Over the course of centuries, and not without some kicking and screaming—for instance, by two-fisted, stout-swilling polygamous Irish bishops—the monks who'd embraced this advice influenced the Church in the West to require this practice of the clergy. The result, where

---

[45] For instance, He did not leave behind a line of divine descendants—whose role in subsequent history would be hard to imagine, wouldn't it?

this discipline was taken seriously, was a ready corps of devoted pastors and preachers, detached from concerns of providing for families or arranging for land their eldest sons could inherit. It is no accident that most of the missionary activity conducted by Christians before the nineteenth century was led by celibate Catholic priests—and where it was undertaken by Orthodox, they sent their monks. It took the rise of the British Empire, and its fleet of protective, avenging gunboats, for married Protestant missionaries to make much impact on the world.[46]

Sometimes people took a good thing a little too far; since monks were the ones writing most of the theology, and they had at great cost followed the Church's Counsels of Perfection (poverty, chastity, obedience), there was an obvious temptation: to read Christ's words "Be you therefore perfect, as also your heavenly Father is perfect" (Matthew 5:48) and draw an unjustified conclusion—that *all Christians really ought to be monks,* and that those who "fell short" were somehow second-class faithful. Early medieval monastic stories are rife with Christian couples who finally took the plunge and embraced "true" perfection, in the form of celibate or "spiritual" marriages. To most of us, this sounds like the worst of both worlds: you can never have sex, but there's *someone else in your house.* But to these monks, this was the coolly logical implication of the gospel. To them, one can answer as follows: If you demonstrated that Jesus really had wished to impose universal celibacy, it would prove just one thing—He was not the Redeemer of the human race, but its enemy, since He sought its extinction by around 100 A.D. Did the God who "created them male and female" send His son to remedy that mistake?[47] That position really would be Gnostic, and so it clearly can't be Christian.

Happily, the Teutonic tribesmen the Church was trying to baptize simply scoffed through their forked, tangled beards at arguments like these, and the pastors who dealt with the laity strongly pushed back against the treatises that trickled from certain rigorist monasteries. By the High Middle Ages, popular Christianity reflected the healthy balance that already prevailed in official Church teaching: Marriage is clearly good,

---

[46] CCC, 1579-1580

[47] St. Augustine gets a lot of heat from modern, liberal scholars who consider him hostile to marital sex. And like most pioneers, he did make a few mistakes (for instance, condemning sex during pregnancy as a mortal sin). But overall, he was concerned that the power of sexual passion could, even in marriage, overwhelm rational and spiritual concerns. (I know, I know, most of you will say, "That's only when you're doing it right.") In an era when girls were still turned over by the fathers for marriages they'd barely or never consented to, Augustine's fears were surely legitimate. He knew this firsthand—having before his conversion kept for more than a decade a lower-class concubine whom he knew it would be illegal for him to marry. Augustine's slightly Stoic views on this subject would find their corrective in the healthy, biologically based Aristotelianism of St. Thomas Aquinas—who held that sexual pleasure was a good created by God and would have been even greater absent the Fall.

and the sexual act is the ordinary means of grace in the sacrament. Sexual pleasure is good, but like every other good thing (such as luxury, leisure, or glory), it is subject to abuse. In fact, the very intensity of our desire ought to render us especially cautious in how we pursue it, knowing our own capacity for ruthlessness. (If there's anything that's more ruthless than the porn or the abortion industry, I really don't want to know about it.) The life of a vowed religious, faithfully followed, is even better than marriage, but it's a comparatively rare calling that only God can issue, and laymen should not view it through a lens of either shame or envy. Those of us in the Coast Guard Reserve don't need to be embarrassed when we meet the guys in Special Forces. But we might want to buy them a drink.

55. Well, that's all very nice for you. But by confining sex within a sacrament and making the act itself a religious prescription, isn't the Church just imposing on a basic, natural drive a strict set of ritual and moralistic controls? Imagine if the Church tried that with eating—if the only food you could have as a Catholic was Holy Communion, or the only way you could wash was with holy water in a baptismal font. It sounds like you're wrapping the whole human race in a tight set of Spanx. No wonder you Catholics are so repressed.

I'm tempted here to make an easy joke about the comparative joie de vivre of the Mexicans and the Swiss and leave it at that. But you raise a point that's too important to fob off with a line about "the Catholic sun" and "good, red wine." Yes, we must learn to repress our sexual urges. Sorry. Toilet training came as a trauma to me, too, but in social terms I think the trade-off was worth it. Likewise, the costs of sexual repression are obvious, and I won't indulge the postmodern reader by ticking them off. The benefits are clear to women who can walk down the street without being mauled by construction workers, to coworkers who don't have to endure sexual harassment, and to spouses who are *pretty sure* their partners aren't giving them either illegitimate children or herpes.

On a deeper level, if sexual intercourse isn't the physical sign of a lasting, loving commitment that's the building block of a family—then what exactly *would* be? If the level of vulnerability and trust entailed in sharing the intimate act does not signify an ongoing personal bond, how then would we signify such a connection? Buy a Manhattan co-op together? Once you inflate the currency of interpersonal intimacy by joining the "hook-up" culture, or designating sex as something you save for someone very special—on your fifth date—how do you trade in that wheelbarrow full of Weimar *reichsmarks* for something solid? Maybe we've just given up on the idea that personal bonds can last for decades, or even years. We might just have embraced the vision Aldous Huxley offered in *Brave New World*, of the bland and neutered pursuit of moment-to-moment cheerfulness, with every sharp edge buffered by consumption and psychiatric soma. It might be worth retrieving that paperback from the box of books you read in high school and thumbing through it again—only this time realizing that it was meant not as a blueprint but a warning.

As a friend of mine, the pro-life leader Jason Jones, once wrote:

> Since the Sexual Revolution and its ugly stepsister, feminism, overturned our assumptions about what sex means and what it's for, we have almost forgotten how to form families, or what they are. Divorce laws have made the contract of marriage laughably easy to escape from, even as we have tightened up bankruptcy laws and canonized student loans as sacramental covenants. Voters—not just judges, real live American voters—have redefined marriage in several states to include homosexual unions. Single people can adopt children, and couples can cook them up in petri dishes, discarding the "surplus" embryos . . . [w]hat agenda is served by all these bizarre acts of rebellion against the plain nature of things and the immemorial structure of human society? Nothing so elevated or insane as Marxist-Leninism. Nothing so cool and mathematical as capitalism. The philosophy underpinning our current crisis, which explains our Keynesian politics and addiction to credit card debt, Europe's falling and our own flat birth rates, our willingness to tax our children (via deficits) instead of ourselves, is a simple creed known to every teenager: *"We want the world and we want it now,"* in the words of Dionysian rock-god Jim Morrison, who died a bloated shell of a man at age 28, leaving behind no acknowledged children, but at least 20 paternity suits filed by women he had abandoned.
>
> Repulsed by the gray "organizational men" who toiled without credit or creativity inside massive corporations, the young (who are now middle-aged) took as their creed a vulgar hedonism, papered over for some by New Left politics. Even when hippies cut their hair and got "real" jobs, the creeds they had popularized changed our economy and politics, all across the Western world. Gone was the stern frugality of the Depression generation, the optimistic fecundity of those who birthed

the Baby Boom. In its place came a cleverly calculating Epicureanism, a breed of men who lived for pleasure but knew how to avoid overdoses and V.D., who relied on now-legal abortion to clean up the unintended consequences of pleasure, who looked to vacant New Age spirituality, or endless acquisition for its own sake, with endorphin rushes from risk buffered by the certainty that their banks were "too big to fail." When the focus of life becomes not pursuing the Good, or even transmitting life so someone else has the chance to, and descends instead to the accumulation of diverse, amusing experiences, man as an organism ceases to function as he was built to. His machines, lazily tended, break down and fall apart. His governments, overburdened and underfunded, welsh on their debts. His countries are either depopulated or colonized by fertile foreigners. He looks around, and he shrugs. If he majored in English, he might use the line, as he shuffles offstage: "Not with a bang, but a wanker."

56. Why are the alternatives so stark? Why did your God make this instinct so insistent and yet so hard to use correctly?

For that, you'd have to ask Him. It would be easy, but not too helpful, simply to blame man's Fall. But there's a fundamental difficulty in the very nature of the thing: One of our strongest natural drives has as its object not a piece of steak or a crate of mangoes but another human being of equal importance to ourselves. That person has similar weaknesses, fears, human rights, flaws, neuroses, and battle scars—and an infuriatingly independent intellect and will. Dealing with him or her is less like scratching an itch than it is like playing Rubik's Cube at gunpoint, or chess in Grand Central Station. But the instincts entailed are nearly as urgent as hunger at nightfall or thirst on a sweaty day. And the consequences, by nature, can be enormous—in the form of that kid who will still be living on your couch at age twenty-eight.

No wonder we tried to wriggle out of this bind and imagined that the rise of penicillin and the Pill were a loophole that science had found in the human condition. In *Humanae Vitae*, Pope Paul VI was put in the unenviable position of reminding the world that things are more complicated than that—and that the rules for fulfilling primal urges *that entail other human beings* are rather tighter than those surrounding beekeeping or botany. The emergence of bold new sex plagues, the collapse of marriage, the traumas suffered by children of divorce, and the hordes of fatherless boys who head every year into prison—all these were actually simple for the Church to predict. Simple, but thankless. Mother Church is the cancer crank who shows you pictures of lungs of smokers.

She's the bedroom mirror you put away in the closet when your waist hits "44." She's the tribune of reason who whispers to you in a still small voice, "I told you so."[48]

57. You Catholics make marriage sound almost impossible to do well. And the divorce stats across most religions do seem to bear you out there, so I guess I'll concede your point. Maybe only a tiny minority of people are really "called" to marriage, and the rest of us weaklings should take on the simpler task of living quietly and alone as hermits, nuns, or priests. Except that you people don't seem to be able to match your own standards in those vocations, either.

You know what it means when someone always lives up to his standards? That they are pathetically low. I'm reminded of an old and beloved college president whose students were sure that he had personally hung the moon. What deeply impressed them about him was how convincingly he flattered them: He assured them that the education they were getting at his college made them better informed and wiser than graduates of Harvard (they weren't); insisted that each of them was sure to become a leader (they didn't); and when it came time for grades, he pretty much sat them in his lap like Santa Claus: "You want an A? Why of course you get an A. *Everybody* gets an A. Ho, ho, ho!" (They did.)

58. But maybe it's time for you people to admit defeat. I can't click on a newspaper without finding another major archdiocese or religious order getting sued to an inch of its life for shuffling sex abusers. The main orders of American nuns have been denounced by the Vatican for trading in rulers and penguin suits for feminism and Wicca. The number of priests is plummeting, and their average age is creeping up toward "Dead." I can't really find any style of life where being Catholic makes for peace and a quiet conscience. But I suppose all you'll say to that is some boilerplate about Christ coming "to bring a sword," and the "straight path" being narrow. To the rest of us, those old comebacks are cold comfort, smeared on toast.

You're right. I'm not here arguing that the Church is a persecuted ethnic minority or a harmless, much-put-upon cult that the state ought to tolerate out of respect for

---

[48] CCC, 2347

the one, true, god Diversity. Unlike an ethnic group or national creed, the Catholic Church makes universal claims—like those in the *Communist Manifesto* and the Declaration of Independence. The Catholic Church doesn't claim to be a nice place to worship for Irish, Croatians, Italians, and Filipinos. It's not a "welcoming praise and spirituality environment" such as offered by Unitarians behind their rainbow flags. It doesn't even say it's the proper faith for a particular people, as the Anglican Church does for Englishmen, and Judaism for Jews.

No, the Church makes a wilder, bolder claim. Without saying that other faiths are devoid of truth, she asserts that she is the "universal sacrament of salvation,"[49] and the mystical body of Jesus Christ, the incarnate Son of God. The one God, the only One. The God perceived more dimly in other faiths whose moral laws are written in the heart of every honest man. Wait, it gets weirder: The Church claims that this incarnate God comes down each day, thousands of times, in a way impervious to the eye, into the flat bread and cheap wine poured out on marble altars and plywood tables across the world by the frequently celibate, grossly imperfect men she anoints as priests. St. John Chrysostom once wrote that he trembled for the salvation of every priest—since their immense importance brought with it the gravest possible burdens. Another sainted priest, John Marie Vianney, wrote:

> If I were to meet a priest and an angel, I should salute the priest before I saluted the angel. The latter is the friend of God; but the priest holds His place. St. Teresa kissed the ground where a priest had passed. When you see a priest, you should say, "There is he who made me a child of God, and opened Heaven to me by holy Baptism; he who puri-fied me after I had sinned; who gives nourishment to my soul."

It's hardly fair to expect the whole world to accept this; it is literally a miracle that over a billion souls now do. As I do. But we cannot blame those who hold the Church to a sterner code than they hold rap singers or NASCAR drivers. Priests who claim to wield this kind of power, who have chosen to take up the cross, *should* behave better than scoutmasters, therapists, cops, and (even) New York City firemen. Catholics should not be angry or defensive or self-pitying when their Church is held to the hard, noble standards that she herself has set. We should be flattered. And then, when we

---

[49] CCC, 776, 779

remember that those standards came not from us but from a just God, we should be scared right out of our pants.[50]

59. So far as I can tell, a priest is just like a minister or a rabbi. They both teach and perform certain special ceremonies only they're allowed to do. What is so elevated and demanding about that?

OK, remember all that there was to say about bishops (chapter 5)—how they're the direct descendants of the apostles, via a laying on of hands, who have passed on the power the first bishops got from Christ at the Last Supper?

Sort of. You just keep piling up mysteries, one on top of the other.

This one isn't all that strange. It's analogous to DNA, in a way. I mean, even though you are a contemporary American—and so, like me, you need to join Ancestry.com to learn your grandparents' first names—you do admit to having ancestors, right? And that those ancestors had their own in turn, reaching back to 33 A.D., and presumably even further back than that, to monkeys and pond scum? In your own body today, there are genes and chromosomes that were present in those ancestors and were passed down person to person by means of activities that entailed the *laying on of hands* (at least). Well, the power of serving as bishop was passed along by one man recruiting another and handing along his powers, which came from Christ. And priests are simply assistants to the bishop, minus some of his powers and privileges. (For instance, they can't ordain other priests or bishops.) So in a real sense every priest is a descendant of one of the twelve apostles. Or I should say one of the *eleven*; Judas did not go off and start his own apostolic succession, tempting as that explanation might be at times (depending on the bishop).

I think the source of your discomfort is this: The leaders of the Reformation, in response to the loathsome corruption and neurotic Pelagianism that pervaded the Church in their time, reinvented Christianity as an *existential religion for individuals*, centered on internal submission to God as He makes Himself known to each believer's conscience. You can learn of the gospel from an apostle in a catacomb, or via a televangelist over the airwaves—it doesn't matter—and so make a perfect act of faith "accepting Jesus Christ as your personal lord and savior." That's how you "get saved." Rituals, sacraments, times, places, things—bodies, in short, and the whole of the material universe—are mere distractions from what happens inside the believer's head or heart. *That's* where the action is. You could describe Protestantism (a little uncharitably) as Stoicism-plus-Jesus. If we see it as a pathway to heaven, it's like the Interstate Highway System, minus most of the roadsigns and the maps.

What Catholics believe is that Christ really founded something starkly different: *a ritual faith for a family*, in fact for a whole new people—a reborn and universal

---

[50] CCC, 1541-1547

Israel, with Christ succeeding Moses as lawgiver, Aaron as High Priest, and every one of the prophets. He passed along His authority to the apostles, which they shared with their priests, to govern and nurture through the sacraments a corporate Body that would be "saved." We each still have to work on our personal relationship with God, but we do so using the tools laid out for us, within a framework we didn't invent, submitting to authorities we never voted on, alongside brethren we'd never pick. Catholicism is a huge, dysfunctional, cringe-worthy family whose infinite sticky tentacles no member can ever escape. It is Mama, it is the Mafia, it's a grueling haul to heaven on the Greyhound that we sit through grumbling about how we "just missed the Acela." There's no quiet car, flush toilet, or Wi-Fi, the whole thing reeks of garlic, and sometimes they plug in a driver who's clearly drunk. But he's the only guy on board with a license. So as the Council of Trent decreed (session XXVI), "Sit back and leave the driving to us."

60. Given the scandals, when you see a priest, you don't wonder if he's one of the bad ones?

Twenty years ago, you would have been right. But today, if there's one institution on earth where the perverts have been hunted down and denied access to kids, it's the Catholic Church in America. For that we have to be thankful to the trial lawyers and the reporters. (And I am—there ought to be some sort of papal medal given the pro-abortion atheists over at the *Boston Globe*. Perhaps "The Order of the Assyrians.") As we speak, those freaks with the urge to molest children will have to find gigs at places that are harder to investigate and less lucrative to sue.

No, when I see a priest—as when I see an American serviceman or a New York City cop—my first thought is "*Thank* you . . ." In fact, just as some patriotic Americans when they meet a soldier or sailor go up and tell him, "Thank you for your service," I think that Catholics ought to offer the same morale-booster to priests and nuns. Maybe we could start a clerical version of the USO—minus the Playboy bunnies, but serving better whiskey.

Flannery O'Connor put it best, to my mind, when she wrote to a soul who complained that priests did not live up to his high standards: "It is easy for any child to pick out the faults in the sermon on his way home from Church every Sunday. It is impossible for him to find out the hidden love that makes a man, in spite of his intellectual limitations, his neuroticism, his own lack of strength, give up his life in the service of God's people, however bumblingly he may go about it."

Myself, I'm especially grateful every time I go to confession. I am also thankful for Mass, of course, but it often seems that the priests are grateful, too. Confecting the sacrament, offering *in persona Christi* the perfect sacrifice, feeding Christ's people the saving Food . . . the priests I've known have told me that this is the high point of their lives. (All the more reason why liturgists shouldn't crowd the sanctuary with laymen poaching on their role.)

I cannot imagine taking the same satisfaction in hearing confessions. In the church where I used to go to be shriven the priest who faithfully staffed the booth each Saturday was clearly in his '70s. His old voice creaked through the grille, gentle but serious, and on my way out after penance I found myself wondering about the man. What path drew him to this place? Is he sick at heart, after all these years, of hearing week in and week out how stubborn and irreformable are our hearts? How is his health? And then, more selfishly: What will we do without him?

The last survey I could find on the average age of American priests put it at sixty, and that number comes from 1999; perhaps we'd rather not hear how much worse the situation has gotten since. A priest in my area told me that his bishop fairly begs elderly clerics not to retire—so most of them don't. They keep on straining to raise chalices, bending old necks beneath the stole, long past the age the rest of us hang up our aprons. They serve generations such as mine that have failed to replenish their ranks. In the year after I was born, 1965, there were 994 priests ordained in America. In 2008 there were only 480. (On the bright side, the dioceses with solid bishops and orthodox seminaries, and the priestly groups who offer the Latin Mass, are bursting with vocations—as are convents where nuns wear their habits and follow their Rules.) Still, for now, the only reason many of us have parish priests at all is that so many men—perhaps too many of the wrong sort of men—were ordained back in the 1950s and 1960s.

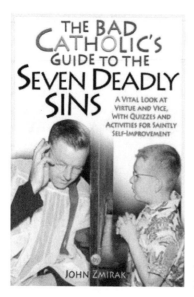

While the number of clergy involved in abuse is a tiny percentage, the ugliness of the crimes and the callousness of their cover-up have for now made squalid and pornographic the public perception of our priests. The media doesn't have to make things up, just highlight them, to drain the Church's credibility, even among believers. For *The Bad Catholic's Guide to the Seven Deadly Sins*, we chose as the cover photo a quaint old 1950s picture of a priest hearing a boy's confession. When I showed the picture to a fervent Catholic friend, he winced. "I don't know. Might people think it's kind of . . . pervy?"

I almost snarked back: "When you hear that someone's Italian, do you assume he's in the Mafia?" But my quick Celtic temper gave way to Slavic sadness, as I thought back on all the good priests I've been blessed to know over the decades. Father Pezzullo, Father Mulloney, Father Grisaitis, Father Hardon, Father Shelley, Father Spriggs . . . I can't list their names without my eyes tearing up. These men deserved better than to land in the ditch where the priesthood seems to lie today— when policemen in once-Catholic countries are drilling into the coffins of dead archbishops in search of incriminating documents. That didn't happen in *The Da Vinci Code*; it happened scant years ago in Belgium. When I read the reports, I wanted to be outraged at the state's incursion on the Church. But I couldn't. My weary thought was, "Was that really necessary? If so, God help us."

Will we ever again have rectories full enough to let our priests live in communities? Not in my lifetime. How many young men today are ready to serve as circuit-riding hermits, living in large and haunted Gothic buildings, driving hundreds of miles every week to say Mass for laymen they'll barely know? It sounds like a stark and comfortless life to me, one I'd have trouble urging on any young man. Maybe I'm part of the problem.

St. Thomas teaches that grace perfects and builds on nature. Spiritual writers assure us that God will provide us the consolations we need to follow the call He sends us. I will take that on faith, and remember to pray that He do that for all our priests. Thinking of the humanly desolate situation so many priests face today helps me to see them in full color and three dimensions—not as the functionaries of a billion-man religion, impersonal channels of sanctifying grace, or even (God forbid), as one nasty sacristy rat I knew used to say, "sacrament machines." Without losing respect for the uncanny spiritual powers with which they have been vested, I have learned to see them more as men. Each one is a priest as my dad was a father, and each one carries a cross.

61. Wasn't the abuse scandal inevitable, given your so-called celibate priesthood?

You're right, of course. Because the first thing that someone attracted to teenaged boys thinks of when he can't seduce one is, "Oh well, I guess I'll just go home and sleep with my *wife*." The only problem is that these priests weren't married, so they didn't have a little lady back at home whom they could dress up in a Boy Scout uniform. What a pity the Church didn't think of this simple precaution—ordaining married men, because *marriage cures men of the urge to have sex with anyone else*, of any age and either sex. Statistics show this, of course. No married men ever cheat on their spouses, not even those so emotionally stunted as to prefer sex with twelve-year-old boys whom they can dominate in a power relationship and shame into secrecy. If only more people understood the *magical* power of the sacrament . . . Next we have to get the NCAA to lift the celibacy requirement from football coaches.

Image courtesy of Wikipedia Commons, uploaded by Mhrmaw.

Russian "Matryoschka" dolls take their name from the honorific title given the typically "formidable" wives of Orthodox parish priests.

62. OK, smart guy. Point taken. But if you opened up the priesthood to married men, wouldn't you attract fewer *weirdos*?

I know what you're talking about. I also know plenty of men who might have made excellent priests who simply couldn't imagine leading the lonely life of a celibate in our sex-drenched society. There is nothing wrong with married priests in principle. It violates no doctrine, which is why the Church has thousands of married priests in Eastern Catholic churches, and among Protestant ministers who converted to Catholicism. In fact, given the desperate shortage of vocations in the West, in order to make sure that the Church kept up her primary mission—which isn't running schools or meddling in immigration policy but *administering the sacraments*—I've sometimes thought it might be smart to cautiously introduce more married priests.

Here's one big problem: If it paid a decent salary (enough to support a family), the priesthood might attract droves of underachieving men with useless master's degrees in things like pastoral psychology or education, great steaming piles of student debt, and the misconception that they were somehow qualified to "counsel and lead." More likely, given the fact that your average Catholic is still dropping in the collection basket that same $1 bill he used to give back in 1979, the priests' kids would simply starve.

So the only way I can imagine a widespread use of married priests in the West would be if we moved from a "tenure" to an "adjunct" model of priesthood: Instead of thinking of priests as *those unmarried Irish guys who drink Jameson's together at the rectory we fund through those bingo games*[51] *and who are at our disposal 24/7 because, face it—what else do they have to do?* the Church might get along just fine with priests who worked full time at regular jobs (I especially like the idea of priests who are also cops), lived offsite with their families, and who once or twice a week came by and heard confessions or said Mass. Each parish could have a team of eight or ten such priests—who wouldn't draw a salary but would do this work as their service to the Church. We'd still want celibate pastors, I think, and by tradition bishops and monks (as in the East) would come from the ranks of those men whose whole lives were wedded to Christ and His Church, and not to the bossy *matryoshka* who's in charge of the parish's potlucks and gossip. And those of you with experience among our separated brethren will know of the perennial problems raised by rebellious randy youths, as noted by Protestant poets John Hurley and Ronnie Wilkins:

> The only one who could ever reach me,
> Was the son of a preacher man,
> The only boy who could ever teach me,
> Was the son of a preacher man,
> Yes he was, he was, oh yes he was.

Consider yourself duly warned.

---

[51] Except in the Diocese of Brooklyn, which at least in my own experience, funded its operations through high-stakes, Mafia-protected, and police-supervised poker games, and high-priced, easy annulments. But that was back in the '70s and things are probably better there now. Especially the hairstyles.

Still, I wouldn't be the least bit upset if we had more married priests. One of the best pastors I ever had was a married priest at a Melkite parish I attended in New Hampshire, and knowing him helped me overcome my resistance to the idea.

There's just one thing I'd like to whisper in the ear of any pope who considered opening the priesthood up to married men: He should include at the bottom of that press release an infallible, ex cathedra statement reiterating the fact that women cannot be ordained. Of course, there's no theological connection between those two issues. They're as different as chalk and chiggers, but Catholic dissenters—ably assisted by the media—persist in linking them. So if a pope were to decide to ordain married men, invincibly ignorant publications like the *New York Times* and the *National Catholic Reporter* would portray it as a "concession" and pretend it was just a matter of time before the pope went ahead and ordained women too.[52]

CBEOCBEOCBEOCBEOCBEOCBEOCBEOCBEOCBEOCBEOCBEOCBEOCBEOCBEOCB

FAQs from Your Stoner Neighbor #8
If you think the priesthood is so marvelous, and there's such a tragic shortage, why don't you consider joining up? Have you ever looked into the priesthood?

If you met me, you wouldn't ask that. Priests to whom I've even mentioned the idea have either—depending on temperament—spat coffee on me while breaking down with laughter or turned white as if I'd trod on their grandma's grave, then whispered: "No, no, *no* . . . " Still, there was a brief episode in my teen years where I was haunted by this idea. Whenever I tell the story it makes my friends gasp over their omelets.

In the bleakness of my post-Catholic high school in the 1980s, one teacher fought for the Faith. I owe a thank-you note to Miss Gertrude Best, a slim and ascetic middle-aged lady who taught us in history class about the communist persecutions of the Church—even as down the hall the jaded ex-seminarians taught us "liberation" in lieu of theology. My friend and I became her acolytes, starved as we were for facts about our Faith.

---

[52] For 497 pages of Teutonic proof that women priests are not an option, see *Women in the Priesthood?: A Systematic Analysis in the Light of the Order of Creation and Redemption*, by Manfred Hauke (Ignatius, Press: San Francisco, 1988), and also CCC, 1577.

To offer us some protein, Miss Best was kind enough to drive us every week to sit in on the theology classes she was taking with Rev. John Hardon, S.J., at St. John's University. While the man was brilliant, the classes were dull—based as they were on impenetrable phenomenological addresses by Pope John Paul II. But I made the most of the question periods, probing that saintly priest with all the Faith-testing, Jesuitical questions that sixteen-year-old smart alecks are driven to ask. And Father Hardon parried them brilliantly, as Jesuits have done for centuries. He shot down in flames every doubt my personal Screwtape had whispered in my ear and built up in my mind solid habits of faithful reasoning. I will be grateful to him in eternity, I hope.

When my high school friend expressed an interest in the priesthood, Father Hardon offered advice: "I wish that I could recommend you apply to the Society of Jesus," he said in his careful way. "I love the order, and wish it could be saved. But I cannot in good conscience send any young man into its seminaries. The closest thing today . . ." And that was how Father Hardon sent my friend and me to visit the Legionaries of Christ. (Yes, that's the order that the Vatican found out sixty years too late had been founded by a sociopathic pedophile. Now may I move on?)

We attended what promised to be an ordinary retreat and were deeply impressed at the hordes of healthy, energetic young men wearing cassocks and playing soccer. The Mass was slow and reverent, though the chapel was modern and hideous. (I'd come to learn later that they built things this way on purpose, which still puzzles me.) Then the high-ranking fortysomething priest came out to address us in the chapel, and I had what some worried friends still call my "James Joyce moment." Perhaps it was his starkly military bearing, the solid jut of his jaw, or his metallic Dublin accent, but that talk in the chapel really does seem in retrospect like a snippet from *A Portrait of the Artist as a Young Man*. I'll do my best, at a distance of thirty years, to reproduce the heart of the rector's remarks and my silent responses.

Before the Lord God created the material universe, He knew one thing. Would you like to hear what it was? He knew the names of every man He would call to serve Him as a holy priest at the altar. He had them written down, if you will, in the Book of Life. He knew that He would create them for that one purpose, and that purpose alone.

Wow . . . I never thought of it that way. Cool!

Now imagine that you're a potter, and you're working with a piece of lowly clay, trying to make it into a coffee cup. That is the purpose for which you got the clay in the first place. You try to shape it to serve its purpose, but this clay says, "I will not serve!" It resists your hand, and insists on turning into an ashtray. Tell me, what are you, the potter, going to do with that rebellious lump of clay?

Um, use it as an ashtray?

You're going to throw it into the everlasting fire, where it will burn up and be utterly forgotten. Then you'll take up a new piece of clay that will be obedient to your wishes and form that into the coffee cup that you wanted.

Gulp. Gag.

Now, I'm not saying that each and every one of you here today is called to serve God as one of His holy priests at the altar. I would not presume to know. But ask yourselves in prayer, in the solitude of your room tonight, why else would God have brought you to this very special vocations retreat?

With that, the priest crossed himself, dipped to the floor in a mechanically perfect genuflection to the tabernacle (which was made, I think, out of Legos), and marched out of the room. And I felt as if the soccer-playing priest had punched me straight in the solar plexus. My rational mind, which Father Hardon had helped me hone, shut down like a busted TV. In its place, I was ruled by my gut, which was twisting the way it did when my father wielded his belt: "Maybe I have to become a priest or . . . go to hell."

I hadn't known this was a vocations retreat. And yet here I was. Did that fact prove that God's hand had moved me here like a chess pawn? (As a teenager I was unusually superstitious.) I had never for one moment been attracted to the priesthood. I'd hated serving as an altar boy, knocking over candlesticks and burning up with self-consciousness every moment I stood in the sanctuary . . . sure on some primal level that I didn't belong up there. As much as I loved some of the priests in my parish, and feared the others, the thought of living in a house full of other men repelled me. The prospect of lifelong celibacy seemed implausible and appalling. Indeed, there wasn't a single aspect of the priesthood that appealed to me, except the prospect of delivering angry sermons that no one would dare to interrupt.

But maybe what I wanted, on any level and with any part of my soul, was completely beside the point. (I would later learn from former students at Legionary high schools that their priests said precisely this, that any repugnance at the prospect of the priesthood was entirely irrelevant to the question of their vocations—and might even be proof of a calling.) The clay that wanted to be an ashtray hadn't been consulted about its wishes, but when it rebelled it paid the price. If I refused this evident call, if not from God then from one of His holy priests, would I be saying, with Satan, *"Non serviam"*? I thought of the Lake of Fire, the Second Death, the worm that does not die, and it was in this spirit of calm reflection that I explored the question of my vocation.

Through my next panicked week, I read every Catholic book I could get my hands on. I raced through St. Augustine's *Confessions*, wondering if my resistance to the rector's speech was akin to the young Augustine's vicious theft of figs. I did my best to understand St. Ignatius's *Spiritual Exercises*, taking from it only a sense of the solemn demands made by the vocation that loomed like a .38 at my ear. I lost sleep, spent hours agonizing before the Blessed Sacrament, and walked through the day as if on a tightrope over the leaping flames of hell. Oddly, it never occurred to me to talk to anyone, priest or layman, about my dilemma. A priest had already spoken to me, and God awaited my answer.

And then it came to me, almost all at once: If an apparition of the Sacred Heart came to me and told me I was called to the priesthood, I know what I would say. *I would say no.*

All at once, I felt light and free. Surely, I reasoned, part of any vocation to the priesthood must be a basic willingness to pursue that vocation, especially if it came in the form of a divine apparition. Having searched myself, I didn't have that docility. Not one tiny speck of it. Thank God! I kept my Faith, decided I was called someday to marriage, and went on with my life, now free of terrors.

Some of my friends have found this story troubling—not that any of them ever thought I was meant to be a priest. Still, wasn't my reaction a little bit . . . Luciferian? Wasn't I warning God not to put me to a test I planned to fail?

No, not a bit. My reaction was the right one, and I'm ready to answer for it on judgment day.

I wasn't saying no to God but to a callously manipulative man who was threatening earnest teenagers with hellfire the better to pad his recruitment numbers. His account of God was ill-suited to Christianity and his recruiting technique better suited to the Communist Party, USA, than to the holy altar of God. The more I've learned since then about Legionary founder Rev. Marcial Maciel's idea of docility—perfect conformity to the will of God as expressed in Maciel's whims—the more thankful

I am that I fought off this moment of cult-style recruitment. It wasn't Satan moving me to refuse. It was my guardian angel, stirring my natural Celtic cussedness and wholesome self-respect to warn me away from a group whose founder saw baptized Christians as Play-Doh to be twisted at the whims of human superiors.

I was always repelled by the cult of idolatrous human obedience that I learned of from friends in the Legionaries or their lay offshoot, Regnum Christi. I winced at stories of young men kept in the seminary for eight, ten, or twelve years—then summoned to hear the news that they "weren't called" to the priesthood but to marriage. And here was a nice, low-paying job working for one of R.C.'s many ministries . . .

I know one laywoman who'd slaved for a year in an R.C. job she hated, who told her spiritual director that she was sliding into depression. He rebuked her for elevating her own wishes over the will of God, as expressed in the decrees of her superiors. The misery she was feeling was the residue of her selfishness being burned away in the crucible of holy suffering. Left aside was the other possibility: that she was suffering because she was in an abusive situation, which the mind the good God gave her was screaming at her to flee. (She did flee, and is now a happily married, faithful mom.)

It's not surprising to me that, in an age where bishops, clergy, and teachers were making up the Faith as they went along, earnest, well-meaning Catholics would cluster around a seemingly solid order staffed with outwardly well-formed priests. I remember daydreaming about the Restoration these cassocked athletes would some-day lead. What has confused me was why orthodox Catholics would embrace a system that so disregarded, even despised, the natural goods of creation—such as the psyches, talents, and freedom of the people recruited by this order. Perhaps it was simply a case of the theological virtues, falsely conceived, eating the natural ones for fiber. Or maybe it was really the ideological mind, best diagnosed by Eric Hoffer in his matchless *The True Believer*, which yoked men to other totalitarian movements, from Nuremberg to Phnom Penh.

I was shocked by the callous way in which the system disposed of seminarians and laymen, treating them like cannon fodder sent to fill the trenches. Of course, it was all in the service of holy and super-natural goods—which would somehow, one had to take on faith, benefit someone's soul at some point. Such rationales also soothed the consciences of bishops who covered up abuses; it's all too easy to glibly conflate one's personal or institutional interest with noble, even eternal motives. That is the heart, I think, of what makes a man a Phari-see. This temptation is certainly not limited to the leadership of an order that is now dis-graced by its founder's hypocrisy.

It is interesting to think: What would make a man like Father Maciel come up with such a system, one designed to hammer and break the human will under the blows of icy obedience? What kind of man would come up with such spiritual Bolshevism? An outright sociopath who craved the power to micromanage souls—and also perhaps a man who knew his own soul to be deeply, almost irredeemably corrupt. Projecting his own sordid state onto the innocents he recruited, he imposed on them the kind of grinding discipline he himself would have required—if he were actually trying to crush his pedophile tendencies. He left his cancerous soul to canker and prescribed chemotherapy to the healthy. He invented a mechanism for taming sex abusers and applied it to everyone but himself.

Mother Shipton?

From an Original Picture in the Possession of Ralph Ouerley Esq.ʳ

Back to my James Joyce moment. Some friends have chuckled at the story, then raised the nervous objection: "But what if an apparition really had come and said you had a vocation? I mean, the Sacred Heart . . ." At this point they'd wince, afraid of blasphemy. I haven't always known just what to say, sure in my gut that I was right but uncertain about the arguments.

Then I did more reading on the nature of apparitions and the Church's rules for discerning spirits. And now I have the answer: If that priest's talk had been followed by an apparition, it would have been a false one. St. John of the Cross warns us (and the Church agrees) that most of them are false—the products either of hysteria or the devil. I hadn't learned all this by age sixteen, of course. Still, I had the good sense to stay away from shrines like "Our Lady of the Roses" in Bayside, Queens—where a whacked-out Catholic housewife claimed that Our Lady showed up each week to condemn documents of Vatican II and individual rock-n-roll albums. These Marian updates had begun at my sister's parish, St. Robert Bellarmine, but at the pastor's request, Our Lady had graciously relocated to the Vatican Pavilion of the 1964 World's Fair. The blessed rose petals from this shrine were a hot item among those seeking miracles in Queens.

Father Hardon himself was sent by the local diocese out to Flushing Meadow Park to investigate this apparition (whose followers still flock to Latin Masses in New York City wearing trademark blue berets). He reported to our class, "These phenomena are not merely hysterical or fraudulent. What I saw there was diabolical." Maybe the formation I'd received from priests like Father Hardon had taught me to sniff out brimstone. That's one thing real priests, with real vocations, are called to do.

CRISO CRISO CRISO CRISO CRISO CRISO CRISO CRISO CRISO CRISO CRISO CRISO CRISO CRISO CRISO

63. So counting down through seven, I guess we're down to the last sacrament.

Indeed we are.

So what's it called?

That *is* what it's called.

What is?

The Last Sacrament.

O for Christ's sake . . .

That is why we engage in it, yes. But also for the sake of a sinner's soul and body—in that order. Performing it edifies the former and sometimes heals the latter.

Performing *what*?

The Last Sacrament. Aren't you paying attention? It's also called Extreme Unction, in case that helps.

64. Oh, loads. I totally get it now. It's some really potent ointment—like Extra Strength Aveeno for Infants with Eczema.

Anointing is involved, so you're getting closer. OK, since this is strictly speaking a catechetical work and not an Abbott and Costello bit: The Last Sacrament is also called the Anointing of the Sick. But for centuries Catholics typically waited to call for it until they were pretty much dying. The Church has tried to restore the more ancient practice, of people receiving this sacrament whenever they're quite ill, either critically or chronically. It entails a priest—not a well-meaning layman or even a sweet-natured nun with a banjo and balloons—visiting a sick person either at home or in the hospital, praying with him and anointing various, symbolically important parts of his body. The effect is to offer him spiritual strength, absolution for his sins, and sometimes even physical recovery.[53]

---

[53] CCC, 1510–1516

65. Symbolically important parts of the body? If we weren't discussing dying, I'd be tempted to ask . . .

The Church is way ahead of you here. According to the preternaturally deadpan 1907 *Catholic Encyclopedia*, the anointing entails:

> the unction with oil, specially blessed by the bishop, of the organs of the five external senses (eyes, ears, nostrils, lips, hands), of the feet, and, for men (where the custom exists and the condition of the patient permits of his being moved), of the loins or reins; and in the following form repeated at each unction with mention of the corresponding sense or faculty: "Through this holy unction and His own most tender mercy may the Lord pardon thee whatever sins or faults thou hast committed [*quidquid deliquisti*] by sight [by hearing, smell, taste, touch, walking, carnal delectation]." The unction of the loins is generally, if not universally, omitted in English-speaking countries,[54] and it is of course everywhere forbidden in case of women.

You really can't make this stuff up. But of course, we never did. Christ set the example for us by pouring out His strength to heal the sick wherever He went, and St. James wrote a fairly explicit description of how we could follow in His footsteps: "Is any sick among you? let him call for the elders of the church; and let them pray over him, anointing him with oil in the name of the Lord: And the prayer of faith shall save the sick, and the Lord shall raise him up; and if he have committed sins, they shall be forgiven him" (James 5:14–15).

The Protestant Reformers came along to deny that this practice was really a sacrament, with Calvin going so far as to call it a "hypocritical stageplay" and insisting that any biblical reference to the apostles' healing the sick referred to the brief period of extraordinary miracles that followed closely on Pentecost. But once the miracles stopped, it was time for Christians to cut it out, lest they "insult the Holy Spirit by making his power consist in a filthy oil of no efficacy" (*Institutes of the Christian Religion* 4.19.20). The trouble is that Christians in the East as well as the West, and even in schismatic groups that had split off in the fourth century, had all practiced the anointing of the sick and given it the kind of importance one gives a sacrament. Such a rite is one of the short list of things that Monophysites and Nestorians, Jesuits and monks of Mt. Athos, all hold in common. So if the Church got this wrong, that means she went astray and started writing "stageplays" pretty early on—right around the same time she decided which books went in the New Testament. Maybe we should reconsider that one too—toss out the weirdness of John's

---

[54] The Brits were not above committing sins of the flesh (see Oscar Wilde and Henry VIII), but their sense of tact and decorum prohibited mentioning them, even to a priest at one's deathbed. The Irish, for their part, averred, "You t'ank I'm touchin' him *there*? You got another thing coming, buddy-boy!"

Revelation, and include something much more obviously edifying, like the *Aeneid*. That way, when a priest came to anoint a dying sinner, he could start off by warning everyone present that what they were about to see was *not* a sacrament, and then recite from scripture:

> A reading from Book Six:
> A further thing is this: your friend's dead
> body—
> Ah, but you don't know!—lies out there unburied,
> Polluting all your fleet with death
> While you are lingering, waiting on my counsel
> Here at my door. First give the man his rest,
> Entomb him; lead black beasts to sacrifice;
> Begin with these amends.[55]
> The word of the Lord.

> R: Thanks be to God.

66. OK, what does the ritual really say?

I'll give you a short selection from the *Rituale Romanum*, in English translation. (Even some Trads prefer that this sacrament be conducted in the vernacular; forcing a dying man to flip through a Latin/English missal is wanton cruelty.)

> We beg you, our Redeemer, to cure by the grace of the Holy Spirit this sick man's (woman's) infirmity. Heal his (her) wounds, and forgive his (her) sins. Rid him (her) of all pain of body and mind. Restore him (her), in your mercy, to full health of body and soul, so that having recovered by your goodness, he (she) may take up his (her) former duties. We ask this of you who live and reign with the Father and the Holy Spirit, God, forever and ever.
> All: Amen.
> Let us pray.
> We entreat you, Lord, to look with favor on your servant, N., who is weak and failing, and refresh the life you have created. Chastened by suffering, may he (she) know that he (she) has been saved by your healing; through Christ our Lord.
> All: Amen.
> Let us pray.
> Holy Lord, almighty Father, everlasting God, in pouring out the grace of your blessing on the bodies of the sick, you show your loving care

---

[55] This is taken from the finest contemporary English version, by Robert Fitzgerald.

for your creatures. And so now as we call on your holy name, come and free your servant from his (her) illness and restore him (her) to health; reach out your hand and raise him (her) up; strengthen him (her) by your might; protect him (her) by your power; and give him (her) back in all desired well-being to your holy Church; through Christ our Lord.

All: Amen.

67. It seems to me that Calvin had a point. If your sacrament had much power to help people get better, why would they hold off on it until they'd pretty much given up hope? Why should we take seriously all those prayers for healing when (as you admit) they seem to have no bodily effect?

At this point, a more philosophically grounded apologist for Catholicism would give you a clear exposition of the mysterious interaction between our prayers for *what we want* and God's providence in giving us instead what we really *need*. But that has already been done far better than I can, in C. S. Lewis's *Miracles*, so I'm tempted to refer you to that. Or simply to invoke the classic headline from *The Onion*:

God Answers Prayers Of Paralyzed Little Boy
'No,' Says God

But instead, I'll just point out the obvious. If God granted the answer we wanted to every prayer of petition, consider the consequences:

- Every little girl in Manhattan would have a pony. And maybe a slave.
- Every boy would have a real, live gun.
- Every teen girl would have Barbie's physique.
- Every boy would be Spider-Man.
- Every fourth-grade math teacher would, at some point, simply drop dead.

- Every eighth-grade boy would in fact get the chance to "date" identical twins.
- Every meter maid would go blind.
- Every member of Congress of the *other* political party would drive off some bridge in Massachusetts or turn up unctioning his loins in JPEGs he accidentally e-mailed to the media.
- No pet would ever die—except those living next door that never stop baying at shadows.
- Your kids really never *would* grow up. They'd stay your favorite age forever.
- Divorce would become unnecessary in a world full of merry widows.
- I'd be paid to play computer strategy games like "Europa Universalis" instead of editing books.

The point is clear: The entire world would come to a crashing halt if God passed along His omnipotence into our sweaty little praying hands. He might not have a watertight plan for each of us that is impervious to our petitions—otherwise, when Christ told us to pray, He would have been simply taunting us. But He isn't going to let us remake the universe to suit our every wish. And part of the universe is this: Material things decay. Our bodies are material things, and therefore each of them will go the way of all flesh, which is, they tell me, grass. And grass gets mowed, by a Swede with a scythe.

As Augustine explained, we were made from the "dust of the earth" and imbued with the Spirit of God. He granted us protection from the fires and falls, sharp teeth and intestinal parasites, that afflict every other living critter. (It's unclear what He had in mind once men got really busy obeying orders to be fruitful and multiply—though the Assumption of the Blessed Virgin Mary, who lacked Original Sin, gives us a tantalizing hint.) But once we made it obvious via Adam and Eve that mankind would prove to be a "high maintenance" species, God withdrew those gifts.[56] We started to die like everything else—like all those animals who never sin, whose death is not a punishment or even a spiritual medicine (Tolkien called death the "gift of men"), but simply the necessary outcome of being born. Animals don't like to die, of course, but they don't spend years consumed with the fear of it, as we do.

We are outraged by our mortality and that of those whom we love. Sure, the people we hate are also mortal, but that is cold comfort. Grave dancing is much less fun than it sounds, even when it's done as an Irish jig. The death of terrorists and dictators in no way restores the lives they have claimed—safe as we feel that they

[56] CCC, 1008

are finally out of the way. The death of anyone seems to diminish everyone, as John Donne pointed out in his classic sermon "No Man Is an Island."

So if God granted our prayers, nobody whom you loved would ever die, heaven would be empty, and there would be no room for new folks to get born. But life and health are good things, and suffering in itself is purely evil—though Christ teaches us how to recycle the toxic stuff. So He invites us to pray for them, even as we accept the fact that at some point each of us will pass his divinely appointed "Sell-By" date.

68. Considering what we're talking about, you seem remarkably chipper. Do you know something I don't? Did the Virgin Mary appear to you and let you know that you'd never have to face illness and death?

Quite the contrary. The men who draw up statistics have told me pretty much exactly how I will die—slowly, of cancer. Both my parents and one of my sisters did, and my other sister fought off breast cancer, God bless her. (After her partial mastectomy, I came by to congratulate her with a box of *Minni di Virgini*, the breast-shaped cookies made by pious, pervy Italians in honor of St. Agatha—who had hers cut off by the Romans during her martyrdom, then restored to her by St. Peter so she could die intact. Sis stared at me in her deadpan way and shook her head: "You're pretty

much the only person on earth who would make this kind of gesture." I answered, "You're welcome!) I've already discussed this subject in public, so rather than reinvent the wheel of Fate, I'll share with you the article I published on it at *Crisis* magazine, when my poor sister Christine got her terminal diagnosis. Its title is one I'm sure my critics will appreciate:

John Zmirak Must Die

No, really. All kidding aside. I mean it. I know it may be hard for some of you to accept. (For others, it might seem too good to be true.) But, barring the Second Coming, it's absolutely certain: Someday, the Zmirak supply will simply run out. Sure, it will be for some the end of an institution, like the last Manhattan show in the Broadway run of *Cats*, or the last Kennedy in congress. But it's really going to happen, and if any of you have strong emotions on the subject, consider how I feel. For me, the prospect looms rather more ominously, acquiring perhaps a spurious air of epochal importance. Think of those creepy History Channel programs that (wistfully) depict a world without people; in one episode, there's a close-up computer rendition of the Chrysler Building collapsing. Now imagine that it's falling on top of me. That's how I'm feeling at the moment.

Because, you see, I just this weekend received the news. Maybe the memo was going to my Spam folder, but I'd never before realized, down deep in the bone, that someday my bones will be gnawed clean by tiny critters and armies of microorganisms. That the self I've spent so many years buffing and honing to a fine polish of eccentricity will simply vanish from the earth, to face one of three grim fates:

(a) Eternal punishment with the devil and all his angels, in the lake of fire where the worm dieth not.

(b) Flames of purgation hotter than any on earth, that will burn away most of what I myself have contributed to the mixture, leaving at best a tiny nub of human identity, probably around the size of a roasted peanut.

(c) Utter oblivion.

Given what I've been taught about options (a) and (b), I find myself daydreaming about ending up with (c)—all of which goes to show you that atheism is the fruit of wishful thinking. When I read St. Thomas Aquinas's account of the theoretical state called limbo—perfect natural happiness, marred only by the lack of the Beatific Vision—I'll confess that my first thought was, "Can't I just pick limbo? I never asked to play at the high-stakes table, and I'm not sure how I got up here. Let me slip away to the quarter slot machines and the skill cranes, and I'll try not to make any noise."

I wonder how many Catholics, if offered the certainty of limbo instead of the fear of hell, would take it, instead of holding out on the off-chance they'll make it to heaven. Those tormented by scruples might even settle for less than an eternity spent playing checkers with Seneca and embrace oblivion, instead of taking chances on hell. But those options aren't on the table. Here we are, at the World Championship of Poker, playing against the Mafia, almost out of chips, and drawing to an inside straight. Still, the Dealer insists He's on our side . . .

What brought these Lenten thoughts home to me this week was the news that yet another close relative of mine has been diagnosed with what is likely a serious cancer—one with grim survival stats. Grieved as I felt for her, I watched with self-disgust as my concerns quickly turned inward. My mind leaped in just a few minutes from the prospect of her suffering to blankly selfish thoughts: "That makes four out of four of my closest genetic connections, stricken with one variety or another. One beat it, but two are dead." Which tells me not just that someday I'm going to die, but very likely how I'll die: Slowly, over months, just like my mother and father did, surrounded by people feeding me false hopes and applesauce, while a TV flickers and the pain gets every single day more crushing, more soul extinguishing.

Because what I've learned from watching cancer is, There's Never Enough Morphine. For one thing, doctors can't give you enough to ease the pain that comes at the end, hemmed in as they are by fear of lawsuits by—get ready—*patients* who miraculously recover and then sue their doctors for getting them addicted to painkillers. Yes, there really are people out there who respond to beating "terminal cancer" by doing this, with the outcome that thousands of patients like my mother end up screaming through some of their final days—until at last the doctors see that there's no danger of recovery, and they open the floodgates of opiates, which typically (and mercifully) slows down

breathing, sometimes stops it. Some persnickety ethicists out there complain that this amounts to euthanasia. I'd like a few moments alone with them in a cancer ward, with a bag of surgical instruments. I could teach them the redemptive value of suffering.

I'll never forget my mother sitting at home on our couch (as she did until two days before she died—through a Catholic home hospice) with the computerized morphine drip that gave her steady, always insufficient doses of the stuff, as the tumor quietly thrived—a tumor she'd earned over decades through the Marlboro "Lungs for Clothing" trade-in program. (Which is really neat, by the way: You send them little pieces of your lungs, and they ship you T-shirts and jackets with their logo. Mom had quite a collection by the end.) Having spent the better part of twenty years at bingo and high-stakes poker games in church basements all through the Diocese of Brooklyn, and slightly addled by the opiates, my mother became convinced that the numbers on the morphine drip were part of a lottery—and if her number came up, she would "win" and get back her health. In her smoke-stained fingers she clutched the sterile medical plastic, squinting at the numbers on the readout. "Come on seven" is the last phrase of hers that I can remember.

My father's end was not much different, except that his doctors were at once kinder and less humane—acting really more like benevolent veterinarians. They gave him plenty of morphine as soon as the pain began and kept him in the hospital. What they didn't do, and his appalling second wife wouldn't let me do, was *tell the man he was dying*. Right up until he went into the final haze of painkillers, he expected that surgeons would find a way to remove the "adhesions" he believed were keeping him from eating. Instead, the stomach tumor had come back and was eating him—not that anybody did him the courtesy of telling him. At least I was able to get a priest in while he was conscious to hear his last confession. I'd managed the same for mom, and knowing that was a small comfort. But I'm still surprised how small.

Likewise, in the past few days as I've felt, in the pit of my stomach for the first time, my own mortality, I've been a bit appalled how little religion has seemed to help. I've had genuine scares before—heavy turbulence in an airplane, highway merges that seemed close calls, a mugger following me into darkened streets in Georgetown. And at those times, at the prospect of a quick and easy end, prayer came almost naturally: I asked for mercy and felt a certain confidence I'd receive what had been promised. Much different have been the past few days, spent in the imagined shadow of a very different kind of death, wondering if what faced my parents will claim yet another of my immediate family.

The pious thought, which some friends shared with me while each of my parents was dying, that they were "doing their purgatory here on earth," seemed to me technically and theoretically sound. But here's a problem that faces smooth-talking apologists like me: Has anything this person did on earth—indeed, all the worst things piled up—really merited the kind of slow anguish that seems likely to lie ahead? As neatly as your mind can fit this notion into its orthodoxy grid, it's hard to wrap your heart in it. It's better, surely, than the secular alternative—that suffering is meaningless, useless, redeemable for absolutely nothing, not even Marlboro sweatshirts. I was helping to edit a self-help book recently, and in it one subject insisted that "God (or the Universe) wanted me to learn from that experience." I hope she clears up which is which, because whatever God wants for that woman, what the Universe wants for each of us is clear: *to break down the subatomic particles out of which each of us is made and scatter them randomly through empty space.*

My intellect points me to the crucifix to show me that our way is not only better, but it is Good. As I am learning, that makes it no less terrible.

So I'm making practical plans. I will offer as much comfort and as many prayers as I can to my sick family member. For myself, I'm planning a steady diet of antioxidants and regular visits to the doctor. But if what's beginning to seem like a family curse does indeed fall upon me, I intend to be prepared. Instead of wheedling with doctors over the legal liability issues that accompany pain management, I will spend my time doing two things: praying, and engaging in the kind of dangerous sports that, while they're not intrinsically evil, up to now I've avoided. In between trips to confession and attempts to gain indulgences, I will sky-dive, base-jump, walk tightropes if I can find them. If all else fails, I plan to sneak into Mecca and preach the Faith. Indeed, I'll read aloud from *The Bad Catholic's Guide to Wine, Whiskey and Song.* It just might be my only chance (quoting my mother) to "win."

69. Given all that, do you think that the Last Extreme Anointing or whatever it is—you've left me hopelessly confused—will do anything for you?

I certainly hope so. I'm hoping against hope not for a cure for cancer but for a really overwhelming attack of God's grace on my deathbed, a dose of divine chemo to counteract my every mutated impulse, metastasized vice, and malignant attachments. We Catholics used to pray (and ought to start praying again) for "the grace of a happy death." That may sound paradoxical to the person who thinks that the best way to go out is either strapped to a bomb among his enemies or "in the saddle" with a high-priced escort like Nelson Rockefeller. Of course, what most of us postmoderns would really prefer—if immortality at least as a ghost downloaded into the Internet isn't yet an option—is a quiet, painless death whose time we chose ourselves, whenever the cost/benefit ratio of staying alive tilted a little too far to the left. Essentially, we want to live for seventy-five or eighty years, proceeding from a Montessori school to the Ivy League and then to a condo in Sutton Place. We'll retire in a "spiritual" place like Taos, then when our bones get a little bit creaky we'll drop by the veterinarian so he can seamlessly put us to sleep. I can sympathize with the sentiment, being a Catholic Epicurean. But as a truly consistent Epicurean, really trying to maximize pleasant experiences and minimize the awful ones, I have to take account of the next life and its prospects. For that reason, I frequent the sacraments as often as possible, thinking of them as supernatural antioxidants. I'm hoping that God will decide, in the end, not to waste all the graces He offered me through those means by letting the Tapeworm get me in the end. Or as the classic Catholic funeral prayer, the *Dies Irae*, puts it rather less digestivally:

On that great, that awful day,
This vain world shall pass away.

Thus the sibyl sang of old,
Thus hath holy David told.

There shall be a deadly fear
When the Avenger shall appear,

And unveiled before his eye
All the works of man shall lie.

Hark! to the great trumpet's tones
Pealing o'er the place of bones:

Hark! it waketh from their bed
All the nations of the dead,—

In a countless throng to meet,
At the eternal judgment seat.

Nature sickens with dismay,
Death may not retain its prey;

And before the Maker stand
All the creatures of his hand.

The great book shall be unfurled,
Whereby God shall judge the world;

What was distant shall be near,
What was hidden shall be clear.

To what shelter shall I fly?
To what guardian shall I cry?

Oh, in that destroying hour,
Source of goodness, Source of power,

Show thou, of thine own free grace,
Help unto a helpless race.

Though I plead not at thy throne
Aught that I for thee have done,

Do not thou unmindful be,
Of what thou hast borne for me:

Of the wandering, of the scorn,
Of the scourge, and of the thorn.

Jesus, hast thou borne the pain,
And hath all been borne in vain?

Shall thy vengeance smite the head
For whose ransom thou hast bled?

Thou, whose dying blessing gave
Glory to a guilty slave:

Thou, who from the crew unclean
Didst release the Magdalene:

Shall not mercy vast and free,
Evermore be found in thee?

Father, turn on me thine eyes,
See my blushes, hear my cries;

Faint though be the cries I make,
Save me for thy mercy's sake,

From the worm, and from the fire,
From the torments of thine ire.

Fold me with the sheep that stand
Pure and safe at thy right hand.

Hear thy guilty child implore thee,
Rolling in the dust before thee.

Oh the horrors of that day!
When this frame of sinful clay,

Starting from its burial place,
Must behold thee face to face.

Hear and pity, hear and aid,
Spare the creatures thou hast made.

Mercy, mercy, save, forgive,
Oh, who shall look on thee and live?[57]

Amen to that.

I can't depict a "happy death," having never seen one. But a really talented writer can. I pray that I may "go out" half as well as Lord Marchmain, in Evelyn Waugh's *Brideshead Revisited*—the only book I have ever read seven times. The priest, Father McKay, wants to offer the Anointing of the Sick to the longtime ex-Catholic adulterer Lord Marchmain. And the narrator, Charles Ryder, wants

---

[57] Translation by Thomas Babington Macaulay.

to stop him—afraid that the sight of her father receiving the rite will awaken the childhood faith of his wealthy, glamorous mistress, Julia. The priest tries to reason with Ryder:

> "Do you know what I want to do? It is something so small, no show about it. I don't wear special clothes you know. I go just as I am. . . . I just want to ask him if he's sorry for his sins. I want him to make some little sign of assent; I want him, anyway, not to refuse me; then I want to give him God's pardon. Then, though that's not essential, I want to anoint him. It is nothing, a touch of the fingers, just some oil from this little box, look, it is pure oil, nothing to hurt him."

When Ryder's best efforts only succeeding in infuriating Julia, she decides to grant the priest access to her now-unconscious father. Ryder explains what happens next.

> I recognized the words *Ego te absolvo in nomine Patris . . .* and saw the priest make the sign of the cross. Then I knelt, too, and prayed: "O God, if there is a God, forgive him his sins, if there is such a thing as sin," and the man on the bed opened his eyes and gave a sigh, the sort of sigh I had imagined people made at the moment of death, but his eyes moved so that we knew there was still life in him. I suddenly felt the longing for a sign, if only of courtesy, if only for the sake of the woman I loved, who knelt in front of me, praying, I knew, for a sign. It seemed so small a thing that was asked, the bare acknowledgment of a present, a nod in the crowd. All over the world people were on their knees before innumerable crosses, and here the drama was being played again by two men—by one man, rather, and he nearer death than life; the universal drama in which there is only one actor. . . .
>
> The priest took the little silver box from his pocket and spoke again in Latin, touching the dying man with an oily wad; he finished what he had to do, put away the box and gave the final blessing. Suddenly, Lord Marchmain moved his hand to his forehead; I thought he had felt the touch of the chrism and was wiping it away. "O God," I prayed, "don't let him do that." But there was no need to fear; the hand moved slowly down his breast, then to his shoulder, and Lord Marchmain made the sign of the cross. Then I knew the sign I had asked for was not a little thing, not a passing nod of recognition, and a phrase came back to me from my childhood of the veil of the temple being rent from top to bottom.

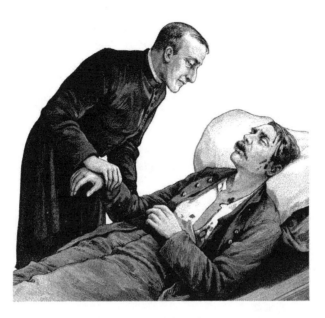

70. So you've hinted at how to die. How then, should we live?

Ah, now you're asking for two books for the price of one. I've already written a morals manual, *The Bad Catholic's Guide to the Seven Deadly Sins*. If you expect to get here what I'm selling there, you really need to read up on Greed.

Acknowledgements

The author would like to thank, first of all, Faye Ballard for her invaluable support and advice through this project, and Gwendolin Herder for her almost Quixotic belief in him, and for her judicious edits. Likewise Anthony Sacramone, for his scrupulous edits and copy-edits. The author also thanks Msgr. Richard Soseman for his patient work vetting the manuscript for orthodoxy, and for his lucid corrections. The author thanks the past editors of *InsideCatholic*, *Crisis*, *Godspy*, *FrontPageMag*, and the *American Conservative* magazines for originally publishing some of the pieces incorporated in this book, and for their permission to reuse those articles here. A small portion of Chapter 6, on the sacrament of Confirmation, was excerpted from the author's own essay in *Godspy*: *Faith at the Edge*, edited by Angelo Matera (Copyright 2008 by Ave Maria Press, P.O. Box 428, Notre Dame, IN, 46556). It is used with permission of the publisher. The author also thanks Susie and Franz Josef Zmirak for their faithful presence, encouragement, and editorial interventions.

For Those Who Love to Laugh

"Humor is the best catechist." –John Zmirak

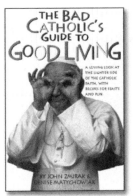

The Bad Catholic's Guide to Good Living

A Loving Look at the Lighter Side of the Catholic Faith, with Recipes for Feasts and fun

Jump right into this hilarious new book and celebrate Catholicism in a whole new way! An indispensable resource for observing the feast days of the saints, The Bad Catholic's Guide to Good Living unveils the history and humor behind the Catholic faith.

978-0-8245-2300-8
$14.95 paperback • 240 pages

The Bad Catholic's Guide to Wine, Whiskey & Song

A Spirited Look at Catholic Life and Lore from Apocalypse to Zinfandel

National bestseller! An intelligent and church-loving introduction to Catholic faith that explains the difference between God and vodka, and why Benedictines make the best beer.

978-0-8245-2411-1
$14.95 paperback • 416 pages

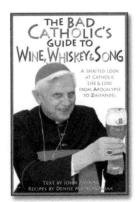

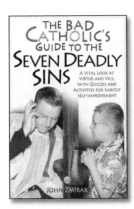

The Bad Catholic's Guide to to the Seven Deadly Sins

A Vital Look at Virtue and Vice, with Quizzes and Activities for Saintly Self-Improvement

Hilarious sketches of history's greatest saints and sinners, theological insights, and cringe-inducing quizzes of virtue and vice so you can discover just how close to the precipice you are. With activities and adventures to help you crawl your way back to solid ground. Self-help has never been so fun.

978-0-8245-2585-9
$14.95 paperback • 240 pages (Spring 2010 Release)

John Zmirak received his B.A. from Yale University in 1986, then his M.F.A. in screenwriting and fiction and his Ph.D. in English in 1996 from Louisiana State University. His focus was the English Renaissance, and the novels of Walker Percy. He taught writing, literature, and screenwriting at secular and Catholic colleges, including Tulane University. He has been Press Secretary to Louisiana Governor Mike Foster, and a reporter and editor at *Success* magazine and *Investor's Business Daily*, among other publications. His essays, poems, reviews and other work have appeared in *First Things, The Weekly Standard, The Atlanta Journal-Constitution, USA Today, FrontPage Magazine, The American Conservative, The South Carolina Review, The Atlantic, Modern Age, The Intercollegiate Review, The New Republic, Commonweal,* and *The National Catholic Register*, among other venues. He has contributed to *American Conservatism: An Encyclopedia* and *The Encyclopedia of Catholic Social Thought*. From 2000-2004 he served as Senior Editor of *Faith & Family Magazine* and a reporter at *The National Catholic Register*. He now serves as Editor-in-Chief of *The Intercollegiate Review,* and *Choosing the Right College*. Read his columns and other new writing at The Bad Catholic's Bingo Hall (*www.badcatholics.com*). He makes his home in New York City.